THE BROTHERS HAMBOURG

Cover photos:
Mark Hambourg (courtesy Remenyi House of Music, Toronto), Jan Hambourg (courtesy Jeanie Hersenhoren), Boris Hambourg (courtesy George Heinl & Co. Ltd., Toronto), Clement Hambourg (City of Toronto Archives)

OTHER BOOKS BY ERIC KOCH

Fiction

The French Kiss
(McClelland and Stewart, Toronto, 1969)

The Leisure Riots
(Tundra Books, Montreal, 1973)

The Last Thing You'd Want to Know
(Tundra Books, Montreal, 1976)

Good Night Little Spy
(Virgo Press, Toronto, and
Ram Publishing Company, London, 1979)

Kassandrus
(Heyne Verlag, Munich, 1988)

Liebe und Mord auf Xananta
(Eichborn Verlag, Frankfurt, 1992)

Work in progress – *Icon in Love* (a novel about Goethe
to be published by Mosaic Press in 1998)

Non-Fiction

Deemed Suspect
(Methuen, Toronto, 1980)

Inside Seven Days
(Prentice-Hall, Toronto, 1986)

Hilmar and Odette (McClelland and Stewart, 1995)
Winner of Jewish Book Award, June 5, 1996

Contents

Preface   vii
Acknowledgments   ix

Mark Hambourg   1
GREATNESS OF NATURE

Jan Hambourg   77
EPICURE, VIOLINIST, SCHOLAR

Boris Hambourg   111
THE TOTAL MUSICIAN

Clement Hambourg   199
THE BLACK SHEEP

*Appendix A: The Bach Solo Violin Sonatas,
   by Jan Hambourg*   233
Appendix B: Recordings   236
Notes   251
Index   273

Preface

The Brothers Hambourg illuminate the relationship between performer and society in England and Canada in the period between the 1890s and the 1960s. The four sons of an adventurous and engaging musician, who left Russia for the West near the end of the nineteenth century, were characteristic of the wave of enterprising artists who fled first from the Tsars, then from the Soviets, and enriched our world with their special brand of cosmopolitan creativity. This books focuses on some of the most significant aspects of their personalities and contributions but does not attempt to present a complete biography of each.

The pianist Mark, the most celebrated of them and a child prodigy who in Vienna was toasted by Brahms, brought classical music to the far reaches of the British Empire before the First World War. He married the daughter of a member of the aristocracy. The chapter about him is based mainly, but not entirely, on his own account of his life as a travelling virtuoso in the early part of the century. An amusing raconteur and enthusiastic clubman, he wrote his autobiography in 1931, almost thirty years before his death. His fame smoothed the paths of the other three.

The second, the violinist and *bonvivant* Jan, made a significant but largely forgotten contribution to Bach scholarship. The chapter about him deals primarily with his marriage to Isabelle McClung of Pittsburgh, the close friend of the American novelist Willa Cather, who used him as a model for one of her characters.

Boris, the third brother, was the director of the Hambourg Conservatory, the unorthodox alternative to the Toronto Conservatory, which brought a worldly flavour to a still largely provincial city and society. For twenty-two years he also played the cello in the Hart House String Quartet, which, on the initiative of Vincent Massey, was funded by the Massey Foundation. The chapter about Boris focuses on these two activities.

In the second half of his life, in the late 1940s and the 1950s, the fourth brother, the pianist and promoter Clement, made an important contribution to the musical life of Toronto. An amiably eccentric personality, he gave an opportunity to talented young jazz performers to perform in the House of Hambourg. He managed this with little money but with great style and high spirits when nobody else showed such flair.

There are a handful of eminent musical dynasties, but can there be four other brothers who achieved comparable distinction in the world of music in Europe and North America?

Eric Koch
Toronto, 1997

Acknowledgments

Two members of the Hambourg family gave me excellent interviews in England in February 1996, Mark Hambourg's second daughter, Mrs Nadine Marshall, in Cambridge, and his niece, Mrs Stella Ryan (Galia's daughter), in St. Albans, Hertfordshire. To both I am deeply grateful.

The *Encyclopedia of Music in Canada** was an invaluable source of information. I was lucky that one of its guiding spirits was Helmut Kallmann, who has been a friend for more than half a century. I am also profoundly grateful for the advice and encouragement Ezra Schabas and Robert Spergel gave me from the beginning. Thanks to my daughter, Madeline Koch, for preparing the index. Thanks to my brave and congenial publisher-editor, Robin Brass, for his help in bringing the book to life.

Finally, a word of apology, and gratitude, to the many dozens of friends, acquaintances and perfect strangers whom I pestered with questions for nearly two years. I hope they will forgive me when they read the book. They certainly cannot be blamed for any avoidable or unavoidable mistakes, nor for the infinity of omissions.

E.K.

---

* Helmut Kallmann, Gilles Potvin, Kenneth Winters (editors), *The Encyclopedia of Music in Canada*, 2nd edition, University of Toronto Press, 1992.

Poster for the tour of 1935 celebrating Boris Hambourg's double anniversary. (Courtesy Toivo Kiil)

Mark Hambourg

GREATNESS OF NATURE

When Mark Hambourg[1] died in England on August 26, 1960, at the age of eighty-one, Neville Cardus wrote in the *Guardian*:

> Mark Hambourg was in his day the average man's ideal and romantic conception of the virtuoso pianist, a complete type of the leonine-maned school. He would nowadays probably be called "ham," as Irving would be so called in the theatre, and MacLaren on the cricket field. Hambourg won his reputation among concert-goers who, before gramophones, radio and television, knew little about music but knew what they liked. He hit the piano hard, straight from the shoulders. Sometimes the right notes actually eluded his expansive and dictatorial hands and fingers. He would hover above the keyboard almost encircling it, and the suspense could become terrific.
>
> It is not, though, to be supposed that Hambourg was not a fine musician, and, in the right place, a sensitive artist. He wasn't a snob, and for the musical starving masses of his period he didn't hesitate to broaden his appeal. He appeared once in the music halls which were then resplendent with last Christmas's principal boys or bawdy and raucous red-nosed comedians. At the Manchester Hippodrome I heard him charge into his customary D minor Toccata and Fugue of Bach, his own arrangement of course. At a concert as exclusively musical I have heard him play the Chopin mazurkas with a mingled grace, poise, and robustness nearly comparable to Friedman's....
>
> He was of his epoch, and none the worse for that. Mark would take it as a compliment to be told that his greatness of nature will be remembered after his piano playing has echoed and died away to a well deserved silence.[2]

On May 30, 1879, Mark was "ushered into the world to the tune of steam and soapsuds" in the steam bath in his uncle's orchard in the rambling village of Boguchar, in South Russia, on the Don River, half way between Moscow and the Black Sea. His mother's brother, who was the government doctor in Boguchar, invited the family to spend their summers there every year. His comfortable house was attached to the local hospital.

For the rest of the year the Hambourgs lived in the small city of Voronezh. Professor Michael Hambourg was only twenty-four when his son Mark was born and had just graduated from the Conservatoire at St. Petersburg, where he had studied the piano under its head, Nikolay Rubinstein. Nikolay was the younger brother of Anton, the pianist and composer whose successor as a pianist Mark – or so many people thought – was destined to become decades later. Both bore a remarkable resemblance to Beethoven of which they were fully aware. Some thought Nikolay was even more gifted than Anton. When Nikolay died in 1881 his friend Tchaikovsky composed his Trio, opus 50, "in memory of a great artist."

The Hambourgs too were a musical family, "just like the Bachs," Mark wrote, "who were so numerous in the seventeenth century in Saxony that it became a habit in that country to call everybody who happened to be in the musical profession a 'Bach.'" Both his uncles were pianists.[3] Mark's mother, Katrina Herzovna, was a singing teacher. When Mark was born, Michael Hambourg had just been appointed professor on the staff of the Conservatoire in Voronezh. Teaching the piano was by no means his only duty. After giving his first public recital at a charity concert in Voronezh six months after Mark was born, he organized musical soirées and choir recitals to raise funds for the education of poor music students and originated the Hambourg Musical Classes.[4]

Mark loved the train journey from Voronezh to Boguchar, even though, when he was little, his mother made him spend the night up on the luggage rack. The train took them to the station nearest to Boguchar. Then, in the spring, when the roads were muddy, they travelled the rest of the way in a wagon pulled by oxen. From time to time the family stopped at post-houses to have tea. If they stayed overnight they shared sleeping quarters with animals, including pigs – "an added joy," Mark recalled.[5]

Mark's earliest recollection of Boguchar was a total eclipse of the sun. To the village priest – the "pope" – this meant the imminent end of the world. To postpone it, the villagers showered him with presents of chickens and eggs and butter.

A particular attraction during the summers was his uncle's troika pulled by three lively little Cossack horses. The uncle often took along Mark and his younger brothers, Jan and Boris, as he sped around the countryside. Another holiday occupation Mark later remembered with nostalgia was fishing in the Don River with his brothers and the village children. When the boys fell in the river the locals were delighted.

The children had a fat nurse. Her drunken husband, Nikolay Nikolayevitch, was in government service. Among the hair-raising stories the nurse told Mark was one about a heretic tied to a tree and tortured to death. He remembered it all his life. When he was four she taught him folk songs, which he used to sing at the top of his voice, beating time on any window he could find.

Mark had already demonstrated at the age of three that he was unusually good at beating time. When he was allowed to accompany his father to the Conservatoire, where the professor conducted an orchestral class, Mark stood beside him at the desk and imitated him.

Michael Hambourg also took him to concerts in the little hall which, as he recalled later, was called by the grand title of Hall of the Nobles, though he did not think many nobles turned up there. It was used for music and other entertainments. There was one traumatic occasion that Mark never forgot. A string quartet was performing. The cellist edged closer and closer to the end of the platform. His father hushed him whenever Mark tried to draw his attention to the danger. Soon the inevitable crash came. The cellist fell into the audience, complete with cello, desk and chair. Later, on the thousands of occasions when Mark himself performed on a platform, he felt nervous whenever his piano was stationed anywhere near the edge.[6]

It was not his father but an aunt who took him in hand at the piano. He was not yet allowed to touch the grand, only a "jangling school instrument." And it was his stern old grandfather's job to punish him if he tried to play on the grand. The aunt taught him a Czerny étude. On his fifth birthday he played it to his father. The professor was delighted and took over his musical education. Mark was now allowed to use the grand for one hour a day. The professor did not believe in children practising more than that. At first Mark hated practising even for an hour, but by the time he was six he could not leave the piano alone. A servant had to lock it up after the prescribed hour, but the boy stole the key whenever he had a chance. When his father did not approve of the way Mark played something, he would simply say, quietly, "I would not do that, Markouscha, if I were you." Mark spent one whole summer practising Beethoven's Sonata opus 49, no. 2. Sometimes, when he looked out of the window he saw village boys stealing apples from his uncle's orchard. They would make faces at him through the window, daring him to come out and stop them. He was strong for his age. He would run out and beat up one of them, seize the stolen apples and eat them. Such were the joys of a Russian childhood.

When Mark was seven, his father was convinced his oldest son was a prodigy. It was therefore essential he obtain the best credentials for him, which meant enrolling him in the Moscow Conservatoire. This had an added advantage: a move to Moscow would give Michael an opportunity to add a degree to a lesser one he already had from St. Petersburg, so that he could be appointed professor of pianoforte at the Moscow Conservatoire, a more prestigious position than the one he had at the small provincial institution in Voronezh. So father and son left for Moscow, and the family soon followed.

While Mark ostensibly took lessons from the director, who "was a devotee of what the French call *des nuits blanches,* so much so that during the day he could not concentrate,"[7] his real teacher remained his father, with whom he studied all forty-eight of Bach's Preludes and Fugues. Forty years later, Mark still thought they were the "basic grounding for every young pianist." On one occasion Mark had to perform a show-off piece by Hummel for Vasily Safonov, the famous conductor and pianist.[8] Safonov was suitably impressed, not only by the boy's musical talent but also by his acrobatic achievement. "What a remarkable *Trefftalent!*" he exclaimed, using a German word. Apparently Russians have no expression for hitting – *treffen* – the right key from a high distance, the target practice of the future virtuoso.

Mark was also supposed to acquire a general, non-musical education. He might well have succeeded if the teachers had not been so impressed by his musical accomplishments that they let him pass examinations which, if there had been any justice, he would have failed. His father had to pass all his examinations the normal way and was duly appointed professor.

When he was ten – in 1889 – Mark was ready to play in public. He appeared in another Hall of the Nobles, this time a concert hall in Moscow holding about fifteen hundred where visiting celebrities like Berlioz and Vieuxtemps had performed. (Before 1917 it was called *Blagorodnoye Sobraniye*. After the Revolution its named was changed to *Dom Soyozor,* House of Unions.) Mark played the Harmonious Blacksmith Variations by Handel and the Concerto in D minor by Mozart and received excellent reviews. Soon afterwards, at a concert the Conservatoire gave for Grand Duke Constantine, the brother of the Tsar, who liked music, he performed John Field's Concerto in E flat, with full orchestra. (Field, Chopin's precursor, was the Irish pianist-composer who spent the last thirty years of his life in Moscow.) At a banquet preceding the concert someone gave Mark a glass of champagne. During the last movement he went blank, lost his place and improvised for at least forty-eight bars, then gracefully found his way back. This impressed the Grand Duke. After the concert, he demanded that Mark be brought to him. He asked the child what he would like to possess most in the world. "A really big toy engine," Mark replied. The next day an imperial courier delivered to his house a really big toy engine. At that moment – or at least so he declared afterwards – Mark decided that being a concert pianist was truly "a fine profession."

Soon after the concert for the Grand Duke, Mark's parents asked a clairvoyante to foretell the future for Mark. In her crystal ball she saw him playing in London. The Hambourgs knew the singer Madame

Eugénie Papritz, who went to London every year to give lessons to the daughters of Society. They asked her what she thought of the idea. She said the English loved music – she was sure Mark would do very well there.

In the spring of 1889, during a drenching rain-storm, Michael and Mark Hambourg, neither of whom spoke a word of English, arrived at Victoria Station. They had left the rest of the family behind in Moscow, including the new baby, Galia. Father and son took a "dingy old four-wheeler" to a boarding house recommended to them in Bloomsbury near the British Museum, at *Dwenty-voor Oupper Bedvoord Pflasse*.[9]

In Mark's account of his Russian childhood there is only one direct reference to the family's Jewish background. When he described the time his father studied in St. Petersburg with Nikolay Rubinstein, he wrote that his father gave Hebrew lessons in the evening. He also did "watchmaking," at which he was very good. (Mark mentioned Hebrew lessons and watchmaking, as it were, in the same breath.) He added that his father "had originally been trained for religion" – in other words, he was to become a rabbi, though Mark did not spell it out – "but the urge of music was too much for him."

It seems clear that neither Mark nor his brothers and sisters had any interest in their Jewish background. At the same time, as far as one can tell, there was never any question of Mark, or any other member of the family, denying it. Religion and specifically Jewish matters simply played no part in their lives.

In the early nineties Mark was studying in Vienna, where the pianist Alfred Grünfeld enjoyed great popularity. Mark respected him greatly. He noted that Grünfeld made a point of playing only once a year in his home town. This event, he wrote, was known as the "Jewish holiday." Grünfeld had such an enormous following "among his co-religionists," Mark explained, that literally the whole of musical Jewry in the city seemed to turn up at this yearly recital.[10] Mark referred to Jews in the third person plural.

There is one indirect, perhaps unintended reference in Mark's autobiography to the Hambourgs' Jewish past. His stern old grandfather, he wrote, the one whose job was to punish him if he tried to play on the grand piano, had one great accomplishment, the preparing of stuffed fish. "Here he was a supreme master, and my treat at five years old was to be allowed to assist him, in the hope of getting hold of any extra raisins which I could pilfer from the elaborate ingredients which he used in his culinary operations."[11]

Clearly, the old man was making *gefilte fish*.

Professor Michael Hambourg was born in 1855 in Jaroslaw in the Ukraine, a market town north of Przemysl, where there was heavy fighting in both world wars. The town is now in Poland and has a special place in the history of Polish Jewry. During fairs in the sixteenth and seventeenth centuries, Jewish leaders in Jaroslaw successfully established working relationships with Christian officials to protect visiting Jewish merchants. This pattern was later introduced elsewhere.[12]

To study music in St. Petersburg, Michael Hambourg had either to be baptized or receive special permission. The capital was outside the "Pale of Jewish Settlement," the area covering parts of western Russia, the Ukraine and Poland in which Jews were allowed to live. However, they could receive permission to live outside the Pale if they fitted into certain categories. One of these categories consisted of people who knew somebody or managed to bribe somebody in the Tsarist bureaucracy. Of the five and a half million Jews who lived in the Russian Empire at the beginning of this century, most lived within the Pale, but surprisingly many lived outside – about 20,000 in St. Petersburg, 150,000 in Odessa and comparable numbers in other cities. Many of these were not distinguishable in education, clothing and speech from the non-Jewish population.[13] But even for the most prosperous and cultivated among them, living in what was, after all, an *officially* anti-Semitic empire was precarious. In 1871 a pogrom in Odessa was so vicious that many Jews began to doubt the possibility of either assimilation or coexistence. State anti-Semitism and pogroms were endemic, particularly after the assassination of

Tsar Alexander II in 1881. Later, the last Tsar, Nicolas II, contributed a large sum from his private purse towards the dissemination of the *Protocol of the Elders of Zion,* a fabricated publication documenting an alleged Jewish conspiracy to take over the world.

In 1827 the first Tsar Nicholas had passed an edict on the recruitment of Jews. Catherine Drinker Bowen described this measure in her book about the Rubinstein brothers:

> Every Jewish male of twelve years, to the proportion of seven in every hundred of population, was to be conscripted for the Imperial Army and to proceed immediately to cantonment school, to remain in the Imperial Army 25 years.
>
> In those schools young boys were fed salt food and denied water. Boys were flogged, dying far from home with the insignia of a soldier on their collars. Children in cantonments wept for their mothers, falling on the drill ground from fatigue. Only the strongest survived.[14]

After the Tsar had passed this edict, Roman Rubinstein, the grandfather of Anton and Nikolay, took precautionary measures. In Berdichev, a town southwest of Kiev, he arranged for a collective baptism for his family of thirty-three.

"My family," he had addressed them *en masse.* "You are the descendants of centuries of Jews. The Tsar has issued a most unjust edict. It will exterminate us all. Take the advice of the head of your family. A live Christian is better than a dead Jew. A little holy water is an ordeal, but better a little holy water than death."[15]

In 1885 Tsar Alexander III attended a performance of Anton Rubinstein's opera *Nero.* He was so impressed that he conferred the title Excellency on the composer, prompting a letter from Anton Rubinstein to his mother: "I have a presentiment that I shall require this *Excellency* some day against the very powers which conferred it upon me. For all your baptism at Berdichev, we are Jews, you and I and sister Sophie."[16]

Anton Rubinstein once made the remark that the Germans called him a Russian and the Russians called him a Jew. Not all former Jews, in Russia and elsewhere, were aware of their lingering Jewishness. Some of those who were aware of it, and were burdened by it, tried to conceal it from their children, to spare them future anguish. The eminent musicologist Nicolas Slonimsky recalled in his autobiography:

> We were fed all kinds of fables to the effect that we were *echt* Russian, with our ancestry going back almost to the founders of the Russian state, and we believed it. But when I was about twelve years old, my aunt, my mother's sister, came to visit us in St. Petersburg. I had never met her before, but I noticed that she was characteristically Jewish. When I said something about our family being of pure Russian stock, she began to laugh uproariously and informed me, rather caustically, that we were Jews, only that we were baptized. For me it was the most terrible shock of my whole life.[17]

There is no evidence, one way or another, that Michael Hambourg was baptized. On the strength of his son's description of him, it is fairly safe to assume that he was an agnostic. In the judgment of Nicolas Slonimsky, the author of *Lexicon of Musical Invective*,[18] most members of the Russian and Jewish intelligentsia were. "Under these circumstances," he wrote, "to persist in the Jewish faith was to condemn one's children to uncomfortable discrimination." Slonimsky, for one, was "baptized with all the due solemnity of the Greek Orthodox ritual," even though the situation was paradoxical, since Jewish musicians received preferential treatment in the Tsar's Empire. Members of the Imperial family, and Russian aristocrats generally, were often music lovers.

Slonimsky presented an illuminating glimpse behind the scenes: "It was an open secret that the Grand Duchess Elena sheltered young Jewish musicians in her own palace to protect them from police harassment. Glazunov, director of the St. Petersburg Conservatoire, was a great admirer of Jews. He used to remark about some non-Jewish Conservatory students that their playing was 'disappointingly Christian.'... More than half of the St. Petersburg Conservatory students were Jewish."[19]

No doubt his father took Mark to London because he thought the chances for him were better there. However, many Jewish musicians of Mark's generation, or the next, began their careers at home in Russia and later prospered. Among these were Mischa Elman, Ossip Gabrilowitsch, Jascha Heifetz, Vladimir Horowitz, André Kostelanetz and Efrem Zimbalist, to name a few. Some of these had diplomas from the St. Petersburg or the Moscow conservatories. These were valuable because they bestowed on their owner the right to live anywhere in the empire – that is, outside the Pale. Michael Hambourg, a graduate of St. Petersburg, was entitled to live in Voronezh, whether he was Jewish or not. If he was still Jewish, which is unlikely, he would have been one of 319 out of a population of 84,000 who in 1874 had permission to live there.

He had his diploma. There was no problem about his returning to the Moscow Conservatoire after leaving Voronezh to study along with Mark. This was just as well since the law required an adult member of his family to reside there while the child was enrolled.

Jascha Heifetz was born in Vilna, within the Pale. When he was ten he was admitted to the Conservatoire in St. Petersburg to study with the celebrated Leopold Auer. Thanks to the enlightened director, there was no *numerus clausus* at the Conservatoire, no limit to the number Jewish students admitted. "Papa Heifetz" came along. The trouble was *he* had no right to reside in St. Petersburg.

Leopold Auer wrote in his memoirs:

> Someone hit upon the happy idea of suggesting that I admit Jascha's father, a violinist of forty, into my own class, and thus solve the problem. This I did... However, since the students were without exception expected to attend the obligatory classes in solfeggio, piano, and harmony, and since Papa Heifetz most certainly did not attend any of them, and did not play at the examinations, I had to do battle continually with the management on his account. It was not until the advent of Glazunov, my last director,

who knew the true inwardness of the situation, that I had no further trouble in seeing that the boy remained in his parents' care until the summer of 1917, when the family was able to go to America.[20]

Assuming that Michael Hambourg decided to go to London not only because a clairvoyante and the singing teacher Madame Eugénie Papritz suggested it, the question arises – leaving the Jewish factor aside – whether he might have had political reasons for leaving Russia.

Mark wrote that his father had always been an adventurous man, full of energy and courage, who understood that conditions at home made life difficult for him and his children. Mark remembered continual rows, unrest and police everywhere, fighting in the streets, people being arrested by the scores and beaten by Cossacks with *naigakas*, long knotted whips. The time was the eighties, when not only Jews but all those who opposed the Tsar were systematically persecuted.

There is only one passing reference to his father's possible political activities in Mark's reminiscences of his Russian childhood, and that reference is far from clear. Shortly after his parents were married, his father was arrested without any warning and taken to prison. The suspicion was that he had a great friend who had another great friend, "and this twice removed friend knew a Nihilist." This was a time when four thousand people a day were being arrested in St. Petersburg alone.

"Had it not been for my mother's energy," Mark wrote, his father, "might have remained in prison for years." But she knew a general, a man of influence, who attained Michael's release *after some months*. Mark added that his father was, of course, completely innocent of any conspiracy, "for he never gave a thought to politics, being entirely immersed in music."

This must have been a slight overstatement. In London, thanks to introductions from Madame Eugénie Papritz, Michael quickly drifted into the circle of idealistic revolutionaries in exile around the great anarchist philosopher and geographer Prince Peter Kropotkin and made friends with Sergei Stepniak and Felix Volkhovsky (more about them later), who became important figures in Mark's early life.

The humanity with which the British welcomed these revolutionaries – they called them collectively Nihilists – was one reason why Mark immediately felt at home in England.

It seems unlikely that his father was drawn to political émigrés who had sacrificed everything for their convictions but had no interest in music *only* because they could converse with him in Russian.

Mark's first stay in London lasted less than two years, from 1889 to 1891, between the ages of ten and twelve.

His father's impractical political friends had no connections in the musical world. So father and son had to spend their time in the British Museum, waiting for something to happen. At last something did happen. They met the London representative of the tea firm of Popoff, who introduced them to the concert agent Daniel Mayer, the man who had just introduced Ignace Paderewski to the British public. Paderewski became "the hero of my earliest youth," Mark wrote later. "The melting tone of his pianissimo I can never forget, and his personality radiated a glow over all he did."[21] Mark's father also admired Paderewski and they became good friends. The music critic Harold C. Schonberg observed that Paderewski's "magnetism, poetry, glamour and mystery" became "pianism personified to a good portion of the globe."[22] It would, however, have been rash of Paderewski's colleagues to go overboard in their praise of him at the time. Emil von Sauer wryly remarked, referring to Paderewski's fashionably pre-Raphaelite pose, "His long, curly blond locks, a kind of melancholy atmosphere that he always surrounded himself with, were just what hero-worshippers were looking for."[23] When another pianist, Moriz Rosenthal, who was known for his sharp tongue, went to hear Paderewski, he shrugged his shoulders and said, "Yes, he plays well, but he's no Paderewski."[24]

Mark played for Paderewski, at Daniel Mayer's request. He chose Chopin's Waltz in D flat. (Before he began, he asked Paderewski, "Do you know this piece, Master?") Paderewski was so impressed that Mayer launched him immediately. Paderewski later said Mark Hambourg was the greatest natural talent he had ever met. To launch him, Mayer chose an unusual technique. At the end of a recital given by the pianist Natalie Janotha,[25] whom he also managed, he jumped on the stage and asked the audience to stay and hear Mark play.

Mark used the name Max, because the family thought this was more British than Mark. For the same reason, Jan was called James, and Boris Bernard. "Galia groaned under the name of Annie," Mark wrote in 1931, no doubt forgetting that Galia was an infant and that if she groaned it was for other reasons. When nearly twenty years later she married Reginald Grey Coke (1864-1930), the second son of Thomas William Coke, Earl of Leicester of Holkham, her name was Galia.

1890 happened not to be the best year for Mark to be launched. A number of "baby pianists" – Mark's expression – were being thrown into the ring at the same time. This greatly aroused the indignation of the thirty-five-year-old George Bernard Shaw, music critic of *The World,* who wrote under the byline of Corno di Bassetto:

> The appearance of young Max Hambourg at the Pavia recital reminded me that I had not exhausted the subject of La Cigale last week. I want to know why the manager of the Lyric Theatre, after making a parade of his sense of social obligation by opening the season with a performance of the National Anthem, proceeded to fill the stage with a troop of children under ten, whose borrowed rouge and bedizenment must, behind the scenes, have presented as grim a contrast to their own pallor.... I warn the Lyric management and my undiscerning fellow-critics that if these senseless child-shows are not stopped by the friends of the theatre, they will be stopped by the theatre's enemies, whose vigilance committees are busily collecting evidence which may be employed not merely to establish the beneficent sway of the factory inspector, but to substitute for him the Puritan censor.[26]

A year later Shaw discussed Mark on his merits:

> Young Max Hambourg gave a pianoforte recital at Steinway Hall [the concert hall adjoining the London premises of Steinway & Co., on Wigmore Street, closed in 1924] and once more played

Bach better than any other composer on his program. With such training as Eugene Holliday has had from Rubinstein, this Russian lad might astonish the world some day; but he does not seem to be exactly in the way of getting it at present.[27]

Mark was soon taken over by another, equally enterprising agent, Narcissus Vert – surely this can't have been his real name – who was managing Josef Hofmann, born in Cracow, three years older than Mark. Mark's father negotiated a three-year contract with the agent, with the stipulation that Mark was to give no more than twenty-five performances in any one year. The professor worked with Mark for three or four hours a day. At the concerts arranged by Narcissus Vert in London, he played Bach's Chromatic Fantasia and Fugue, Mozart's Piano Concerto in D minor, Beethoven's Sonata no. 12 in A flat major, opus 26 (the sonata with the funeral march), and pieces by Schumann and Chopin.

Two men took over Mark's non-musical education, Prince Peter Kropotkin and Sergei Stepniak.

Kropotkin had arrived in England in 1886 three years before the Hambourgs. Born in 1842, he was a descendant of an ancient family and had served as an aide to Tsar Alexander II. In due course he became an army officer in Siberia. There, apart from his military duties, he studied animal life and engaged in geographical explorations. This and other research won him immediate recognition. He could have pursued a distinguished scientific career had not the events in Paris in 1871, the year of the Commune, made him renounce his aristocratic heritage and dedicate his life to social justice. He soon joined revolutionary groups, was imprisoned, made a sensational escape, moved to Switzerland, was expelled and went to France, where he was convicted of sedition and spent three years in prison, writing. His books were designed for the ordinary man. Emile Zola called *The Conquest of Bread* a "true poem." Unlike Tolstoy, Kropotkin did not accept the doctrine of non-resistance to evil, but believed that there were times when violence became the only means of protesting against tyranny and exploitation. In June 1917, after an exile of forty years, he returned to Russia at the age of seventy-five, was warmly greeted by the crowd, his hopes for a libertarian future never brighter. Spontaneous communes and soviets were emerging, very much along the lines he had been advocating. These, he expected, would be the basis of a stateless society. But soon his enthusiasm turned into bitter disappointment. He wrote to Lenin in March 1920 that "Russia has become a Revolutionary Republic only in name." He died the next year.[28]

Unlike the scholarly saint Peter Kropotkin, his friend Sergei Stepniak ("man of the steppes," a pseudonym for Kravchinskii), who had been in England since 1884, was a charismatic revolutionary propagandist. A year before his death he revealed that, with a dagger he had concealed under his coat, he had stabbed to death the notoriously brutal General Mezentzev. Since Stepniak was a quiet man whose warmth inspired all who met him with confidence and affection, this revelation was a great shock to his many British friends.[29]

George Bernard Shaw knew him well:

> No doubt his massive head, his black hair, his powerful shoulders, his immense concentration of expression, used to impress people and even overawe some of them. But if he ever made any deliberate dramatic use of his formidable aspect, I never detected it. On the contrary, his charm in private intercourse was that he betrayed the heart of an affectionate child behind a powerful and very lively intellect.[30]

In December 1895, when Mark was no longer in London, Stepniak was run over by a train at the only remaining level-crossing in London, at Woodstock Road in Chiswick. The ceremony at Waterloo Station, before the coffin left for the crematorium, was almost a state funeral. "It was a significant and striking spectacle," *The Times* wrote, "this assemblage of Socialists, Nihilists, Anarchists, and outlaws of every European country, gathered together in the heart of London to pay respect to the memory of their leader."[31]

The *Weekly Sun* carried this story:

> There was a red flag draped in black, a large wreath from the German Communist Party. There were speeches in English, French, Italian and Yiddish. Volkhovsky spoke "under much emotion," and the other speakers included William Morris [making his last public appearance out of doors before his death the following October], Kropotkin, John Burns, Keir Hardie, Eleanor Marx [Karl Marx's daughter] and many others. The weather was very unfavourable, and much discomfort was experienced from the steady fall of rain and sleet.[32]

Mark used to talk to the "venerable William Morris, with his enormous white beard,"[33] the famous painter, poet, furniture designer and socialist, who often wrote, as one of his biographers observed, "with a fervour of which Stepniak would have approved."[34]

By 1890, thanks to the concerts arranged by Narcissus Vert, Mark was earning enough money to enable his father to travel to Moscow to pick up the rest of the family – one wife and three children, Jan, Boris and Galia – and bring them to London. At that time Felix Volkhovsky, a friend of Kropotkin's and Stepniak's and the man who later arranged Stepniak's funeral, was planning the rescue from Russia of his daughter, Vera, whom he had reason to believe the Tsarist authorities would use as a pawn against him. He had been pulling strings to get her out of Russia.

The Volkhovsky story is truly amazing. Felix Volkhovsky had first met Stepniak in Russia in the fall of 1873 and sheltered him from the police. A year later, when Volkhovsky himself was arrested, Stepniak tried to rescue him but the plan failed. Volkhovsky was imprisoned three times on suspicion of belonging to a secret society and spent six and a half years in solitary confinement in the Peter and Paul fortress in St. Petersburg. In the fortress he lost his hearing and his hair turned white. After his release he was condemned to eleven years in Siberia. His family was allowed to join him, but it seems – the evidence is conflicting – his wife soon committed suicide and two of his three daughters perished. Only Vera survived. In 1889 – at about the time Michael and Mark Hambourg came to England – Volkhovsky escaped from Siberia, leaving Vera in the care of friends.

Volkhovsky had been in touch with the activist New York journalist George Kennan, a cousin of the grandfather of our contemporary George Kennan, also a great American Russia expert. The elder Kennan was the centre of a network of anti-Tsarist operatives. He published in the *Century Magazine* a number of exposés of the exile system in Siberia. These articles became Volkhovsky's passport to freedom.

Once he reached Vladivostok Volkhovsky rushed aboard an English ship. "After explaining to the captain that he was a fugitive without papers he produced a photograph of Kennan bearing a warm endorsement which the latter had sent him in Irkutsk. On the strength of this unorthodox documentation, he was smuggled below and kept hidden until the ship cleared port."[35]

Volkhovsky reached New York, where he stayed only a short time. Then Kennan sent him to, of all places, Berlin (now Kitchener), an Ontario town with a large German-speaking population, where he wrote and lectured about his revolutionary career, using the pseudonym Felix Brant, and planning a movement anticipating the Friends of Russian Freedom which he later formed in England. No evidence of his stay seems to have survived. Volkhovsky gave up after eight months and went to England, where he spent the rest of his life. He edited *Free Russia*, which he took over after Stepniak's death, until his own death in a modest flat in Fulham Road on Sunday, August 2, 1914, the day after the First World War broke out.

Today, Felix Volkhovsky is very much forgotten, not being "fated to take his place alongside Kossuth, Mazzini, Herzen and the rest of the company of exiles that it was England's pride to harbour and encourage."[36] In his day, however, he was well known and he deserves to be remembered.

Felix Volkhovsky fits into the Mark Hambourg story in a manner straight out of popular melodrama. His daughter Vera was exactly the same age as Mark. In Michael Hambourg's travelling papers there happened to be space for *four* Hambourg children, for Jan, Boris and Galia and "Max." Michael offered to smuggle Vera into England disguised as his child "Max." In Mark's judgment, his father was an impulsive, quixotic man who did not understand the risks he was running. The ploy worked miraculously. In Moscow Vera's curls were cut off, and she was dressed in pants and arrived in England with the Hambourg family as *Max* Hambourg.[37] But this is not the end of the story.

At the end of the short passage in his autobiography about his father's heroic mission, Mark wrote (in 1931): "The second 'Max Hambourg' was landed safely in London, and is now, I believe, a distinguished woman professor at Oxford."

Well, not quite.

Vera went to Somerville College at Oxford when she was twenty, in 1901, but became ill after two years and was unable to take her examinations.[38] She then took training as a dancing teacher, but changed her direction when she decided to embark on a literary career. This led nowhere and she made her living "on the borderline of medicine and education." During the First World War she worked in the Women's Land Army, at the same time involving herself in Russian émigré politics. After the war she became a teacher.

In July 1920 she met Bertrand Russell and being, as she put it to him, "a woman of great emotional capacity," she fell deeply in love with him. Twenty-two of her letters to him have been preserved in the Bertrand Russell Archives at McMaster University, Hamilton, none of his to her. We just have one direct observation from him about this relationship, affixed to Letter 20, presumably for archival purposes: "This letter is from a woman I saw something of for a brief time. This letter sounds as if I had an affair with her. But I had not."

When Vera met Bertrand Russell in the summer of 1920 he had just returned from Russia and was writing *The Practice and Theory of Bolshevism*. Unlike Kropotkin, Russell was a pacifist who rejected the use of force altogether, even against tyrants. He had always been an opponent of Tsarist rule, but he believed what was happening in Russia now was even worse.[39]

One reason why Vera fell in love with Russell was that she thought he had "very accurately ... got the feel of Russia – more than anyone else I know of." She once wrote to Russell that, when she was a teenager, Sergei Stepniak, a great favourite of hers, had lifted her up to the ceiling and said, "'Do you know, Verotchka, why I love you so much? It's because you're so very Russian!' and I nearly burst with pride."

But on ideological matters Vera and Russell did not see eye to eye. "I believe," he wrote, "that while some forms of Socialism are immeasurably better than capitalism, others are even worse. Among those that are worse I reckon the form which is being achieved in Russia."[40]

Vera's attitude towards "Bolshevism," however, was ambivalent. During the war she had been a London representative of the Social Revolutionary Party, of which her father had been a member. She had friends on both sides and considered herself an interpreter between Russia and England.

After Russell's rejection, Vera, deeply depressed, married Montague Fordham, a widower and an expert on agriculture whose practical good sense she admired. She married him on condition that she was free to leave him any time. This was a wise precaution, because she soon went her own way. In 1923 she received permission to go to Russia, her "spiritual home," where she stayed for a year and adopted two Russian Civil War orphans. "They let me have them because I was my father's daughter," she wrote. In the thirties, she was passionately opposed to Fascism. In 1938, after the Munich Agreement had virtually handed Czechoslovakia to Hitler, she was a co-signatory of a letter H.G. Wells sent to ex-president Eduard Beneš expressing shame for the manner in which the Western democracies had betrayed his country.[41]

Vera Volkhovsky died in 1966, at the age of eighty-five, six years after the man she had so successfully impersonated in 1890. She must have known that he had become a world-famous pianist. But she was as little interested in him as he was in her.

In London late in 1890, the nine-year-old Vera was back with her father, whom she had last seen the previous year in Siberia, the nine-year-old Mark had his mother with him again, and his brothers Jan and Boris, and the baby, Galia. Michael found the family a place to live in Teddington, but after eight months they moved to "a nice little house with a little garden" in Hammersmith. To save the bus fare, father and son often walked from there to the St. James Hall – between Piccadilly and Regent Street, where the Piccadilly Hotel is now – to hear a concert. They got on so well that they were hardly aware of any age difference, and his father's "exuberant optimism," Mark wrote, "was infectious."

Mark continued performing under the management of Narcissus Vert, while his father sometimes played the orchestral part of Mozart's Piano Concerto in D minor, one of Mark's show pieces. The professor was beginning to have more than one student, so when Mark played in Birmingham or Leeds and his father couldn't come along – Mark was still too young to travel only with his manager or his representative – his mother came. He also performed in schools, often to assemblies of children his own age. This he disliked intensely. Sometimes they hissed at him and taunted him: "Good little Russian, works so hard at the piano, doesn't he? We'll show him just what we think of the piano." And they did so, vigorously. He was strong for his age, and there were fights. Equally distasteful were gushy old ladies who would kiss him and pinch his cheek, murmuring, "What a dear little fellow!" Narcissus Vert had to tell them they could pet him only if they brought him boxes of chocolate. "So my patronesses," Mark reported gleefully, "were asked to bring sweets to tame the little wild Slav boy."

One afternoon, Stepniak took Mark along to the new studio of his friend the painter Felix Moscheles, on Church Street in Chelsea, to play for him. Moscheles soon became Mark's third mentor, with Peter Kropotkin and Sergei Stepniak.

Felix was the son of Ignaz Moscheles (1794-1870), one of the great pianists of his age, a student of Beethoven and among the first to play his sonatas in public, and a teacher and great friend of Mendelssohn.

In fact, Ignaz Moscheles's friendship with Mendelssohn was, in one scholar's view, "one of the most beautiful relationships in music."[42] Felix Moscheles, who was of course named after Felix Mendelssohn, edited Ignaz Moscheles's voluminous correspondence with the composer. Mark called Felix Moscheles "Uncle Lix." Seventeen years later Uncle Lix gave Mark as a wedding present the fragment of a Beethoven autograph "virile in writing but unreadable ... believed to be the thirty-two bars for the beginning of a Tenth Symphony," as well as two Chopin studies "written for Ignaz Moscheles's school of piano playing ... showing Chopin's exquisite fine and clear calligraphy."[43]

Felix Moscheles was an adherent of every conceivable progressive cause. He believed in the brotherhood of man and in the universal language Esperanto and ran a newspaper called *Peace*. His wife, Grete, born in Berlin, mothered Mark. When he stayed in the studio overnight, she gave him a good scrub in the morning and made sure his neck was clean.

Uncle Lix was an immensely useful connection for Mark; in the Moscheles studio he met a number of people prominent in musical and intellectual life. He played for the young Frederick Delius, who had married a niece of Felix Moscheles, for Robert Browning, for Keir Hardie,[44] for Ellen Terry and for Bernard Shaw. (It is not clear whether this was before or after Shaw heard him play in public. Stepniak had written to Shaw that he knew a "wild Russian boy" who might interest him.) Mark also met Hans Richter, the Austro-Hungarian conductor whose concerts were the outstanding events in London's musical life and who was one of the best known conductors of his day. He had conducted the first performance of Wagner's *Ring* cycle in Bayreuth in 1876 and was to introduce it to English audiences at Covent Garden in 1890, *in English*. Richter belonged to the first group of international "celebrity" conductors, men like Hans von Bülow, Arthur Nikisch, Felix Mottl, Hermann Levi and Karl Muck, who had shed the relative anonymity of conductors in previous generations. Richter was to become a major figure in the next chapter of Mark's life.

Then there was Oscar Wilde, one of Stepniak's innumerable friends. Wilde was deaf to music but his aristocratic socialism made him welcome in the Moscheles circle. It happened that Wilde's life too had been touched by a Vera. Eight years earlier, in 1883, his first play, *Vera, or the Nihilists* – about the assassination of a Tsar by a Vera – was performed in New York, in the author's presence. A character in the play, no doubt speaking for Wilde, says, "In a good democracy, everybody should be an aristocrat." The play illuminates the extraordinary influence Tsarist tyranny and Russia's Nihilists had on the imagination of the intelligentsia at the time. The play was a failure.[45]

Among the Americans Mark met in the Moscheles studio was the enthusiastic advocate of universal peace Andrew Carnegie.[46] Moscheles had met him in the United States, as well as his associate Henry Phipps and the journalist and diplomat Whitelaw Reid,[47] all of whom remained friends of Mark's for many years. Phipps invited Mark to spend a weekend with his family and other guests at Knebworth, the estate he had rented from Lord Lytton. Mark was met at the station by two tall manservants with an enormous two-horse wagonette and a luggage cart. Grete Moscheles had wrapped Mark's things in brown paper.

"Where's your luggage?" a manservant asked. Once he grasped the facts he tossed the parcel on the luggage cart "without relaxing a muscle of his perfectly controlled countenance."

Stepniak did not approve of Mark having contact with "the flesh-pots of the rich." Moscheles also frowned on Mark being "thrown into dissipated society life." The time had come for a radical change. The boy required serious training, they thought, in different surroundings, preferably on the Continent. Stepniak suggested that perhaps Hans Richter could choose for Mark a family of artists as superior as he could find – and as poor as possible. He supposed in Vienna, for example, such a combination could be found, a family which would "keep the boy strictly within the artistic circle." Felix Moscheles wrote to Hans Richter, who agreed that he would be very sorry if "young Hambourg of whose musical gifts I have a very high opinion should have to go on working as an infant prodigy and virtuoso in order to gain a difficult existence." The boy needed a good school, so that "in a few years' time he would become an able and serious artist."[48]

Moscheles and Stepniak approached a number of rich people in whose houses Mark had played, requesting financial help. At first, none was forthcoming. Only after Paderewski had given nearly half the required amount did other donations follow.

In the summer of 1891, at the age of twelve, Mark, escorted by his father, went to Vienna to study with Paderewski's teacher, Theodor Leschetizky. Paderewski had been twenty-eight when he came to Leschetizky, and everything he did seemed wrong – too much pedal, not enough rhythm, no sense of style – yet Leschetizky recognized immediately, as Mark put it, "the power and charm" of his playing. It was Leschetizky's success with Paderewski, and the generosity with which Paderewski always spoke of him, which "put him securely on the map as a teacher."[49] When Mark played for him soon after arriving, Leschetizky said to him, "I see that teaching in London is as good as anywhere," which was a tremendous compliment to Mark's father. Up to then, Leschetizky must have thought Vienna was "the only city in the world for learning."[50]

Michael and Mark arrived in Vienna still in time to be fascinated by another pianist, one reputed to be the last living pupil of Beethoven, Antoine de Kontski, "the Lion of Poland" the press called him. He had an enormous beard and played the Moonlight Sonata with all the lights down and a piece of fleecy white felt stretched over the keys "to produce the pellucid atmosphere of the moon."[51]

"From battle, murder, sudden death, and from the Lion of Poland's piano-playing," one critic wrote, "Good Lord, deliver us."[52]

There has been much pondering about why Theodor Leschetizky was such a legendary, revered teacher. Was it a matter of personality? Did he have a system? Artur Schnabel, Alexander Brailowsky, Ossip Gabrilowitsch, Benno Moiseiwitsch, Mieczyslaw Horszowski, Ignaz Friedman, Elly Ney, Paul Wittgenstein – all studied with him. What did he have that made them play so well? Whatever it was, Harold C. Schonberg wrote, "it seemed to work," and it seems that most of his students developed a lifelong affection and admiration for him.

Mark was his student from November 1891 to April 1895, from the

Mark Hambourg, photographed as a little boy in Russian dress – in a London studio. (From his autobiography)

Professor Michael Hambourg, father of the Brothers Hambourg and founder of the Hambourg Conservatory.

Mark Hambourg with his teacher Theodor Leschetizky. (From the autobiography)

Mark Hambourg – the budding pianist.

age of twelve to fifteen. His stay in Vienna was the happiest time of his youth.[53]

Naturally, Leschetizky was careful in the selection of his students. He asked each candidate three questions: "Were you a child prodigy? Are you of Slavic descent? Are you a Jew?" If all three qualities came together, he would rub his hands in glee. He himself was not Jewish.[54]

He was a martinet and a despot. He was also loving and sweet, generous, amusing and humane. By 1891 he was in his early sixties and looked like an old Russian peasant. He was stocky and had a white beard, a double chin, and the round, shiny face of a man who ate and drank a lot. Born in Galicia in 1830, then part of Austria, he was taught music by his father, also a musician, and made his first public appearance in Lemberg (Lwow) at ten. He then went to Vienna, where he studied with Karl Czerny (1771-1857), Beethoven's friend and pupil, who had given the first public performance of the Emperor Concerto, on February 12, 1812. Czerny was also a teacher of Franz Liszt. Leschetizky studied philosophy at the University of Vienna and in 1849 moved to St. Petersburg and became a close friend of Anton Rubinstein, deputizing for him as a teacher and conductor – whence his famous quote "It is harder to play six bars well on the piano than to conduct the whole of the Ninth Symphony." He returned to Vienna in 1878 and lived and taught there until his death in 1915 at the age of eighty-eight. A monument was built to him in his lifetime. He left forty-nine compositions, among them two operas.[55] He destroyed a piano concerto he had composed because he thought it was not up to standard.

Leschetizky stressed complete concentration on the music and a thorough knowledge of every detail. He valued the quality of sound above everything else and did not demand long hours of practice. He was a mortal enemy of all pedantry and rigidity and thought these were typically Teutonic characteristics. His "special bugbear was the Berlin *Hochschule*," Mark wrote, "whose teaching he considered unprogressive and Philistine."

The Viennese, commented Artur Schnabel, considered the Germans "barbaric and boorish in comparison with the beauty, elegance and culture of the Viennese, with their charming (though empty) politeness – in the upper classes – and their soft speech. Nevertheless a niggling inferiority complex slightly disturbed their self-esteem."[56]

Leschetizky paid close attention to "moulding the hands to the contours of the keyboard"[57] and taught students tricks to make seemingly impossible passages easy. Sometimes it was just a matter of tilting the hand a little. He showed them how to play certain melodic passages on the black keys with flattened fingers. In the Chopin Scherzo in B flat minor he had pupils strike the high F – a fortissimo after a treacherous leap – with the tip of the fifth finger, with the hand held flat and used like an axe. He himself had thin bony hands like Liszt's, good for lightness and brilliance. Such hands should press the keys down, he found, caressing the notes to make them sing. Short fat hands, like Anton Rubinstein's, should be trained to exert as little pressure as possible.

Just as important as these musical and technical matters was his psychological approach. He studied intensively the individuality of every student and became much more involved in their personal lives than was customary in teacher-student relations, then and now. He was married four times, three out of four times – not surprisingly – to a student. (The first wife was a singer.)

Ossip Gabrilowitsch, who later married his fellow student Clara Clemens, one of Mark Twain's two daughters, found Leschetizky's close attention to the personal lives of his students admirable. They were all great individualists, he wrote. Leschetizky developed their musical and pianistic gifts "without destroying that which is more precious than anything else in art – individuality." Leschetizky had an *attitude*, he wrote, not a method. It was an "attitude towards music and indeed towards life itself."[58]

Artur Schnabel wrote, "He succeeded in releasing all the vitality and *élan* a student has in his nature, and would not tolerate any deviation of what he felt to be truthfulness of expression."[59]

In his first year Mark had one class-lesson a week, on Wednesdays at five. After the class everyone was invited to a supper party at Leschetizky's house, when there were more student performances.

Invitations to these parties were keenly sought, perhaps because sometimes they were occasions for high drama. A public performer, Leschetizky taught, had better get used to criticism. It was survival of the fittest. But to survive a Leschetizky outburst – not just criticism – one had to have a very thick skin. On one public occasion, Leschetizky "almost killed Mark Hambourg for playing bad at a concert."[60] (This Mark did not report.) On another, when a girl student displeased him, Leschetizky picked up the music and threw it on the floor. She then had to endure a diatribe lasting twelve minutes, witnessed by Mark Twain, who came to Vienna for extended periods of time to be with his daughter.[61]

A pupil of Leschetizky was Prinzessin Elisabeth zu Wied-Neuwied, a small principality near Koblenz, who was also a student of Clara Schumann. (We will meet her again as an old lady.) At one of his Wednesday soirées Leschetizky asked her to play Mendelssohn's Concerto in G minor. However much she worked on the concerto, she had trouble hitting the low D near the beginning. In her private class Leschetizky had her play it twenty times. At the soirée she missed it. Leschetizky became apoplectic – or pretended to. He ordered her out of his sight and declared he never wanted to see her again and she left the room in tears. Immediately afterwards she opened the door again, looked in and asked for forgiveness. Leschetizky threw a book at her. Then he declared to his guests that he hoped this would cure the girl of wanting to play in public. She would never overcome her stage fright and therefore would never be a pianist.[62] Leschetizky himself had been a great success in his youth as a performer, but as he got older he became so nervous that he had to give up playing in public because he could no longer face the footlights.[63]

The princess became Queen of Rumania instead of a pianist.[64]

Mark reported a contretemps of his own with Leschetizky. He had to learn a new piece each Wednesday. For his first class he played Beethoven's Sonata in C major, opus 2, no. 3. Leschetizky did not interrupt. When Mark had finished, he said, "You made hundred and twenty-two mistakes." Mark, who had been warned, was "disconcerted but not discouraged." Still, the time came for him to hit back.

Leschetizky had a formidable musical memory. On one occasion he played *by heart* – for Mark alone – Thalberg's Sonnambula Fantasia. He said he had not played it for fifty years. When he had finished he asked Mark what he thought of it. Mark said it was splendid but he had noticed "a few mistakes." Leschetizky had a spasm. He called him "impudent." As long as he was his pupil he, the teacher, *could not* make a mistake. That was all there was to it. He would not give him another lesson for a month.

Once, a girl – older and taller than Mark, who liked her – had a lesson ahead of him. He was waiting outside when suddenly the door was flung open. She was turning on the Professor in a white fury. Mark could not help seeing it. "To my horror," he reported, "and yes, I must confess to my fearful admiration, she seized him by the shoulders (a sacrilege which took my breath away), shook him thoroughly and cried: 'You rude, intolerable little man! If you were not so small and ridiculous I would throw you down the stairs for daring to speak to me like that! I would rather die than study with a creature like you!'"[65]

The family chosen for Mark to live with was the Kurzweils, evidently not as poor a family as Sergei Stepniak and Felix Moscheles had wished. They had a charming villa opposite Leschetizky's on the Carl Ludwig Strasse and became "rare friends who lavished goodness" on him. Their housekeeper, a virago named Hannah, had worked for Brahms. She slept on the ground floor and was a real terror. It was her job to lock the door at ten in the evening. She had strong views on the wickedness of young boys "which views she was in the habit of airing in the most forcible language." Leschetizky was just as frightened of her as Mark was when the two of them returned together late in the evening after playing billiards. But Leschetizky usually managed to calm her down "by pressing two shiny florins into her palm."

Once, there was a fancy-dress ball in the Redouten Saal. The dance was called *Siebter Himmel*, Seventh Heaven. A condition of admission was a "disguise as an immortal of sorts."[66] Leschetizky arranged to attend the ball, accompanied by some of his pupils dressed up as

The Brothers Hambourg

ERIC KOCH

ROBIN BRASS
Toronto

Passages from *Unfinished Journey* by Yehudi Menuhin Copyright © 1976 by Yehudi Menuhin and Patrick Seale and Associates Ltd. Reprinted by permission of Alfred A. Knopf Inc.

Excerpts from the works of George Bernard Shaw are reprinted by permission of The Society of Authors, on behalf of the Bernard Shaw estate.

We are grateful to the Trustees of the Savage Club in London for permission to publish material they made available to us.

Permission for quotations from the Vincent Massey Papers in the University of Toronto Archives has been granted by the Master and Fellows of Massey College, University of Toronto.

Copyright © Eric Koch 1997

All rights reserved. No part of this publication may be stored in a retrieval system, translated or reproduced in any form or by any means, photocopying, electronic or mechanical, without written permission of the publisher.

Published 1997 by Robin Brass Studio
10 Blantyre Avenue, Toronto, Ontario M1N 2R4, Canada
Fax: (416) 698-2120 / e-mail: rbrass@astral.magic.ca

Printed and bound in Canada by AGMV Marquis,
Cap-Saint-Ignace, Quebec

Canadian Cataloguing in Publication Data

Koch, Eric, 1919–
    The brothers Hambourg

Includes bibliographical references and index.
ISBN 1-896941-05-2

1. Hambourg family. 2. Musicians – Ontario – Toronto – Biography. 3. Hambourg Conservatory of Music. 4. Hart House String Quartet. I. Title.

ML395.K6 1997   780'.92'2713541   C97-931830-0

members of a heavenly fire brigade, "with himself as chief and most infinite Fireman." Mark wanted to take a pretty girl to the dance, but he had no money for the cab. It was unthinkable for him, dressed as a fireman, to take the girl to the ball by streetcar. The problem was still unsolved in the afternoon. But then the door bell rang. It was Hans Richter, who announced that Mark had just been awarded the Liszt scholarship of five hundred marks.[67] On the strength of the new collateral Richter advanced the money.

At Hans Richter's invitation Mark frequently attended orchestra rehearsals at the Grosse Musikverein, where he often saw Brahms. The rehearsals took place in the morning. Brahms usually sat in the same box to the left of the conductor's desk, in a characteristic attitude "with his leonine head sunk on his elbows."

"All eyes were fixed on him," Mark wrote, "for he was the most arresting figure in musical Vienna at that time."[68] In due course, they met. Brahms once gave Mark a small cigar cutter which he treasured all his life. Many years later, he went to see a film about Schumann, with Arthur Rubinstein playing Schumann's piano music and Katherine Hepburn impersonating Clara. He was surprised to see in the film the young Brahms "depicted as nursing with expertise and tenderness Schumann's first baby! Nothing could have been less like the Brahms I knew later. He must have changed a lot through the ages!"[69]

In April 1894 Mark was paid for the first time for playing at a private concert. The occasion was a party in the magnificent, art-filled palace of Prince Pallavicini. He received gold pieces, which his mother set in a brooch.

In 1895 the time came for Mark to make his proper début. So Leschetizky said, and so did his father in London. This was duly arranged. In March he performed Chopin's Concerto in E minor with the Vienna Philharmonic under Hans Richter.

Even the virago Hannah shared the excitement before the concert.. He had no *toilette de cérémonie* – tails – and no money. The eldest Kurzweil son lent him his outfit, but it was much too large, so there was much emergency sewing and squeezing.

The debut was followed by several concerts. At a recital in the Bösendorfer Saal he played the piano part in the Septet by Hummel with the celebrated Rosé Quartet and two other musicians. Rosé's wife, Justine, was the sister of Gustav Mahler.

But these concerts, however well received, were insignificant preliminaries to the great event, on April 3, 1895. He was still asleep at seven in the morning when an agent asked him to appear *that evening* at a concert of the visiting Berlin Philharmonic. It was Gala Week in Vienna, and the soloist – Sophie Menter, famous for her robust, electrifying style, and a great favourite of Liszt, was suddenly indisposed. Mark was to play Liszt's Hungarian Fantasia under the conductor Felix Weingartner, the *Kapellmeister* of the Berlin Opera among other things and the man who in 1908 was to succeed Gustav Mahler at the Vienna Court Opera. Leschetizky had recommended Mark to the agent because he was the only one of his pupils who could play the required Fantasia. The performance was a huge success. After the concert the organizers of the Gala gave a banquet which Brahms attended. He proposed a toast to the "youth who had played at that evening's concert."[70]

Mark had made history and was now ready to return to London. He paid Leschetizky a farewell visit

"I have a little present for you before you go," Leschetizky said, and gave him a purse containing all the money Mark had paid him since his arrival three years earlier. "You will need it more than I do. I have kept it for you all this time, to prove my affection and interest, and my regard for your future career."[71]

After his return to London in the spring of 1895, "this Russian lad" was at last "ready to astonish the world," just as Shaw had predicted when Mark was ten. He was sixteen now and it could no longer be said that he did not "seem to be exactly in the way of getting it at present." After the rigorous but uplifting Leschetizky school and his recent triumphs in Vienna with Hans Richter and Felix Weingartner, "getting it" was no longer the problem. Making money was – for himself and for his family. After all, his two promising brothers, Jan and Boris, needed an education, and his father's income was meagre.

Mark – in his own words "very small, very thin, very weedy, but full of youthful fire" – was practising in the studio of the piano-makers Erard's in Great Marlborough Street when two men arrived, the skinny Australian P.D. Howell and the rotund C.D. Stevens from Birmingham. They were agents looking for a pianist to join two well known singers on a concert tour to Australia. Mark's (and Paderewski's) agent Daniel Mayer had recommended him. One of the singers was Evangeline Florence, who had a lovely voice and shared with May Yohe the distinction of being able to reach high notes normally attainable only by "the cry of the bat" – she later married the owner of the Hope Diamond. The other singer was the red-haired Fanny Moody, who in 1892 had sung Tatiana in the first English performance of *Eugene Onegin* at the Olympic Theatre in London. Mark was offered four hundred pounds, which seemed an enormous sum to him, and expenses. On June 28, 1895, they sailed on board the SS *Orient*, after he had been less than two months in London, "amidst the lamentations of my mother who thought I was going far beyond the limits of the civilized globe, and the rejoicings of my father, who felt that I should return with my fortune made!" He stayed away until the end of November.

Mark enjoyed his first world tour so much that in the decades to come a long string of others would follow, often to areas where no European performer of classical Western music had ever been. Few, if any, other pianists of his stature were as enterprising. Perhaps they did not have his appetite for travel, his curiosity, his generous love of people, his jovial good humour – nor, of course, his stamina.

A constant problem throughout his career as a world-touring virtuoso was the supply of first-class pianos. Erard's sent five pianos along with him on his Australian tour – the first of four – and sold them all. Later, in 1921, Steinway's sent four or five pianos with him to South Africa, and also sold out. Blüthner supplied him with pianos all over the continent of Europe, while in North Africa and Egypt the French piano-makers Pleyel and Gavreau usually supplied him with excellent instruments.[72]

When he first went to Australia he was only fifteen, "surely," he wrote, "the youngest boy to go so far afield alone for a concert tour." In Sydney he joined the Star Concert Company for twelve appearances. Then, after the two singers had gone home, he gave his own recitals and earned his first big money.[73]

Any musician of any standing in Australia, he reported, was either a *Herr* or a *Signor*. One of his press notices identified him as Herr Hambourg of Boguchar in South Prussia, and on one occasion a German of twenty-five challenged him to a fist fight on the grounds that Mark had flirted with his fiancée. Mark pleaded that he was underage, regarding both flirting and fist-fighting. He also met a German piano-teacher who took the view that his elementary pupils should be given the most difficult pieces first; the rest would follow. Instead of five-finger exercises and Czerny studies, he gave them Beethoven's Sonata opus 111 and Liszt rhapsodies. Mark was amazed to discover that this teacher "turned out some very good students."

He played mainly in towns and saw little of the country. Only during his second and third tours did he learn to enjoy the amenities of the big sheep stations and the free wild life on horseback of the Australian Outback, admittedly only as a spectator.

The first thing Mark did on his return to London was to give solo recitals in the old St. James's Hall, as well as several concerts with orchestras, among them the Philharmonia Society. *The Times* referred to him as "the clever young pianist who has lately returned from a successful tour in Australia,"[74] and the *Daily Mail* observed that "Mr. Hambourg has made a considerable mark in Australia, but the eulogies of the *Sydney Bulletin* do not appear to have spoiled him. He is earnest, free from affectation – which is saying a great deal for the average pianist."[75] The *Morning Post* wrote that Mr. Hambourg "is entitled to aspire to a high rank among contemporary pianists, and this he will surely in time attain."[76]

Mark played in Saint-Saëns Piano Quartet opus 41 at the Monday "Pops" with the sixty-four-year-old violinist Joseph Joachim and the seventy-three-year-old cellist Alfredo Piatti, both venerable superstars. (The name of the violist is not readily available.) Joachim lost his place in the intricate fugato because, as he explained, "he did not know much about this modern music."[77] Later, Mark barely avoided bumping into Piatti with his bicycle in Hammersmith. When Piatti noticed who it was who had nearly killed him, he said, "Boy, learn to ride your bicycle more slowly and your scales more quickly."[78]

At this time, Mark became interested in composing. He made friends with Clarence Lucas (1866-1947), who most likely was the first Canadian he met. Lucas was one of the most versatile and prolific Canadian composers born in the nineteenth century. He dedicated his Prelude and Fugue, opus 38, to Mark, and Leschetizky pronounced it the best modern fugue written for piano. Mark often included the work in his recitals and it is singled out in some of his reviews, both in England and during his first American and Canadian tours. Evidently, Lucas was an eclectic, competent composer whose style cannot be compared to any one particular contemporary. The fugue Mark played so often may well have been his best piece.

Mark studied composition with Lucas and in due course began composing himself, pieces which he later published and which he played in concerts, often as encores, including his Variations on a Theme by Paganini, *Volkslied, Espièglerie* (Mischief) and *Impromptu Minuet.*

Clarence Lucas (about whom we shall hear more in the next chapter) also became a friend of Jan Hambourg. He was almost forgotten until May 26, 1997, when, according to a press release, "a new old composer burst on the Canadian music scene." In a ceremony in Ottawa, his family gave some three hundred and fifty of his manuscripts to the National Library of Canada. They had been gathering dust in their homes in England and France.

Before setting out for Australia again in 1897, this time with his fifteen-year-old brother Jan, Mark performed on the continent, in Brussels and in Berlin, where Hermann Wolff, in Mark's view the greatest concert impresario in Europe, took him on. Wolff was Anton Rubinstein's agent. Rubinstein had heard Mark play at Leschetizky's in Vienna and had spoken to Wolff about him. Who would be more suited for the German market than Mark Hambourg, obviously a younger version of the immensely popular Anton Rubinstein, who was a late-century concert-hall version of Ludwig van Beethoven himself? However, the stuffy and chauvinistic (Mark's word) German musical public did not take to him. To explain this in his memoirs, he quoted an article which had appeared in the German paper *Der Montag*:

> Berlin is the Monte Carlo of the virtuosi. The amount of money that is lost here in piano playing is incredible! The most celebrated virtuosi meet with defeat when they come to Berlin! Paderewski does not play any more in Berlin, neither does Hofmann, and Kubelik vanished after he had given one concert. Hambourg and Rosenthal did not seem to do much better! An inverse ratio: the more celebrated the artist, the greater the failure.[79]

Two experiences are worth reporting from Mark's second Australian tour. His manager was the remarkable Greek flutist John Lemmone, the best flutist Mark had ever heard. Lemmone used to play flute obbligatos to Nellie Melba, and the result was "exquisite."[80] Secondly, he met Mark Twain, who was on a lecture tour.

They must have met before in Vienna, where Mark Hambourg and Twain's future son-in-law, Ossip Gabrilowitsch, studied together with Leschetizky. This time, they met at the Yorick Club in Melbourne on the day of Mark's concert, which Twain intended to attend. The latter was looking for his seat in the concert hall just as Mark was coming on the stage. The public began applauding. Twain took the plaudits as a compliment to himself, smiled and bowed to the audience while Mark, unaware of Twain, bowed to the audience as well, from the stage. "I must say," Mark observed, "he sat down hurriedly and began studying the program with minute attention, leaving me master of the situation!"

Mark met Twain again in Vienna in the following year, in 1898. He had gone there to study again with Leschetizky, having first spent a few months in London after his return from Australia. Twain was staying with his daughter Clara Clemens. "I was by no means the only young man in Vienna," Ossip Gabrilowitsch wrote in his memoirs, "whose head was turned and whose heart sorely needed mending. Leschy, with his usual keenness, quickly sized up the situation and made a witty remark to a group of young fellows gathered about him: 'Boys,' he said, 'it seems to me that you are all suffering from the same trouble – Delirium Clemens.'"[81]

Mark was often invited to Twain's quarters in the Hotel Metropole for lavish meals, together with other artists. While they ate, Twain sometimes walked around the table, sipping a glass of red wine, telling stories in his slow drawl. Sometimes he sang "queer old river songs of the Mississippi" while strumming on the piano. He sounded "like a dog howling," Mark reported. Twain smoked cigars known as "twofers" – two for five cents, he explained to his Viennese guests. On Sundays he would relax and give Mark a Rosa di Santiago, his favourite smoke. In a letter of introduction addressed to a Mrs. Laffen, Twain wrote that Mark had "more musical ability than I have, but not as good a complexion."[82]

During the summer Mark visited Leschetizky in the resort Bad Ischl. Leschy was spending much of his time playing the card game Tarok with Brahms and Johann Strauss, "a jolly old fellow, full of the peculiar Viennese sparkling gaiety which he so well imparted in his compositions." Brahms, Mark reported, was "often grumpy." It was the last year of his life.

At the end of October 1898 Mark arrived in New York for his first American tour. He was struck immediately by the importance of advertising. Piano firms "fought for possession of the artists," and the success of the pianist depended more on the advertising efforts of his supporting piano firm than on his intrinsic merits. Knabe was the firm which had got possession of him, and he took his Knabe with him everywhere, as well as Heinrich Hochmann, the delightful tuner who often slept with the instrument to make sure that no harm came to it. He played in New York with the Boston Symphony Orchestra under William Gericke. This was before conductors were treated as stars, and often Gericke's name was not mentioned in the program.

He also played with the Kneisel Quartet, in his view the finest string quartet at the time. In New York he stayed at the Hotel Martin, where the Café Martin served excellent dinners for $1.25 a person. People stood in queues waiting to get in. "I could not help reflecting sadly," Mark wrote, "that I saw no such queues for our good concert fare."

In the Middle West he was impressed by the pioneering efforts of the Chicago Orchestra under its veteran conductor Theodore Thomas. However, he took a dim view of the big hotel in Chicago, the Auditorium, which struck him as "no better than a second-class boarding house." In Pittsburgh, Victor Herbert, "the remarkable cellist who also excelled in the writing of musical comedy," rescued him from a hotel where some time earlier, "the local bishop had fallen through its lift, owing to his great weight."

In San Francisco – this was before the 1906 earthquake – there was a general feeling of "devil-may-care and cowboy gallantry" in the air, and an eccentric Englishman of his acquaintance "rode his fiery steed fifty steps up the staircase of the smart club for a bet." The Palace Hotel was grand in the extreme to the outward eye but its sanitary arrangements were "primitive" and its cleanliness "doubtful." In Los Angeles there had been a calamitous flood and only three piano students attended the concert. They spread the word that Mark had played the whole program just for them. A day or two later he gave another performance. The whole city turned up.

Mark wrote that, back in London, he met Lenin, but he was confused about the dates. Mark wrote that he met him in the summer of 1899, at the height of the Boer War. At that time Uncle Lix's – Felix Moscheles's – studio on Church Street in Chelsea was a meeting place for opponents of the war, and Lenin certainly would have fitted in. Lenin, Mark wrote, had just arrived from Sweden, where he had been attending a big socialist congress. Lenin had run out of money, and the soap-millionaire Fels had advanced him enough to reach England. But Mark's memory was flawed when it came to the timing. According to Lenin's biographer Louis Fischer, Lenin was in London in May 1907 to attend the Congress of the Russian Socialist Party. The delegates ran out of money and Joseph Fels of Philadelphia helped them out.[83]

Uncle Lix lost many of his friends through his uncompromisingly pacifist opposition to the Boer War. When he spoke to crowds in Trafalgar Square he looked "the absolute personification of goodness and benevolence," but on one occasion somebody hurled a brick at him. Among his guests on Sunday afternoons was the young Ramsay MacDonald, Gladstone's son Herbert (an amateur cellist), a Belgian lawyer who was among the first to make a case for an International Court of Justice, and – again – the idealistic steel magnate Andrew Carnegie, who listened solemnly to Mark's playing, though Mark did not think he knew a lot about music. If Carnegie had met Lenin in Uncle's Lix's studio, and if Mark had remembered what was said, the exchanges might have been an inspiring source for Tom Stoppard, who in his play *Travesties* invented a similarly incongruous gathering in 1917 between Lenin, James Joyce and the Dadaist Tristan Tzara when the three men happened to be in Zürich at the same time.

Another event had more lasting consequences for Mark than the encounter with Lenin. In August 1901, Mark met the forty-three-year-old Belgian Eugène Ysaÿe, the pioneer of twentieth-century violin-playing. The composer-pianist Ferruccio Busoni[84] was to play a series of joint recitals with him at the Glasgow Exhibition, but he fell ill. Mark was asked to help out.

One of the many consequences of this last-minute arrangement was Mark's marriage six years later to a student of Ysaÿe's. Another consequence was that, more than a quarter of a century later, in 1928, Mark's brother Boris invited Ysaÿe's daughter Carrie, a pianist and a singer who was married to the Hungarian violinist and engineer Erwin Harisay, to open a studio of her own at the Hambourg Conservatory in Toronto. Carrie returned to Belgium early in 1931 to be with her father, who was mortally ill, but it was too late – he died before she arrived. She herself had not been well when she left Toronto and died soon after her father. Her four daughters are still living in or near Toronto.[85]

In 1901, Ysaÿe, revered by Kreisler, Thibaud, Szigeti, Enesco and many others, was in his prime. He had played the violin since he was four. In 1882, when he was twenty-four, he studied with Henri Vieuxtemps[86] in Paris and received Joachim's enthusiastic praise. Then he toured Scandinavia with Anton Rubinstein and subsequently gave concerts with him in Russia. From 1883 to 1886 he lived in Paris and formed close ties with César Franck, Ernest Chausson, Vincent d'Indy, Gabriel Fauré, Camille Saint-Saëns and Claude Debussy, becoming an ardent interpreter of their violin music. Franck dedicated his Violin Sonata to him, Chausson his *Poême* and Concerto, and Debussy his String Quartet. In Glasgow, Mark performed with Ysaÿe the Franck Sonata, and they also played Beethoven's Kreutzer Sonata.

The twenty-two-year-old Mark and Ysaÿe had a great time together. After their first recital in Glasgow they went on tour in the English provinces. One day, when they wanted to catch an early train back to London, they played the Kreutzer Sonata in the record time of thirty minutes. Another great event was a concert in the Queen's Hall attended by King Edward VII and Queen Alexandra, the first time royalty had been at a concert there on a Sunday afternoon. The hall was sold out. The doorkeeper suggested the two men climb up to the organ loft. They did so and made themselves comfortable. Suddenly the door was thrown open and a man dashed in. "Do you mind," he said in some agitation, "if I stand in front of you?" It was a detective who had taken them as dangerous anarchists. Perhaps somebody had overheard Mark's Russian accent.

A little later, Queen Alexandra heard Mark play in Lady de Grey's lovely villa in Kingston-on-Thames. "The Queen," Mark observed, "was reputed to be deaf but she seemed to take a real musical interest in what I played, as though she both heard and enjoyed it. She continually asked that I should perform special pieces of which she was fond. Altogether she showed surprising knowledge of pianoforte literature." Mark was often engaged to play in "smart society" but found it had little influence on the musical life of London. Its members, he wrote, were not sufficiently serious – they only wanted their "patronage fanned by continuous flattery."

He also spent a good deal of time in Paris, where a friend initiated him into the art of good living. He frequented the salon of Madame

Dorian Menard in the rue de la Faisanderie. Before her marriage she had been a friend of Manet, who, whenever he was hard up, sold her one of his paintings for very little. As a result she had a magnificent collection of his masterpieces. In her salon he also met Colonel Picquart, the head of the Information Branch of the Ministry of War, who was playing an important role in the Dreyfus affair. He had informed his superiors that he was convinced of Dreyfus's innocence, but they were unwilling to reopen the proceedings. Madame Menard's guests, most of whom sympathized with Dreyfus and admired Emile Zola's courage, "crowded around Picquart and hung on his words, hoping to hear him divulge something which they could spread abroad among their friends, and thus acquire prestige as being in the 'know'." On the other hand, at the house of the Marquise St. Paul, Mark met Colonel Marchand "of Fashoda fame" – Fashoda was the conflict in 1898 between France and England over Sudan – "who inflamed passions to boiling point by his constant cry of *À bas les Juifs!* (Down with the Jews!)"

The Marquise St. Paul was an amateur pianist. Once she played for Anton Rubinstein and asked him what he thought of it.

"Do you want my opinion of your playing as marquise or as a pianist?" he asked.

"As a pianist, most certainly, *Maître*," she replied.

"Then, madame, I am sorry to have to tell you that you play very badly indeed."

Another time the marquise insisted on playing for Saint-Saëns. When she started playing for him he whispered audibly *"Merde!"*

To mollify the wounded marquise Saint-Saëns had to compose for her a long set of variations for two pianos.

During his second North American tour in the winter of 1902-1903, Mark played for President Teddy Roosevelt at a concert in the White House. A member of the audience asked the president, after Mark had played a piece, whether he knew who the composer was.

"I do not know who it was," Mr. Roosevelt replied, "but it was something which he has made himself."

Nothing was interesting to the president, Mark explained, which was not an act of personal creation. The president was very cordial to him, radiating vigour of character.

At his farewell recital in New York on February 24, 1903, Mark played the Prelude and Fugue by Clarence Lucas, the Fantasia by Schumann, six preludes, a nocturne and the Berceuse by Chopin, Valse in A flat by Anton Rubinstein, his own Variations on a Theme by Paganini, *A Midsummer Night's Dream* by Mendelssohn-Liszt and some small pieces.

The *Musical Courier* wrote:

> The young Russian pianist has never here displayed himself to better advantage than he did in the Schumann Fantasia. The first movement was broad in conception, dignified in form and impassioned in execution. There were moments that must have surprised those who have hitherto classed Hambourg as a mere technician. The tremendous middle section was taken with large grasp and temperament, culminating in a rousing climax with the difficult finale. The skips usually prove a technical Waterloo for pianists, but Hambourg climbed over most of the peaks with safety. The only infallible performance of that tricky finale ever heard in New York was given by the sorcerer Rosenthal. The last movement of the Fantasia revealed Hambourg as a tasteful master of tone and of the pedal. The Chopin Nocturne was not over sentimentalized. Indeed, on this side of the musical ledger Hambourg rarely errs. He always preserves a sane balance between rhythm and rubato. The Preludes were one and all delightful, and several had to be repeated. In the F major number there was a variation from the conventional tempo, but the piece seemed to lose neither its outline nor its charm. The B flat minor Prelude induced demonstrative applause.
>
> Hambourg's own variations are musical and full of technical tracery. Their brevity is also greatly in their favour. The day of the inordinately long piano piece is about over. Hambourg promises well as a composer, and should be heard from more frequently in this direction.

The "virtuoso" numbers were dashed off with all of Hambourg's accustomed brilliancy and spirit. Applause was insistent and the encores were many. Hambourg's playing always arouses discussion. That is a good sign.[87]

In his memoirs, Mark did not mention his first visit to Toronto. In the chapter on concert halls and audiences, however, he wrote that "Massey Hall, Toronto, though far too large for solo playing, is held in high esteem by the Canadians, who, being accustomed to wide expanses, do not find them bleak when listening to music."[88]

The Toronto *Mail and Empire* wrote:

Mark Hambourg, the great Russian pianist, played a brilliant program in Massey Hall last evening, it being his second appearance this season. The audience was not large, but it was most appreciative, and the virtuoso could have no complaint at the warmth of his reception.

No words could adequately describe the infinite variety of Hambourg's playing. Although the very embodiment of power, and a technician of unexampled ability, he is nevertheless an artist in expression and in his playing of Schumann's dreamy *Des Abends* [from *Fantasiestücke*, opus 12] he showed the poetic temperament and a perfect legato touch. His penchant, however, is for stormy chords and crashing fortissimos....[89]

All Mark wrote about this tour was that it was very long and that by the time he reached the Pacific Coast he did not want ever to see a piano again. From there he went on to Hawaii, where he was lavishly entertained by the "short, fat and ugly" Queen Liliuokalani, the last Hawaiian monarch, who had been at his White House concert and naturally had to compete with Teddy Roosevelt. The Queen, he was told, had the heads cut off ladies of the court on whom her seafaring European husband had "cast his roving eye." From Honolulu he continued his journey to Australia and New Zealand, where he was impressed by the geysers and thermal waters. He envied "the natives their natural solution to the economic problems connected with heating and cooking."

When he returned to England he found that violinists were at a premium but the stock of pianists was low. At evenings in London society he recalled that he sometimes played the works of the gifted young composer Baron Frédéric d'Erlanger,[90] a rich man about town, and could not help wondering whether, if he was given a choice, he might not prefer to exchange his life, with its "aesthetically satisfying uncertainty," with that of a prosperous business man.

Late in 1903 he gave concerts in Poland and Russia. He had an especially enjoyable time in Warsaw, being entertaining by Countess Potocki, the star of Polish society, whose loveliness was so disturbing that if she was at a concert and the performer had "the good or the bad fortune" to see her, he would certainly forget what he was doing. Mark was spared such humiliation. Her husband the count was reputed to have lost more money at baccarat than anyone had ever done before. The dinner the countess gave for him was served on gold plates by a hundred retainers, but the petit-point chairs on which the guests sat were full of holes and the gorgeous carpets threadbare.

At a musical party in Moscow Mark met another countess – Countess Tolstoy. She invited him to a family party at her house. He was thrilled at the prospect of meeting her famous husband. When he went there, Tolstoy was embroidering, not speaking a word to anyone. No one among his family took the slightest notice of him. "Such is the fate of great men," Mark concluded, "in the bosom of their homes!" Mark was too timid to speak to him without encouragement. "I do not know how much he was interested in music."[91]

In Moscow, where he performed Rubinstein's Concerto in D minor – it was his first trip back since he left thirteen years earlier – Mark met some people who remembered him. He toured with the Spanish diva Maria Gay, who had made a sensation in the operatic world "with her virile [sic] performance of *Carmen*."[92] When she sang with Mark in Paris, she was generally escorted by three extremely handsome brothers, all young, all tall, all three with powerful hands. "They proved a valuable asset," Mark recalled, "for they were the best unpaid *claque* imaginable, and whether our concerts were full or not we had the agreeable impression that there was a large and enthusiastic audience whenever the brothers Gay came to hear their sister sing."[93]

In Brussels a few months later – by now it was 1904 – he played the Tchaikovsky Concerto in B flat minor and the Saint-Saëns Concerto in C minor, with Ysaÿe conducting. (On a subsequent occasion in Brussels, when he played Beethoven's Concerto in C minor, Ysaÿe was so absorbed in the beauty of the music that he forgot to continue conducting and just stood there, raptly listening.) Brussels, Mark wrote, was a delightful city in those early years of the century. From there he went on to Berlin and renewed his friendship with Ferruccio Busoni, spending much time with him in his splendid library. Mark was struck by Busoni's musical memory – he knew by heart every work of Liszt and most of the compositions of Bach. Busoni only went out at night, to sit in cafés, smoking heavy cigars, and to wander about the streets "like Haroun at Rashid," looking for adventure. His interest in music was entirely intellectual, Mark observed. The grandiloquence of Liszt and the majestic structure of Bach appealed to him, while he found the romanticism of Schumann and Chopin distasteful. Mark was proud that Busoni dedicated his Second Sonatina to him, "for he was such an apostle of the unusual that any sign of appreciation from his keen and critical mind was a thing to be valued."

In Frankfurt he met Percy Grainger[94] and Cyril Scott,[95] who were studying at the Hoch Konservatorium, as were his brothers Jan and Boris, aged twenty-two and twenty. The five of them made music and "had adventures together." Mark neglects to tell us what kind of adventures.

Later that year he played with the violinist Jacques Thibaud[96] at the Salzburg Festival, which was held in honour of Mozart, though only one work of Mozart's was performed. The festival had not yet attained the glory of its peak in the thirties under Bruno Walter, Clemens Krauss, Arturo Toscanini and Wilhelm Furtwängler. Jacques Thibaud is perhaps best remembered as the violinist in the great Thibaud-Cortot-Casals Trio.

On March 16, 1945, two months before the end of the Second World War, Mark's sister Luba, who was living with Jan in London, wrote to their younger brother Clement in Toronto:

> We have been entertaining Jacques Thibaud – he visited direct from Paris and stayed about a month. He is a *very* great player and do tell Boris better than ever, although he looks worn and weary after five years of Paris and having lost a son killed in fighting. His pianist Tasso Janopoulo is a darling and we all had a glorious time – Tasso becoming a very good friend and Jacques the charmer as ever.[97]

By 1904, Mark informs us in his memoirs, his father had acquired a comfortable house in London, where at monthly musical evenings he entertained his students, friends and "most artists of note who happened to be in town. Every section of society came to these gatherings, as my father had the talent for collecting people around him, and was also able to provide interesting music for their enjoyment. Anyone who had a new composition to present was sure of a sympathetic and attentive audience at my father's parties."

These social events were a considerable achievement since the professor's income was uneven, even though, according to one of his obituaries,[98] he had already in London named his teaching studio the Hambourg Conservatory of Music. He also taught at the London Academy and the Guildhall School of Music. Still, it is likely that without Mark's help it would have been impossible for the family to achieve a respectable standard of living. There were even times when the family did not have enough money to buy proper food.[99] The professor's children learned at an early age that keeping up appearances was more important than living within your means if you wanted to get ahead.

In December 1904 a long article by William Armstrong appeared in *The Étude* entitled "Professor Michael Hambourg on the Modern Pianist and his Art." It is apparent that by "modern pianist" Professor Hambourg meant his son Mark.

It is to Professor Hambourg that the career of his son, the pianist, is largely due. From the outset, he not only carefully watched his development and directed it, but impressed him with the fact that no matter how well he did a thing, he might still do it better. He believes, too, that music is too live and vital an art to be stopped by any bonds of convention, and because a thing has never been done before is no reason for its not being good.

The home life of the Hambourgs is an ideally happy one. They live in a big, old-fashioned house in St. John's Wood, London. It opens at the back on to a large garden. There, father and sons, three of them musicians – pianist, violinist, and 'cellist – have their walks and talks on music, so many brothers in their relations with each other.

It was there that Professor Hambourg talked with me on *the Modern Pianist and his Art.* He was spending his vacation at home, "Because," as he explained, "I am a year behind in my reading: this is the only chance I have to catch up." This reading, as it turned out, was not only on music, but on all that had gone on in the world and its advancement during the months that teaching had kept him in the studio.

Our conversation touched mainly on the things that go to constitute a good technic; the best way to apply to our own needs the teaching of great pianists; the difference between the teacher and the concert performer, and attitudes towards the public.

"The word *Technic* is too often looked upon wrongly," he said, after we had got comfortably seated under a big tree in the garden, the house back of us in unusual quiet for the three sons were just then making chamber music with Ysaÿe in Brussels. "Many look upon *Technic* merely as runs, but that is a very small part of it. *Technic* is the sum total of the means of execution: tone production, beautiful quality, equality and modulation of it in hundreds of shades, and velocity. Taken all together, that is *Technic*....

"Having all these means, and coming to the highest step, Interpretation, you have to follow the course of the good actor. That is to say, you must first read the composition through, then analyze every beat, and try to find its meaning. That is really what the actor does: he learns to pronounce his words so that he can be heard in a great hall; and to modulate his voice in difference shades; then he tries to put into those words the exact sense of each, to express it in the fullest and clearest.

"On these lines the modern pianist must work. In his playing he tries to give a thought which carries through the biggest space, always endeavouring to make the tone beautiful.

"Now what is beautiful tone? Many call beautiful tone what is not beautiful. The old pianist did not use big *fortes* and big climaxes. He thought these things ugly. The pianist of the old school looked upon music as a means to tickle the ear, and the more softly he played, and the less sense he put into it, the more he was considered a dreamy player.

"I remember that here in London, fifteen years ago, when that style of playing was in vogue, every third or fourth man in the audience at a popular concert was asleep. If an interpreter with more fire happened along the public peace was disturbed, and critics cried out 'How dare he do that in music?'

"Now, the modern pianist is quite another proposition. He tries more or less to present a problem that is in his mind. Consequently he uses all the means in his execution as a great actor would in the drama he is playing. That is why the modern pianist uses big climaxes and big contrasts, giving way to his temperament, hurrying, dragging, making pauses where none are written. Everything that he does he does to express the emotion that feels in the moment. For that reason the very great pianist will never repeat a thing the same way.

"Take Rubinstein, for instance. He never played a thing twice alike, even on the same evening. The mood of the great artist is so changeable that he may think one way now and five minutes later he will think differently. The ultra-orthodox say that he is extravagant, that he has too much originality, or that he changes the composer. That is nonsense.

"The strangest part of the situation is that the same orthodox musician will see five different actors on as many occasions play an identical role, and play it quite differently. The one plays the role one way, the other another; yet the ultra-orthodox musician grants the actor his freedom of thought, while he denies it to the pianist.

"Orchestral conductors are allowed the same privilege. Richter, Weingartner, Mottl and Nikisch each give a different reading to Beethoven's Fifth Symphony and yet each will be accepted as beautiful. Now, if a pianist plays a work in a manner that is admired and liked, why not recognize his right to freedom of thought and individuality? To play like so many do and send the audience to sleep required no great talent; but to play like Rubinstein or Paderewski requires not only talent, but genius."

On June 18, 1906, in the Queen's Hall, Mark gave his one thousandth public performance. After that, he embarked on his first South African tour, for which he received a thousand pounds expenses, plus fifty percent gross – always, he was discovering, a better arrangement than a straight lump fee. After the first three concerts in Cape Town his manager had already made enough to cover Mark's thousand-pound expenses. There were no orchestras in South Africa yet, and people flocked to hear Beethoven and Chopin played on the piano. He played in the new City Hall, with the scaffolding still up, without roof and without doors. In one month he gave nineteen recitals in ten towns, travelling with his piano from Cape Town to Natal and back. The railways, he wrote, were remarkably comfortable, even though it was so soon after the Boer War. There were scarcely any roads; you either went by rail or "by animals." In Johannesburg, still an overgrown mining village, he stayed in the pleasant home of a kind friend, Sir William van Holstein, where he had many merry evenings, making music and playing poker, and performed in an enormous skating rink called Wanderer's Hall. Twelve "Kaffirs" hoisted the piano on the platform, "straining, grunting and groaning." Evidently, the piano had not been sold this time; on the way home it was nearly dropped in the sea in the port of East London as it was being hoisted from the tug to the liner, and one black man tumbled overboard. No one made the slightest effort to rescue him, however much Mark protested. "Either he'll swim and get ashore, or he won't," he quotes an English shipping hand. "It isn't worth worrying about. One more or less of them kind, what's the difference?"

Two years later Mark went to South Africa again – with his new wife.

In the summer of 1907 Mark fell in love with Dolly. He was visiting his brother Jan, who was studying the violin with Ysaÿe, as Dolly was, at his summer school in the village of Godinne-sur-Meuse in the Belgian Ardennes. Students and artists from all over the world flocked there to attend Ysaÿe's master classes. The place "was racked from morning to night by the strains of Vieuxtemps concerti, while the studies of Kreutzer and the Chaconne of Bach pealed from every cottage window – the cacophony was complete!" In the evenings, the students assembled at Ysaÿe's house, where he conducted them in impromptu orchestras and chamber ensembles. Visiting artists – Mark, for one – often performed with the students.

"La Dolly" lodged in the house of the village shoemaker, who was also the village poacher. "Many a succulent meal of game did I enjoy in that cottage stimulated by the pangs of love.... It was indeed a perfect setting for an artist's romance."

Dolly was the daughter of the sixty-two-year-old Sir Kenneth Muir Mackenzie, Permanent Principal Secretary to the Lord Chancellor and Clerk of the Crown in Chancery. Later, at his retirement in 1915, having been the right-hand man of five successive lord chancellors, Muir Mackenzie was created a peer. His wife, Amy, had died in 1900. She was the daughter of William Graham, MP for Glasgow and a noted art collector who had commissioned his great friend the pre-Raphaelite painter Burne-Jones to design a Broadwood piano with "a lovely light wood case, elegant in shape and covered all over with a pattern of leaves and flowers in raised gesso work and gilded ornamentations." The piano – later in the Hambourg house – survived the Blitz when Mark thought "every bomb was coming straight for it." It is now in the Birmingham Museum.

William Graham's wife – Dolly's grandmother – was, Mark believed, the first woman to bring a grand piano to Africa, when it was carried on the heads of Arabs across the Isthmus of Suez, for shipment to India, thus anticipating Mark's pianistic pioneering.[100]

Mark went to see his future father-in-law, a true Victorian "at a time when practically all musicians were addressed as *Signor* by the ruling classes and dimly connected in their minds with Italian street-organ grinders." Muir Mackenzie said he was delighted his daughter was bringing a musician into the family. "But at the same time I must tell you that you must not expect my friends to be your friends."

Things did not turn out that way. He and Mark formed a warm relationship, and so did many of Muir Mackenzie's friends – "bishops, cabinet ministers, lord chancellors, diplomats, generals, heroes, and Mr. Winston Churchill as a young man."[101]

Dolly's father lived with the Hambourg family from the beginning of the First World War until his death at the age of eighty-four in 1930. He never missed a London concert of Mark's. He had a deep love of music, "and an insight," Mark wrote, "which was an inspiration to me."

Two months after they were married, Mark and Dolly sailed for his second South African tour, two years after the first. At one of his concerts in Cape Town he started to play Schumann's Fantasia. In the second movement he wandered off into the *Faschingsschwank aus Wien*. As far as he could tell, only Dolly noticed, and she was horrified. From now on his public and private mistakes, anxieties, triumphs and tribulations were shared. For Dolly, the world revolved around Mark. It was, from beginning to end, an excellent marriage.

In South Africa, they travelled together to many remote places where, in his words, the hoofmarks of hippopotami were freshly minted in the mud of the dripping woods and where he would not have been in the least surprised to see Dr. Livingston emerge from the undergrowth, dressed in the skins of wild beasts, saying, "Mark Hambourg, I presume."

Mark was in the United States when the first of their four daughters was born. While he was in New York his mother arrived on some family business. He had to leave her while he went on a short tour with the highly successful violinist Jan Kubelik, who was travelling in great state with a servant and numerous secretaries, accompanists and helpers of various kind, playing among other pieces – what else? – the Kreutzer Sonata.[102] Mark told his mother to order whatever she wanted. He would settle her account when he returned, but "my mother was a thrifty Russian woman with the selflessness of the best kind of simplicity. The extravagance and luxury of the American hotel seemed wicked to her, and when I came to look at the bill she had incurred for food during the three or four days I had been away, I found the whole amount did not come to more than one dollar ten cents!"[103]

In the summer of 1908, after giving a farewell performance in the Albert Hall attended by over six thousand people, Mark left on his fourth tour to the Antipodes. Dolly and the baby came along, together with the baby's nurse. After giving sixteen recitals in Melbourne, Mark and his retinue went to New Zealand, where in Dunedin in the South Island they met Hugo Görlitz, the once-prosperous concert agent, who was travelling across the country on a motorcycle. Görlitz had been mainly responsible for engineering Jan Kubelik's artistic and financial success in Europe and America. Now he was selling gramophones for a firm in Christchurch at the southernmost end of New Zealand. "A nasty turn in the wheel of fortune," the former manager explained stoically. "Please take me to your concert tonight and let me hear some Beethoven. I'm starved for good music."

Hardly had he arrived home in the middle of the winter of 1908-1909 than he was engaged to tour Canada, where often as not his hosts were Methodist clergymen and YMCA secretaries, the principal sponsors of his concerts. Their womenfolk would have frowned heavily had they known that their honoured guest, not used to peanut butter sandwiches and ice cream for supper, sometimes sought out a local men's club where he could procure a whisky and soda along with more substantial fare.

On this trip he skipped Toronto. In Winnipeg he spent several entertaining evenings with Sir William M. Whyte, vice-president of the Canadian Pacific Railway,[104] and Sir William van Horne, the president,[105] "men who thought in thousands of miles of railroad, as compared with the hundreds of our little Europe, and envisaged millions of bushel of wheat and whole forests of timber." He also met Sir Augustus Nanton, "whose kindness was as far reaching as his financial operations."[106] Another new acquaintance was Sir Daniel McMillan, lieutenant-governor of Manitoba, who "had a charming old-world manner which made him a perfect host."[107]

On to Regina, where it was forty below and the citizens were selling to eager buyers ice-covered, bleak, undeveloped land, talking as if it were easily equal in value to the lots around Piccadilly Circus. In Moose Jaw music lovers turned up in great numbers at Mark's concert, even though the brand-new town had developed so quickly that it had outgrown its water supply and everybody was only allowed a tumblerful a day, and in Vancouver buildings were springing up overnight, with sprigs of the British nobility dabbling in real estate. Mark played poker in the Hotel Vancouver with a charming irresponsible young man who was killed five years later in the first weeks of the war, while his concert agents nearly persuaded him to rush up to the Klondike. He had visions of himself and his poor piano "being hauled over ice-bound trails by teams of furious dogs." Fortunately reason prevailed. In Victoria he admired Craigdarroch Castle, the extraordinary stone mansion the Dunsmuir coal and railways family had built facing the snow-capped Olympic Mountains. It all was, he wrote, like a hectic dream.

After giving a recital on the way home at the other side of the continent, in Newfoundland, where he stayed with the genial governor Sir Ralph Champneys Williams, who had held posts in Gibraltar, Barbados, Bechuanaland and the Windward Islands and who regaled him with amusing stories about his career as a colonial administrator, Mark arrived back in London just in time to witness the funeral procession of King Edward VII.[108]

An account of Professor Michael Hambourg's departure in 1910 from London for Toronto will follow later. He was fifty-five, Mark thirty-one. In his book Mark dealt with it only briefly. "My gallant old father," he wrote, "being ever of a restless temperament, made up his mind to go out to Canada and settle in Toronto and see if he could found a school of music there. Off he went by himelf at the age of sixty and when he had been in Canada for a few months he sent for the rest of the family." This was a lapse. Mark revered his father, so he made him five years older than he was. He may also have confused this exodus with his father's departure from Russia two decades earlier, when the professor first came alone with Mark, and a year later picked up his family. This time, it seems, the family came together, leaving Mark and Galia in London, while Boris was on a concert tour.

In October 1911 Mark sailed to Canada again, for another coast-to-coast tour, and to see how his father was getting on. For some reason, he discussed this trip in his autobiography but failed to report on his visit to Toronto.

For once, Mark did not have any amusing stories to tell about his voyage across the Atlantic and the train journey from Halifax west. Instead, he gave us a vivid account of a surprising and upsetting death.

There was fog as the ship sailed up the Gulf of St. Lawrence. He had asked the captain to let his party – Mark, Dolly and his manager – go ashore at Rimouski on Quebec's South Shore on the tug that picked up the mail from the ship. That was the only way Mark could reach Halifax in time for his opening concert. So at ten o'clock at night the tug took them and the postal officers ashore, and they went to the station to wait for the midnight train from Montreal. There had just been an election. The platform was crowded with excited people seeing off the successful candidate. There had been a lot of drinking. The train arrived. Mark and Dolly went to their compartment in the sleeping car. The manager said he would just go down the platform to the telegraph office to send a cable to his wife reporting his safe arrival, before going to his compartment.

Just as the train was about to start, a guard rushed in and said, "Mr. Hambourg, you are wanted on the platform. Something has happened to your manager." Mark and Dolly rushed out. Indeed, something had happened. The manager had been shot dead.

"There," wrote Mark, "stretched out on the ground in front of us, lay my wretched manager, with his brains blown out." The local police chief, "half-seas over," i.e., drunk, was among the crowd. He promptly arrested Mark and Dolly. The corpse was taken to a room in an "unappetizing hotel." The woman in charge insisted Mark and Dolly sleep in the room next door. Mark declined. The woman said, "*Comment?* You dislike sleeping next door to a corpse? What are you afraid of? The dead don't bite!"

The train left without them. The concert in Halifax took place without Mark. The lawyer in town happened to be the American consul. He took Mark and Dolly out of the hands of the drunken police chief. They were detained in Rimouski for several days while the lawyer was investigating. An inquest was held. People in Rimouski, it appeared, had been in the habit of carrying firearms. A law had recently been passed making it illegal. Still, on political occasions people fired exuberantly in the air just to make a noise. Mark's "wretched manager," who was a tall man, had got in the way.

The priest in Rimouski wouldn't bury him because he was a Protestant. They had to go to Rivière du Loup for the funeral. In due course, the exuberant man responsible was found and convicted and apparently spent several years in prison.

The horror of this death lingered in Mark's mind for the rest of his Canadian tour, while he was playing for the Duke and Duchess of Connaught at Rideau Hall in Ottawa, while he skated on the Bow River in Calgary – he had never been on skates before – and while he enjoyed Vancouver, which was "much milder in spirit" than it had been two years earlier because people were already feeling not quite so rich and were wondering whether they had been wise to buy so many lots of real estate.

Maybe, for some deep obscure reason, the lingering horror was the reason why Mark forgot to report on his visit to Toronto.

In 1912 Mark and Dolly bought a house on Cumberland Terrace in Regent's Park, near Ignaz Moscheles's residence where Liszt had stayed when he was in London. That summer, Ignaz's son Felix celebrated his eightieth birthday and asked Mark to play Ignaz's Concerto in A minor, a charming Mendelssohnian concerto largely forgotten. He also played at a concert honouring the seventy two year old sculptor Auguste Rodin on a visit to London, certainly a memorable occasion, but perhaps not quite as memorable as his dinner party on board the yacht *Enchantress* with Winston Churchill, who had just been made First Lord of the Admiralty. "I enlivened the party after dinner doing card tricks," Mark reported, "in which Churchill was quick to join me, and showed some good turns himself. Distinguished as he is for his versatility, he seemed to be as adept at conjuring as at other things." Mark wrote this in 1931.

In the summer of 1913, in Berlin, he saw his old teacher Leschetizky again, now over eighty, nearly blind. (He had two more years to live.) He was "wonderfully lively." They sat in cafés until the early hours while Leschetizky told stories about Czerny, Brahms and Rubinstein. Mark gave a recital in the Beethoven Saal which Leschetizky attended. After the concert he told Mark, "You play more like Rubinstein than anybody I've ever heard." This gave Mark immense pleasure.

In 1951, in his chapter on program-making in *The Eighth Octave*, Mark wrote: "Anton Rubinstein, who may be considered Liszt's successor, played with great volume of tone and swept his hearers off their feet with his power and intensity. He was, notwithstanding this, a very inaccurate performer, owing probably to his spiritual excitement, and his critics said that one could make another sonata with the amount of wrong notes he performed in Beethoven's Appassionata."[109]

It is not impossible that, at least subconsciously, Mark was aware that in the later stages of his own development Leschetizky's comparison was to have a validity his old teacher could not have thought of at the time he made it in 1913.

On August 4, 1914, Sir Kenneth Muir Mackenzie, Clerk of the Crown, was playing golf. A special messenger came looking him. The Proclamation of War had to be issued from his office.

In the four years to come, when railway and car travel in the U.K. was limited, Mark often rode in the big Steinway van with two gigantic piano men. They could be relied upon to get the heavy instrument unaided to the highest platform, or through any windows, or up the steepest staircase, without scratching a wall or jolting the instrument.

Other obstacles, the result of war hysteria and spy fever, were more difficult to overcome. In several towns Mark's posters were torn down because a newspaper had announced that Mark was merely pretending to be a Russian while "his true nationality was well known." Mark brought action in the High Court for libel.

"I had to go into the witness box to be cross-examined," he wrote. "Though my case was as transparent as the day, I would rather have faced a thousand big audiences with my piano than that one clever lawyer whose business it was to find something in my words to confound me." He need not have worried. He was awarded substantial damages. The case received wide publicity. After that, every hotel keeper registered him as "British subject, Russian born" the moment he came through the door. They knew how expensive it was to question his citizenship.

In November he sailed to the United States on board the White Star liner *Adriatic*. He could not afford to refuse the offer of work, however dangerous the crossing. At Euston Station he was delighted to meet Pablo Casals, who subsequently turned out to have been endowed with an extraordinary aptitude for the game of patience, or solitaire as it is called in the U.S. Mark said he was a mere baby compared to Casals. The cellist taught him so many variations during that anxious voyage that Mark's head reeled. For the rest of the time Casals stayed in his cabin, near Mark's, practising Bach's unaccompanied Suite in C major. "By the end of the voyage I began to feel that Bach was indeed a heavy burden."

Shortly after his arrival in New York, news came of the first Zeppelin raid on London. The aggressive wife of one "one of our most distinguished artists" – one wonders which one, he does not say if he was German or Austrian – "came to me and said, 'There, you see, your wonderful London will shortly be a mass of ruins. Nothing can save it.'"

He described the musical life of New York after the outbreak of the war in terms comparable to those used a generation later after the rise of Hitler. Many artists who came to the U.S. never went home again. "It will not be at all surprising," Mark wrote in 1931, two years before Hitler came to power, "if by the next generation the musical centre of the world will have become New York, rather than the capital cities of the old world.... It is not the first time in history that the immigration of artists, due to war conditions or persecutions in their own countries, has caused a new birth and vigour of artistic endeavour in their adopted land."

Mark spent many hours with fellow artists of every nationality, "held together as we were by the bond of mutual respect, and by the principle that art has no boundaries but is a universal brotherhood."

He saw a great deal of Josef Hofmann, who had been a prodigy in Cracow and had given his first performances in London at the age of ten. There was Fritz Kreisler, limping on stage on December 12, 1914, only three months after having been wounded in the leg as a lieutenant in the Austro-Hungarian army fighting the Russians on the Galician front, and having been reported dead. (The New York *Evening News* headed an editorial about the concert "Fritz Kreisler Very Much Alive."[110]) The Italian Berliner Ferruccio Busoni was in New York for awhile, cadaverous and tired-out, and so was Carl Friedberg, another student of Clara Schumann's, whom Mark greatly admired. From France came Jacques Thibaud, Alfred Cortot and the Flonzaley Quartet, and from Belgium Eugène Ysaÿe. Mark wined and dined – and made music – with the twenty-three-year-old violinist Mischa Elman, a refugee from the Tsar.[111]

Just before Christmas 1914 Mark went to Canada on a concert tour with the English soprano Maggie Teyte.[112] Considering that Canadians, unlike the English near the southeast coast, did not hear the sounds of guns across the water, he was impressed by their spirit of patriotism and self-sacrifice. All Ontario was a training camp, and

Mark Hambourg ~ Greatness of Nature

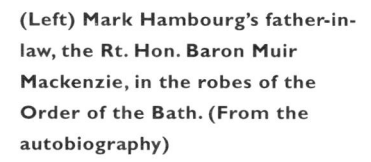

(Left) Mark Hambourg's father-in-law, the Rt. Hon. Baron Muir Mackenzie, in the robes of the Order of the Bath. (From the autobiography)

Dolly Mackenzie as she appeared when the wedding was noted in the *Illustrated London News*.

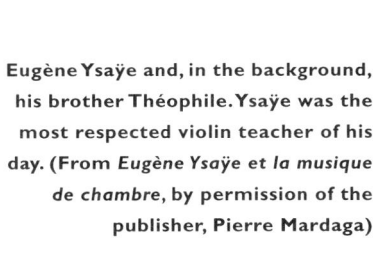

Mark in a drawing from *Bookman*, 1930.

Eugène Ysaÿe and, in the background, his brother Théophile. Ysaÿe was the most respected violin teacher of his day. (From *Eugène Ysaÿe et la musique de chambre*, by permission of the publisher, Pierre Mardaga) khaki was everywhere. Once again he had nothing to say about meeting his family in Toronto.

On April 17, 1915, he left New York on board the American liner *St. Louis*. He had made the booking at the last minute, at the urging of a friend who was head of the shipping and banking firm which owned the ship and who wanted Mark to keep him company. He offered Mark the best accommodation available. Originally Mark was to cross the ocean with a group of artists and writers who were members of the Lotus Club, the New York affiliate of the Savage Club, an essential part of his life in London. They wanted Mark to go with them on the British luxury liner *Lusitania*, which was to leave New York after the *St Louis*. Mark was anxious to get home. He left with his friend.

The *Lusitania* was torpedoed on May 7. None of his friends survived.

Mark was certainly of military age. It is not clear what physical disability – he mentions this as the cause – kept him out of the army. But he certainly did his bit for the war effort – to provide the consolation of music in four years of gloom and horror. In the fall of 1915 he organized a series of afternoon recitals in the Aeolian Hall in Bond Street primarily to perform the Elizabethans and Henry Purcell and other later composers who had seldom been revived, to remind the public that England, too, had "a fine tradition of noble music." In 1915, 1916 and 1917 he gave twenty-three concerts in the four weeks before and after Christmas. He also played frequently with orchestras, in Eastbourne and Bournemouth among many others.

One great pleasure during the long war winters was to make music with Belgian musicians who had fled to England, with Eugène Ysaÿe, with the violinist Désiré Defauw, who became the artistic director of the Montreal Symphony Orchestra from 1940 to 1952, with the violist Lionel Tertis[113] and with many others. Defauw became known in London because he solved his transportation problem – taxis were "rare, rude and exorbitant" – by constructing an ingenious bicycle with a trailer behind for his wife and little boy, in which he rode about with his hair flying, "followed by a crowd of astonished and admiring street urchins."[114] The musicians usually met in Mark's house on Sunday afternoons and played for their own pleasure. Chosen friends were sometimes invited to listen, among them a "rare bird," a British general who was musical, General Ashmore. He happened to be involved in the defence of London against air raids and gave them a sense of security. Sometimes, when he was called to the telephone while they were playing, they had to control their trembling.

One forgets today how frequently London was bombed in the First World War. Once, at a concert in the Coliseum during one of the worst raids, Mark selected Chopin's Nocturne in F sharp minor to play while guns went off overhead. No one moved, he reported, no one fidgeted. "It was a remarkable tribute to the controlling power of a beautiful melody."

Mark also played in hospitals. It was marvellous for him to see how much the men suffering from war wounds enjoyed serious music. The Moonlight Sonata was much in demand – he knew that his recording of it was often played on gramophones in the trenches and in rest homes. He wrote that he played it on Beethoven's hundredth birthday, but this was an error – he probably meant the ninetieth anniversary of Beethoven's death, on March 26, 1917. (Beethoven was born on December 17, 1770.) His recording of Rachmaninov's Prelude in C sharp minor was also popular. He could never understand why it had such universal appeal.

There was a limit to which music could provide comfort during the war years. It was not until November 1918 "when one could draw the blinds from one's windows and once again look the moon freely and fearlessly in the face" that Mark, and the rest of mankind, could become human beings again.

The slaughter which began in 1914 marked the end of the nineteenth century. The romantic virtuoso belonged to that century. The year 1914 was, in musical terms, the end of the essential Mark Hambourg. The twentieth century's demand for simplicity and austerity in performance made the florid and individualistic Liszt-Leschetizky tradition of performance seem self-indulgent and anachronistic. Though Mark had a good life for forty-two years after 1918, full of music, family, friendships, club life, good humour and many pleasures, he lived off capital. The only Leschetizky students who succeeded in managing the transition to modern austerity – these are highly subjective judgments – were Artur Schnabel, Benno Moiseiwitsch,[115] Alexander Brailowsky and Mieczyslaw Horszowski.[116]

Schnabel devoted a paragraph to Mark in his autobiography, published in 1961, ten years after his death. Leschetizky had said to Schnabel, "You will never be a pianist. You are a musician."

> My rival at Leschetizky's was a youth three or four years older than I. To him Leschetizky could have said: "You will never be a musician; you are a pianist." His name was Mark Hambourg. He really had elemental qualities. His thunderous octaves, incomparable ones, had real fire, were not mechanical. He made a big career, was a very popular virtuoso. He retired many years ago. His style fitted a young man. If, getting older, one remains as one has been as a youth, the effect will not be to appear young but out of date – which sounds like a paradox.[117]

Arthur Rubinstein – no relation to Anton – was only eight years younger than Mark but managed the transition more successfully. In London during the First World War, he heard Mark play, with Ysaÿe and others, Mozart's Piano Quartet in G minor. He described Mark as a kind man but found him old-fashioned: "Hambourg was a pianist of the old virtuoso school; his percussive tone and his freelance treatment of the work was wholly unadaptable for Mozart."[118]

Mark and Benno Moiseiwitsch were fellow members of the Savage Club. They were life-long friends and Benno was to deliver a loving eulogy at Mark's funeral. There were more stories about Mark and Benno at the club than about any other "Savages."

> On one occasion Benno found Mark (whose range of tone included an exceptionally loud fortissimo) absent from the poker

table. He enquired about Mark's whereabouts and was told he was playing in Newcastle. "Really?" said Benno, cupping his hand to his ear. "I can't hear him."[119]

Mark had joined the club in 1904 or 1905. His father had taken him there in 1891 when he was twelve. The club sponsored "crankism together with high literary, artistic, musical and scientific achievement, characters of all kinds galore." He remembered that he was "so little when my father brought me in after dinner to play that I had to be stood on a chair for the members to see me.... It was still the fashion in the nineties for men to wear beards and whiskers, but these hirsute creatures sitting about appeared to me veritable antediluvians, monuments of antiquity."[120]

Mark waxed lyrical when, twenty-five years later, he described the card room: "Time loses its meaning in that sanctum; the pale dawn, the twinkling stars, follow each other in lightning succession in that concentrated fanciful kingdom of aces and kings."[121]

One day, Mark dropped his wallet as he left the club. The old porter ran after him. "Ain't it lucky for you, sir," he said, "that it was me as found it, and not one of the members?"

In the winter of 1918-1919 Mark crossed the English Channel at least sixteen times, usually in rough weather. In Paris, the old Proustian salons to which hostesses had invited artists like him to perform had vanished. Success had become the function of advertising. Furthermore, he was appalled to find so much anti-British sentiment. From the way the French spoke, no one would have imagined that a single British soldier had ever crossed the waters to share with them the horrors of war.

Being singularly gregarious, Mark enjoyed meeting celebrities and he met them everywhere. At a party in Berlin he met Einstein. He was surprised that Einstein did not treat him with the contempt he thought his scientific ignorance deserved. Mark did not know that Einstein played the violin. Einstein expressed his regret at not being able to come to Mark's concert, but on that evening he was giving a recital of his own, for charity.

Throughout the postwar period, Mark's travelling schedule kept him on the move. In 1920 he played over one hundred and twenty recitals in Great Britain alone. While in London, one of his students was the twenty-year-old Gerald Moore, the future accompanist of rare distinction. "Mark taught me for a considerable period without a fee. But I still had not found out for myself how to practise and could not be roused from my lethargy. To wake me up Mr. Hambourg – as I naturally addressed him – would roar at me. In an endeavour to spur me he would manifest utter impatience. I am convinced that he finally made a nominal charge for his tuition for my own good, because he found me so unrewarding a pupil."[122]

In spite of this, and the age difference, the two formed a close friendship. Forty years later, at Mark's funeral, Gerald Moore was another old friend who delivered a eulogy.

In postwar Toronto, where Prohibition still held sway, Mark attended a New Year's Eve party.[123] His host said to him, "I'm making a nice ginger ale cup. Come and see how I mix it." His friend poured four bottles of rum into a bowl, followed by a bewildering succession of all kinds of liquor, culminating in a generous provision of whisky. Mark delicately tasted it and was knocked over. The other guests tossed down many glasses with the greatest of ease. Next time he visited Ontario Prohibition had been rescinded and Local Option established.

Mark found life in Canada much more Americanized than the last time he had been there in before the war. The public gaze was concentrated on New York as the source of everything worth considering in art, fashion and literature, rather than on Europe. But musical life, and especially musical education, had made tremendous strides. He was much impressed by the achievements of his old friend the piano teacher W.O. Forsyth and by Ernest MacMillan, who was resuming his career in music after returning from four years as a prisoner of war in Germany. He also admired the musical establishments of the University of New Brunswick and of Queen's and McGill universities, which were always anxious to invite artists touring the country to perform. It may have been on one of these occasions that

Mark became aware of a man reading a newspaper in one of the front rows while he played. He stopped and stared at him. The man look up, smiled, and said, "Please go on playing, you do not disturb me in the least."

> This made me think of the time when Franz Liszt played by request before the Emperor of Austria at the Palace of Schönbrunn in Vienna. The Emperor kept up a running flow of conversation with those around him while Liszt was playing, so that at last he could bear it no longer and stopped.
>
> "Please continue to play, Herr Liszt," said the potentate graciously. "You do not inconvenience me at all."
>
> "I am sorry indeed, Sire," replied Liszt," for you do inconvenience me greatly."[124]

But not every place in Canada was as civilized as the universities in which Mark played. In a small place "on the Pacific slope" – he did not name it, he only played there because it was on his route – the mayor had to issue a licence to make it possible for Mark to perform. Ambulant pianists were unknown. No activity on the list applied. Mark was not a "performing animal." He was not among "people who were exhibiting themselves for the purpose of making money." He was not "the fattest woman," nor a dwarf, ventriloquist or siamese twin. "Sleight of hand" tempted him but in the end he decided on "conjurer." One is reminded of another Western mayor – or maybe the same one – who after a concert said to Mark's brother Boris, the cellist in the Hart House String Quartet, probably around the same time, "That was a great concert. I hope your little group will grow so that soon it will form a big band."

In South Africa Mark found the atmosphere quite different from before the war. The old settlers who had seen rough days and who had cared intensely for the softening pleasures of music had died out. The Jazz Age had arrived. A new generation was being spoon-fed with every kind of entertainment. That was bad enough, he thought, but the older generation had not changed enough – some of its members still hung on to the worst aspects of prewar society. In the Orange Free State, whenever he addressed anybody in English, he was answered in Dutch. The bitter feeling between Boers and British lingered on.

New roads had been built everywhere. He could travel from the Cape to Johannesburg by car without difficulty, unthinkable when he had been there before the war. Mark relished social life in Cape Town, and in Salisbury he played golf with the governor of Southern Rhodesia and enjoyed the hospitality of his music-loving family, thinking himself lucky to find spiritual friendship so far away from Europe. On the way home he met a Belgian District Commissioner from the Congo, who complained to him that he had not included Elisabethville (now Lubumbashi in the Democratic Republic of Congo) in his concert itinerary.

"Oh no," Mark thought to himself. "That would be going too far, playing the piano so close to the equator. Soon I shall be trekking from the Cape to Cairo, stopping every twenty-four hours playing Beethoven in the outposts of the White Man." Playing in the tropics had its drawbacks. At a recital in Lahore, he had to stop in the middle of a sonata because two of the keys refused to move. Eventually, someone extracted two enormous cockroaches from inside the piano with a pair of pincers. They had been enjoying a good meal on the felts.

He had wanted to go to India for a long time. Before being able to go he visited Morocco and Egypt. At last, on the boat to Australia in 1931, the secretary of one of the most popular entertainment clubs in Bombay asked Mark to let him know when he was coming back so that he could arrange a concert for him during the ship's stay. This was done – Mark cabled the date to the secretary from Fremantle, but fog delayed the ship. The audience had to wait till midnight to hear him play. Mark was surprised to note that among the exquisitely dressed and bejewelled Parsee ladies there were so many who were just as keen about his classical program as any Westerner.

The experience was so gratifying that in the following year an extended tour was arranged. He usually stayed in Government Houses, and once with the Commander in Chief. The P&O Shipping Company provided him with a personal servant, Rawdi, who took great pride in beating down the swarms of porters who fought for his luggage at every place they stopped.

"I may rob you, Master," Rawdi told him, "but no one else must." Rawdi bought him a posy of flowers for Christmas. Mark was really touched. At the end of the week Rawdi presented his account. "For Christmas present to Master – 2 rupees."

In South America Mark played in Buenos Aires, São Paulo and Rio de Janeiro. Everywhere he went he was impressed by the depth of the musical culture. Rio possessed one of the largest music schools in the world, and the highest percentage of its students were budding pianists. Windows were open on account of the heat, he wrote, and the dissonance which resounded all over the place would have satisfied the most atonal composer. "The only conservatory that I know of which is even larger," he said, "is that of Toronto, Canada."[125]

In 1924 the first Labour government under Ramsay MacDonald came to power in the U.K. Mark's seventy-eight-year-old father-in-law, Lord Muir Mackenzie, put his services at the disposal of the new government, especially of the Lord Chancellor Lord Haldane, an old friend.[126] He had always been sympathetic with the cause of the moderate left and now agreed to act for some time as Whip in the House of Lords, as chairman of countless committees, and as Lord-in-Waiting at Buckingham Palace. When he died in 1930, having held the office of High Bailiff of Westminster, he was buried in the Cloisters of Westminster Abbey.

Through his father-in-law Mark moved in exalted circles. At least once he spent a weekend at The Wharf, Asquith's place in Oxfordshire.[127] He was surprised to note that husbands and wives were never put together to sleep but were given rooms at opposite ends of the house. Lady Oxford introduced him to someone as "Sir Mark." He remarked, "Not yet," to which she replied, "I was not certain if you had sunk or not."

Mark recalled, "I had a reputation for being good-tempered at cards, so I was put at the great man's table during a whole weekend at his country house. It was trying both to my pocket and to my manners, but Mr. Asquith enjoyed his game so much and opened such a first-rate bottle of brandy for me that his lack of card sense became obliterated in a happy haze of good fellowship."[128]

In the twenties Mark made recordings and played on the BBC. He was fascinated by performances other than "live," a word he did not use. He saw that the new technology would vitally affect the future of making and listening to music. His views were the opposite of Glenn Gould's a generation – and monumental advances in sound editing – later: "The term 'engineer-musician' which I believe exists in the radio world, and even possibly at the gramophone companies, is an indigestible one for an artist to swallow. Can one reconcile the artist-musician with his fantasy and the engineer with his mechanical expediency in the realms of art?" He went on to state that on the gramophone nothing can be altered once it is recorded. "There stands the music as the artist played it, and if mistakes are made there they remain to convict him."

In matters of musical taste Mark had an open mind. He did not by any means play only the classics. He liked a great deal of contemporary music. He gave the first performance of the piano arrangement (by Leonard Borwick) of Debussy's *Prélude à l'après-midi d'un faune*. To Ravel personally he expressed an interest in giving the first performance of his Piano Concerto in G major (see below in the Boris chapter). He included in his recitals Ravel's *Jeux d'eaux* and *Gaspard de la nuit* – "such a foreign idiom to me until I got acclimatized." He played works by many of his Spanish and Italian contemporaries. He introduced Manuel de Falla's *Fantasía Bética* to Canadian audiences in a recital at Massey Hall in Toronto.[129] He made a point of performing Malipiero's *Barlumi* twice over, so that audiences could take it in. It was "weird harmonically (if the word harmony can be applied to it at all!)."

He writes that he played Busoni's *Klavierkonzert mit Altsolo und Schlusschor,* opus 39, composed in 1904, in London, with the composer at the conductor's desk: "He persuaded me to learn it, and a hard time I had of it! To begin with, it was very long; to go on with it was very difficult; and to end up with, it was so fatiguing to play that I nearly lost my health in mastering it.... However, I learned it out of affection for him."[130]

In Mark's obituary in the *Guardian* on August 29, 1960, it is stated that Mark performed this work in 1912:

> Busoni not only dedicated his second sonatina to Hambourg but asked him to play the solo part of his piano concerto which he himself conducted in the Queen's Hall in 1912 after which Liszt's concerto for two pianos was performed by the two virtuosi with the instruments so placed that they had to turn their backs on each other.
>
> Busoni considered that Hambourg was the only player to whom he dared to entrust his concerto and Hambourg realized that he alone, after doing so, had sufficient stamina to dare to match Busoni at the keyboard. It was an astonishing evening for connoisseurs of the piano.

It may have been Busoni who stimulated in Mark an interest in non-Western music. He observed in 1931 that the Indian scale "is divided into measurements between which most Western ears are not yet capable of differentiating.... Even up to quite recently Indian and Chinese music has been considered barbaric by Westerners. How if it is we who are the barbarians, with our system of tonics and dominants, and the Orientals whose ears are really advanced?"[131]

At the Savage Club this story made the rounds:

> The excitable Mark came charging into the Club, encountering Benno and pitchforked out his news.
> "Benno, Benno, they are to make a film of the life of Beethoven and I am to play Beethoven!"
> "So!" Moiseiwitsch replied in his slow guttural speech. "And who is to play the piano?"[132]

This film turned out to be one of the great disappointments of Mark's life. Everything had been prepared. Artists had been brought over from Hollywood to London. Mark was engaged at a retainer for nine weeks. But in the end the studio was not ready, or so he was told, and the whole thing was called off. "Such a sublime project shattered on so small a rock!" Mark lamented. "Perhaps it was just as well because the producer was insisting on a ballet to be introduced into the film to make it less highbrow, in which he wished Rossini to be seen playing the music for the dancers. He also had the idea that the Countess Guiccardi, Beethoven's girl friend, was to dance in a cabaret scene with myself as Beethoven."[133]

But he did star in other films – above all in Moonlight Sonata (the opening movement only), which "was produced with rather grotesque scenery – the moon rising on a rippling lake, and then disappearing to show the various positions of my hands on the keyboard. It was ridiculous but certainly effective, whilst Beethoven's slow legato melody could not have been bettered for the purpose."[134]

There was another, less effective film of Schubert's *Moment Musical*. He had a part in *The Common Touch*, in which he played a broken-down old street musician, with uncomfortable make-up on his face, who had to play the first movement of the Tchaikovsky Piano Concerto in B flat minor. He actually played it on a first-class concert grand, not on the terrible old piano shown in the film. "The result was successful and the recording brilliant even if I did not look as glamorous as I had imagined."[135]

Shortly before the outbreak of the Second World War, the Hambourgs sold their house on Cumberland Terrace, Regent's Park, in which they had lived since 1912. They moved to a smaller place at 43 Grove End Road in St. John's Wood. They made a handsome profit thanks to the Duchess of Windsor, or rather thanks to Mrs. Simpson, as she then was. She had taken a furnished house on their terrace. Her sudden fame and King Edward VIII's visible car when he came on a visit had driven the price up.

In September 1940, when the Blitz began, they moved their beds into the basement of the new house, while Mark's brother Jan slept under the heavy wooden kitchen table, with his Amati and Stradivarius violins. In the passage next to the larder "snored" two very fat maids whilst various relatives lay around on mattresses. A large explosion demolished a mansion just behind theirs. When they looked out in the morning they saw a pair of ladies' pink corsets hanging on the tree opposite. "They remained hanging there till long after the war," Mark wrote, "as a reminder of human frailty." "As a sedative," Mark took to composing and remained day after day in his studio with his manuscript in front of him, writing studies and mazurkas.

Sometimes he emerged. He was playing for a BBC overseas broadcast in the Paris Cinema, which was so far below ground it was thought safe from bombs, when there was an explosion so close it made the piano move. "I went on playing but the BBC telephoned from Broadcasting House asking angrily who the devil had knocked against the microphone? No enquiry as to the safety of the thirty men working in the theatre with me. All they thought of was the machine!"[136]

Wherever Mark and Dolly went, the bombs followed them, to Brighton, to Torquay, to Pulborough, where a dogfight took place above them and a German plane came down in a garden nearby. After the Blitz came the doodlebugs and they were worse still. Some of these flying bombs came whizzing over a theatre in Wimbledon where Mark was playing a Beethoven concerto with full orchestra, but luckily the conductor, who was a bit deaf, did not notice them. But the audience did and was "restless if manful."

Throughout the war there was unprecedented enthusiasm for music. For many musicians – and for a public living under enormous stress – it was an extraordinary time. Dame Myra Hess started the Lunch Hour concerts at the National Gallery. They were such a success that various other public places copied them. Mark's own contribution began in November 1939 when he played the Tchaikovsky concerto at the Queen's Hall, his cousin Charles Hambourg conducting.[137] The hall was sold out. At the end of June 1941, when he was about to perform in Bournemouth with the new Wessex Symphony

Orchestra, the news of Paderewski's death in New York was announced. Mark played Chopin's Funeral March "in memory of a great artist and my early benefactor."

In eighteen months Mark played Beethoven's Emperor Concerto and Tchaikovsky's Concerto in B flat minor a hundred times. It took him "three months' rest on top of a hill in the country to get over the effort."

Soon after the war he made a pilgrimage to Bonn in the British zone of occupation to visit the house in which Beethoven was born.

> The elderly caretaker seemed to me to be a bit crazed by all he had gone through, and I think he had the puzzled idea that I must be some distant descendant of Beethoven, for he followed me out into the street with an air of veneration and exclaimed with passion:
>
> "*Herr Professor,* Beethoven declared that all men should be brothers, but we appear to be more and more like wild beasts!"
>
> "It is only governments and politicians who cause this," I said consolingly. "We artists, we musicians, are still men of peace, and Beethoven's house still survives."[138]

In 1949 Mark came to Toronto and opened the summer season of Prom Concerts at the Varsity Arena on May 5. Pearl McCarthy reviewed the concert in the *Globe and Mail*.

> The Opening had high adventure, for, in addition to the fact that the orchestra had just recently reassembled, there was the excitement of having two men of intense and individualistic personality collaborating – Frieder Weissmann, conductor, and Mark Hambourg, pianist, as soloist.[139]
>
> Out of that collaboration, a fascinating experience was afforded for listeners. There was Mark Hambourg, one of the few big men of the old school of the grand manner who is still before the public, a pianist from the day which condemned regimenta-

Mark was a devoted member of the Savage Club.

Mark and Dolly.
(International Piano Archives, University of Maryland)

Mark late in life, cane close at hand.
(International Piano Archives, University of Maryland)

tion and, especially in tempi, believer in letting inspiration be their artistic guide. And there was the younger Frieder Weissmann, himself no robot, but with the touch of the gallant cavalry officer in his command over his own sensitive artistic fire.

Those talents came together in Tchaikovsky's B flat minor Concerto, and there was nothing dull about sitting in that arena while it happened.

Mark Hambourg's romantic zest and basic musicality went to people's hearts. They liked him and his music and gave him an ovation both respectful and affectionate. They seemed to find it a great relief to listen to a man whose performance was not coldly correct and who smiled at them as if they were people and not mere box office. In his solo numbers he played Chopin and Liszt, which they welcomed.[140]

In Toronto Mark gave a master class of ten sessions, an evening class to professional teachers, and the next morning the same class for students. Each session was devoted to one masterpiece, the Appassionata sonata of Beethoven, the *Wanderer Fantasie* of Schubert, the Bach Chromatic Fantasia and Fugue, Chopin's Funeral March sonata and Schumann's Fantasia.

One Saturday afternoon, May 14, Mark, his brother Boris (cello) and James Levey (violin) gave a recital at Eaton Auditorium. Mark played two Beethoven sonatas, opus 31, number 3 and the Appassionata.

After drawing attention to certain liberties Mark took, Ronald Hambleton wrote in the conclusion of his review in the *Globe and Mail*. "The towering moment of the whole afternoon came with his playing of the Appassionata sonata. There was the same disregard of exactness, but once you fell into that tidal wave of sound Mr. Hambourg produced it didn't seem to matter. For sheer passion it was unlike any other performance we have had in Toronto. Mistakes and all, it was a highly enjoyable afternoon."[141]

On October 22, 1950, Mark's Diamond Jubilee – sixty years of performing in London – was celebrated at Covent Garden. He played Beethoven and Chopin.

M ark called his collection of essays published in 1951 – nine years before his death – *The Eighth Octave*. Seven and a quarter octaves is the range of the normal piano. But, thanks to the blessings of his exciting life, the allotted span of *his* piano was stretched, metaphorically speaking, to eight octaves.

In his last essay he described a "crock party" at the Savage Club:

> I myself was leaning on two sticks which in my exuberance I dropped on my gouty toe as I clutched my hopeless cards and exclaimed in agony: "Hells Bells, that! as well as losing!" Next to me was Teddy, sitting on a rubber cushion to relieve his condition. Behind him More wielded an ephedrine spray which he puffed with a loud gasp every time he took a card. A fourth player, Joe, was accompanied by a hot water bottle, pressing it alternatively to his arm or his chest to relieve his dicky heart. A fifth, Duggy, used a large asthma puffer to pump up his nose like a pair of bellows whilst he abjured everybody to play faster and declared that he was losing his shirt....
>
> We may be seared by autumn, but we are not fallen leaves yet.[142]

On August 28, 1960, two days after Mark's death in Cambridge, his sister Luba wrote to Clement in Toronto:

> I write to you with a heavy heart about dear Mark who as you will have heard from cable and no doubt press died on Friday last. I spent last Wednesday with them when he so gladly passed me on the card from you to me, and also read me your note to him on same. He had a good laugh about it. I must tell you he was complaining then of pains across his chest and thought it was rheumatism and although we played our usual game of 66 he was groaning a little at the time. They started off early Friday

morning to go to Cambridge to stay with Nadine and Tom [Mark's daughter and son-in-law] who have just bought a house there. After lunch they settled down to a mild game of bridge to take his mind off. He just lay back in his chair and within minutes was no more.[143]

Jan Hambourg

EPICURE, VIOLINIST, SCHOLAR

"**J**an was an epicure," the accompanist Gerald Moore wrote. "His interests were bestowed in equal proportions on Bach, Burgundy, the French impressionists and racehorses."[1]

Jan was the most intellectual of the Hambourg brothers, the one most interested in ideas. He was thirteen when Olive Garnett met him in Bloomsbury at the Stepniaks.

"John Hamburg [sic]," she wrote in her diary, "was there. We had supper. He speaks English well. He came part way home with me and talked about music, music criticism, Max (his brother), etc. All the Hamburgs seem to think that musical taste is a matter of development, apart from a natural gift or a good ear, etc."[2]

In 1910, after the Hambourgs' arrival in Toronto, Donald H. Sinclair of the *Canadian Courier* found them living in a big west end apartment house.

> Their flat was a treasure house of art. For instance, on the walls, I saw original sketches of those geniuses of pen and ink – Du Maurier, Tom Browne and the artist Thackeray, also autographed photographs of celebrated musicians, and the original of "The Cherry Girl" sculpture of Albert Taft.
>
> Why did the Hambourgs come to Canada?
>
> The other night I asked Mr. Jan Hambourg to explain.
>
> "We came to Canada because my brother Mark urged it," he said. "Lately my father has suffered from rheumatic trouble – which is fatal to a musician. We blamed damp, foggy London for it. We had to go somewhere. Mark suggested Canada. He was greatly impressed by this country – of course enormously from the commercial point of view. But we Hambourgs are mostly interested in things aesthetic, though the money, too, is an attrac-

tion, isn't it? Well, Mark said there was appreciation of art and money in Canada – especially in Toronto, which he considered was the foremost musical city in Canada and showing the best prospects, indeed, in that respect of any city in America. Here we are!"

Mr. Jan Hambourg showed me his two concert violins, one a Nicolo Amati, grand pattern 1664, valued at $5,000, the other a Giuseppe Guarneri valued at $3,500.[3]

"With these instruments I wish to become acquainted with Canadians," he laughed. "I come to Canada as the missionary of the Ysaÿe-Kreisler, Belgian and French school. I hope that pupils from all over America will come to me here at Toronto for instruction. We expect to find fine material here in Canada to work with. So far you Canadians excel in execution and you have some fine names." He mentioned Donalda, Parlow, Edmund Burke and other Canadian musical friends of his.[4]

Mr. Jan Hambourg is an alert athletic young Russian of twenty-eight years. He plays tennis, chess and billiards besides the violin – and would like to play rugby football. I do not think he has what they call a "temperament," which is not to say, however, that he is not wedded to his art. He is. And he has some triumphs, too. Ysaÿe said of him once, "Since the death of Wieniawski I have heard no one who has reminded me so vividly of that master's playing as regards poetic interpretation, tone, colour and rhythmic brilliancy."

Two years ago, he created a sensation by rendering at five recitals sixty-five pieces from memory.... Jan speaks four languages. He discusses literature with glee....

Yes, he knows something of Canadian literature, too. His favourite author is Sir Gilbert Parker,[5] whom he knows quite well – both his books and the knight himself. Mr. Jan Hambourg has always regretted that his concert managers have not arranged a tour for him across this country or "continent," as he prefers to call the Dominion. His experience of the colonies so far has been confined to South Africa and Australia. Commenting on conditions there, he remarked that Canada was miles ahead of her sister colonies in aesthetic development.

Even in the primitive western towns where Mark played, after each succeeding tour, there was a noticeable improvement in the musical intelligence of the audience. The song of the prairie, the woods and the mountains – throbbing young life hammering out the destiny of a great country – this is a song these European masters have come here to learn. And perhaps they will soften it.[6]

Jan had studied in London, Frankfurt, Prague – and with Ysaÿe in Godinne, where Mark, on a visit to him, had wooed and won Dolly Mackenzie. He had made his debut in Berlin. After a few years as a concert performer, he had joined his father and brother Boris in Toronto in 1910 to establish the Hambourg Conservatory, becoming head of the violin department.

In 1916, the year of his marriage, Jan Hambourg was thirty-four, Isabelle McClung thirty-nine. She was tall, a society lady, an amateur musician, passionately interested in the arts, the daughter of Judge Samuel A. McClung, a strict, conservative, wealthy Calvinist who had lived with his wife, son and two daughters in a large house at 1180 Murray Hill Avenue, in fashionable Squirrel Hill in Pittsburgh.

Isabelle "was the most beautiful girl I had ever seen," wrote a friend, "large of mind and heart, entirely frank and simple with natural dignity of manner. Not an artist in the sense of producing, she could identify herself wholly with the artist's efforts and aims. She had an infallible instinct for all the arts. She never mistook the second-best for the best."[7]

At the time of his marriage Jan was described as "a cultivated musician of mixed Russian-Jewish-English background, a sensitive performer, an avid reader, particularly fond of the French novelists, and a man of considerable general culture."[8]

When Yehudi Menuhin was asked in a letter what it was in Jan that drew Isabelle to him, he replied, "I can only say that a violinist possesses irresistible attraction – even Jan Hambourg!!"[9] Menuhin had been a friend and admirer of both Jan and Isabelle, a friendship he described extensively in his autobiography.[10]

The two exclamation marks at the end of his reply suggest that he was not altogether serious when he wrote it. This is entirely natural. The question put to him was mischievous. It did not mean what it said. It meant, "What made Isabelle decide to get married in the first place, after fifteen years with Willa Cather? And in the second, why did she pick Jan Hambourg?"

Menuhin knew what everybody else knew. He had been asked an unanswerable question and evaded it with wit and grace. The *even* merely meant that Jan Hambourg was an acquired taste. Menuhin certainly knew that he could not throw any light on the mystery why, eighty years ago, Isabelle married at all, or why she married Jan.

For fifteen years she had been an intimate friend, the "one great romance,"[11] of the novelist Willa Cather, a writer of such distinction that Sinclair Lewis, when he received the Nobel Prize for Literature in 1930, called her "the greatest American novelist," who should have won the prize instead of him,[12] so eminent that Rebecca West compared her to Marcel Proust,[13] and so remarkable that Katherine Anne Porter concluded her essay about Cather with this statement: "She is a curiously immovable shape, monumental, virtue herself in her art and a symbol of virtue – like certain churches, in fact, or exemplary women, revered and neglected. Yet like these again, she has her faithful friends and true believers, even so to speak her lovers, and they last a lifetime, and after: the only kind of bond she would recognize or require or respect."[14]

The precise nature of the relationship between Willa Cather and Isabelle McClung remains a matter of conjecture. The early twentieth century was a time when closets were still firmly shut. There is a conflict of views on whether, during the five years beginning in 1901 when Willa Cather lived in the McClung house, at Isabelle's invitation, they had separate bedrooms.[15] During this time, and for another

Jan Hambourg, in a rare photograph of a violinist-scholar in repose.
(Courtesy Jeanie Hersenhoren)

ten years until Isabelle's marriage to Jan, the two travelled widely together in the U.S., Canada, England and France.

"If I had to guess on the basis of the evidence," Joan Acocella wrote in the *New Yorker,* "I would say that Cather was a homosexual in her feelings and celibate in her actions."[16]

Hermione Lee commented that Willa Cather did not call herself a lesbian, which, however, does not mean that we could not now describe her as a lesbian writer: "If we can't say anything about writers which they would not have said about themselves, then there is no use in writing about them. But it is important not to collapse Cather's imaginative life into a simple matter of repression, nor to condescend to her for lack of 'openness.'"[17]

If Joan Acocella was right and Willa Cather was homosexual in her feelings, we may make the same assumption of Isabelle. Why then did Isabelle marry at all – and why did she marry Jan? And what did Willa Cather think of the marriage?

Two admirers of Willa Cather had views on these questions:

> Willa supposed she [Isabelle] had wanted a home.... [Isabelle] had evidently wanted companionship with an understanding member of the opposite sex. She had wanted to ally herself with Jan in particular because he represented the arts and the arts were her love. Jan Hambourg was not a great artist and never would be but he had other attributes, Willa admitted. He was kind to Isabelle. In return, Isabelle certainly had gifts for him – a cultural background, sensitivity, financial security, the charm of an experienced, gracious hostess – and Isabelle was a giving person.[18]

For students of Willa Cather the question of Isabelle's marriage to an artist was of special interest. In her third novel, *The Song of the Lark,* she had the main character, the opera singer Thea Kronburg, say to a man who wanted to marry her:

> I don't see why anybody wants to marry an artist, anyhow. I remember Ray Kennedy [another suitor] used to say he didn't see

how any woman could marry a gambler, for she would only be marrying what the game left.... Who marries who is a small matter, after all. But you've cared longer and more than anybody else, and I'd like to have somebody human to make a report to once in a while. If you're not interested I'll do my best anyhow. [19]

She then excuses herself. Her car is waiting. She's singing Sieglinde on Friday and she has to get her rest.

"In the bulk of literature about women," Joan Acocella wrote in the *New Yorker*, "who marries whom – or at least who goes to bed with whom – is not simply a small matter, it is the subject." This scene was a "turning point in the history of literature."[20]

With *The Song of the Lark*, H.L. Mencken wrote, Cather, who had grown up in Virginia and Nebraska, "definitely stepped into the small class of American novelists who are seriously to be reckoned with."[21] Joan Acocella called it the first portrait-of-the-artist-as-a-young-woman in which the woman's artistic development is the whole story, with sex an incidental matter. [22]

For each the other was certainly somebody "human to make a report to." Whether sex was an "incidental matter" in their relationship – or any matter at all – their marriage, which lasted for twenty-two years, appears to have been excellent. After her death in 1938 Jan was unhappy and lonely throughout the war in London until he died in 1947.

Jan's niece, Mrs. Stella Ryan, visited the couple in Paris in 1930 with her mother, Galia. She was eighteen at the time. It was her first visit to Paris. The Hambourgs had an elegant apartment at 46 rue du Bac, on the Left Bank, across the river from the Louvre. Mrs. Ryan was too young to appreciate him. Jan intimidated her, she said, as he did other young members of the family. But she was fascinated by Isabelle, "a large, formidable woman, highly coloured, with black hair and sparkling eyes."[23]

Music had much to do with the novelist's subsequent relationship to Jan, which evolved from cautious coolness to friendship and respect.[24]

Music was essential to Willa Cather, wrote Richard Giannone in *Music in Willa Cather's Fiction:*

> It was an emotional experience that had a potent influence on her own imaginative processes – quickening the flow of her ideas, suggesting new forms and associations, translating itself into parallel movements of thought and feeling. I think no critic had sufficiently emphasized, or possibly recognized, how much musical forms influence her composition, and how her style, her beauty of cadence and rhythm, were the result of a sort of transposed musical feeling, and were arrived at almost unconsciously, instead of being a conscious effort to produce definite effects with words.[25]

In successive vivid episodes in *The Song of the Lark,* Willa Cather described how a gifted, ambitious young girl from "a little desert town whose people live by the railway and order their lives by the comings and goings of trains" became a first-class artist – in a world not far removed from what Jan had described as those "primitive western towns where Mark played" and where there was, "after each succeeding tour, a noticeable improvement in the musical intelligence of the audience." Another theme in *The Song of the Lark,* also present in Olive Garnett's diary entry about Jan, is the "preoccupation with musical achievement and musical standards, which sets the whole story against a background of musical endeavour."[26]

Curiously, Willa Cather had met *Mark* Hambourg some fifteen years before she met Jan. When she was a twenty-six-year-old reporter for the *Lincoln Courier,* she joined Mark and the young pianist and composer of songs Ethelbert Nevin for lunch at the Hotel Schenley in Pittsburgh. Nevin too had been an infant prodigy and was very well known at the time. He had grown up near Pittsburgh but lived in Italy. Cather knew his songs and "was half in love with him."[27] In 1925 he was the subject of her story *Uncle Valentine.* Mark was on one of his early American tours.

"We sat down at the table," Cather wrote, "and the grapefruit turned Hambourg's conversation upon India and the strange sights one sees there, and the good things one gets to eat there." As the men debated the relative merit of talent and art for the performer, Nevin cooked a "complicated omelette" in a chafing dish."[28]

In the spring of 1899, Cather met Isabelle McClung in the dressing room of the actress Lizzie Hudson Collier, the leading lady at Pittsburgh's Avenue Theatre Stock Company, whom she knew and admired. The two women were immediately drawn to one another and discovered that they shared a passionate interest in theatre, music and literature. Though Cather had already achieved "a certain celebrity," she still lived in rooming houses.[29] Two years later Isabelle invited her to move to the family's residence on Squirrel Hill.

The novelist Dorothy Canfield Fisher remembered:

> The McClungs had a great rich house, with plenty of servants, conducted in the lavish style of half a century ago. Isabelle was simply devoted to Willa always, and was sweet, warm-hearted and sincere – as well as very beautiful, at least I used to think her so, in a sumptuous sort of way. There was a great deal of stately entertaining carried on in the McClung house too, the many-coursed dinners of the most formal kind, which seemed picturesque (and they really were) to Willa.[30]

Judge Samuel McClung is specially remembered for having presided at the trial of Alexander Berkman, the anarchist who shot and wounded the industrialist Henry Clay Frick in 1892. (Incidentally, when Frick was shot, he insisted that none other than Dr. Lawrence Litchfield look after him. Litchfield's wife Ethel, a friend of Isabelle's, had been a student of Leschetizky. In the Litchfield house Jan first met Willa Cather.) Judge McClung sentenced Berkman to prison for a maximum of twenty-two years, the harshest possible sentence. Berkman was an associate of Emma Goldman, "Red Emma," who spent the last year of her extraordinary life in Toronto. (She died on May 10, 1940, at the age of seventy-one, on the day the Nazis invaded Holland, which is one reason why the Toronto papers did not carry any obituaries.) Cather had sympathized with Berkman before she ever met the judge (later in life she became very conservative). One would assume she kept her opinion to herself while living under his roof.

The judge and his wife had considerable doubts about the propriety of having Willa Cather reside in their house. But Isabelle, who "had been challenging the judge's orthodoxies by hobnobbing with Bohemians,"[31] may have threatened to leave if she could not have her way. In any case, she prevailed.

Cather had fallen in love with Isabelle, or, to put it more precisely, in the phrase used by William Godwin of Mary Wollstonecraft's relationship with Frances Blood, "she contracted a friendship so fervent, as for years to have constituted the ruling passion of her mind."[32]

Isabelle converted the sewing-room on the top floor to a study for her friend. There, Cather composed the first volume of her prose fiction *The Troll Garden*. Though her presence caused some strain, she became so much part of the family that *The Social Directory of Greater Pittsburgh* listed her among the six members of the McClung household.

Jan had met Isabelle in London several years before he proposed. They were married on April 3, 1916, at the Church of the Messiah in New York City. Only relatives of the bride were present. The *New York Times* identified Jan as a violinist and a Russian, the brother of Mark and Boris. It did not mention Clement. Mr. Hambourg, the paper wrote, "met his wife while playing in London several years ago. Four years ago he went to Canada and started a school of music there, which he will continue to direct."[33]

Jan was much nicer than his brother Mark, Cather wrote to her friend Dorothy Canfield Fisher. She was glad of the marriage because Isabelle was very happy. Whether it was Cather who had found the minister to perform "the Protestant-Jewish" wedding was not known, but she may well have done so, and also arranged the reception. Cather admitted that she and Jan were not very congenial, but the letter revealed no hostility, and there certainly was no seething anger.[34] On the other hand, another friend, Elizabeth Sergeant, wrote in her memoir that Jan and Isabelle would not desert American shores during the war but that Cather was afraid they would end up in Europe after it was over – which indeed they did. Cather's "eyes were vacant and her natural exuberance drained away" when she heard about Isabelle's proposed marriage."[35]

Cather and Isabelle remained friends for life. After Isabelle's death Jan sent to Willa Cather all her letters to Isabelle. Cather burned them. One of the surviving few letters from Isabelle in Paris ended like this:

> Jan cleared about $1,000 on his "cave" of old wines…. We were keeping them for you, but you did not come. Now the Cave is empty.
> So lovingly to you,
> Isabelle.[36]

As to "the Protestant-Jewish wedding," whatever the documents said about Jan's religion, Jan was evidently perceived to be Jewish, so much so that one biographer commented, "Willa Cather's nasty portrayals of predatory Jewish men in stories written after she knew of Isabelle's marriage plans *(The Diamond Mine* and *Scandal)* were in part motivated by the unfortunate anti-Semitism Cather shared with many American writers of her generation, and in part by her hostility to her victorious rival. Later Cather seemed to announce her affection for Hambourg…. In life, if not in fiction, Cather achieved an amicable relationship with Hambourg, possibly because she recognized that – if she were to retain a close friendship with Isabelle – she simply had to accept her husband. Hambourg, in turn acknowledged Cather as his wife's dearest friend, and the three spent a good deal of time together over the years." [37]

Literary pictures portraying Jews as outsiders, another writer observed, and identifying Jewishness with "commercial exploitation, secularization, and destruction of traditional values" were drawn by "stellar members of Cather's generation (Anderson,

Willa Cather (left), in a portrait taken in Omaha, Nebraska, and Frances Isabelle McClung (below), close friend of Cather and wife of Jan Hambourg.

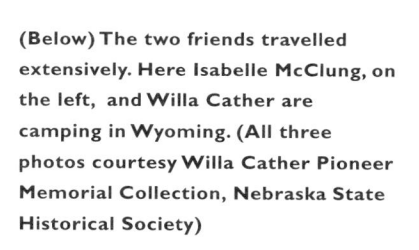

(Below) The two friends travelled extensively. Here Isabelle McClung, on the left, and Willa Cather are camping in Wyoming. (All three photos courtesy Willa Cather Pioneer Memorial Collection, Nebraska State Historical Society)

Dreiser) and of the generation succeeding (Hemingway, Fitzgerald, Eliot, Pound)."[38]

A student of Cather's fiction summarized her position as follows:

> The moral absolutists, who find any expressed consciousness of otherness evidence of racism or elitism, will find many instances of distancing, if only in the epithets Jew, Jewess, Hebrew. The rest of us must read and ponder. We can at least agree that Cather was aware of Jews as a presence in American life and, more than any other writer of her time, chose to register that presence in fiction.... She witnessed, and put in her fiction, the anti-Semitic prejudices of the dominant culture. In her way, she combated this bias, but hers was not the direct way of the social protest novel, and, clearly, she did not make it an overriding concern. She put the need of the work first.[39]

Willa Cather invented Louie Marsellus, a cultivated, suave, materialistic Jew, for one of her most personal works, *The Professor's House*. It was published nine years after Isabelle's marriage. In the opinion of some of Cather's biographers, Louie bore a distinct resemblance to Jan Hambourg.

Louie bore a distinct resemblance to Jan Hambourg. The central figure in the novel is Louie's father-in-law, Professor St. Peter. Louie's wife Rosamond, the professor's daughter, had been engaged to a gifted protégé of the professor, an inventor called Tom Outland who was killed in the war. Louie profitably exploited the invention of his predecessor – a man who had died a hero's death. Louie's and Rosamond's wealth, therefore, was based on what critic Leon Edel called "an ethically dubious foundation." At first the professor considered Louie an upstart and disliked him intensely, though his wife was very fond of him and in particular liked his European manners. Later the professor softened.[40]

In the view of a student of Willa Cather's "Semitism," her portrait of Marsellus was actually not anti-Semitic but, on the contrary, designed "to explode the stereotype" and to show that Marsellus's "energy and zest for living (what the professor, with unconscious bias, calls the 'florid' style) make him, after all, the true inheritor of the Outland legend."[41]

> Most interesting in these familiar knots is St. Peter's reluctant but increasing fondness for the thick-skinned, irrepressible Louie, at first an unwelcome substitute son-in-law, but eventually acknowledged as generous and benign. It is as though Cather's own tendency to anti-Semitism ... is being argued with and overcome. Jan Hambourg, the dedicatee in the first edition of *The Professor's House* was probably on her mind.[42]

Leon Edel comments on the dedication to Jan:

> As we compare the somewhat glib and pretentious Louie with the real-life musician, we recover similarities or exaggerations at so many points that we are prompted to conjecture whether the novelist did not find it necessary to write this flattering dedication *For Jan – because he likes narrative* to overcome her guilt over the unflattering portrait she had painted, or to disguise what she had done. Behind the ambiguous compliment to a man who had taken her loved one from her, we may read a considerable infusion – and confusion – of emotion, jealousy, guilt, anguish, and downright hatred.... However much she found Jan Hambourg a civilized and cultured being, she would have preferred to have him as a friend rather than as a consort and husband of Isabelle-Rosamond.[43]

There is a significant moment in the novel when the professor's negative feelings towards Louis are overcome, the moment when it is discovered that his other son-in-law, the unsuccessful, restless, anti-Semitic journalist Scott, had Louie secretly blackballed from the Arts and Letters Club.

Louie has this to say:

"As for Scott, I can understand. He was the first son of the family, and he was the whole thing. Then I came along, a stranger, and carried off Rosie, and this patent began to pay off so well – it's enough to make any man jealous and he's a Scotchman! But I think Scott will come around in the end; people usually do, if you treat them well, and I mean to. I like the fellow. As for Rosamond, you must not give that a thought. I love her when she's naughty. She's a bit unreasonable sometimes, but I'm always hoping for a period of utter, of fantastic unreasonableness, which will be the beginning of a great happiness for us all."

"Louie, you are magnanimous and magnificent!" murmured his vanquished father-in-law.[44]

When Jewish characters in American fiction are tormented and they don't fight back, they are often despised for their spinelessness, for example Robert Cohn in Hemingway's *The Sun Also Rises*. It is a measure of Cather's unwillingness to follow stereotypes that the Professor, after he has overcome his initial dislike of Louie, praises him for his forbearance.

Jan was head of the violin department at the Hambourg Conservatory in Toronto for four years. When he and Isabelle came to Toronto after they were married, they lived on St. Vincent Street, not at the conservatory, where his mother and his brothers Boris and Clement lived. Vincent Street, later swallowed by provincial government buildings, was south of Wellesley Street and east of Queen's Park. Willa Cather had been right – they left for Europe at the earliest opportunity once the war was over. It is to be assumed that the wealthy and art-loving Isabelle did not feel entirely at home in Toronto. After his father's death in 1916, two months after Jan's wedding, Jan left the job of directing the conservatory to his younger brother Boris. It seems to have been understood that Jan and Isabelle did not intend to stay.

In 1920 they left Toronto for a luxurious apartment on the Left Bank in Paris, near the rue de Sèvres. In the summer they joined

Willa Cather on a two-week journey to the battlefields, still devastated by war, and found the grave of her cousin who had been killed in 1918. Jan had arranged all the details of the journey. She wrote a long letter to her cousin's mother about the grave. In 1923 she published her war novel, *One of Ours,* for which she was awarded the Pulitzer Prize.

One of Jan's students at the Hambourg Conservatory, Samuel Hersenhoren, followed him to Paris. Sammy was twelve at the time. He stayed in France from 1920 to 1925, first in Paris, and after 1923 in Ville d'Avray, a wooded and pleasant suburb where Jan and Isabelle rented a villa. Later, Hersenhoren became a noted violinist and conductor in Toronto. For nine years he played second violin in the Parlow String Quartet (1942-1951). He conducted premieres of many Canadian works, in live concerts and on the CBC. In 1950 he conducted the orchestra for the first Canadian ballet festival. Many Canadians also remember him as the music director of *The Wayne and Shuster Show*. He died in 1982.

His widow, Jeanie Hersenhoren, of course, did not know him as a boy, but later in life he often spoke to her about those "incredible years":

> Every day Sammy had his lesson, and every day he practised for a few hours. And for the rest of the time he walked. By the time the five years were over he knew Paris better than Toronto. He also spent some time in Florence, and in other places. Can you imagine what this meant? Isn't it an amazing story – for this boy from this modest, if not to say poor, Polish family? His father worked in the rag-business on Spadina. And there was his youngest son, Sammy, with his dome-top trunk, going off to Europe for five years! His two older brothers were quite resentful of this – into adulthood. Sammy never saw his family for five years – his father may have visited him once, I'm not sure. When he came back, his first job was to play with Percy Faith, Percy on piano, Sammy on violin, in a silent movie house on St. Clair Avenue – he never looked back! Jan's wife taught him table-manners, and he came

Jan Hambourg ~ Epicure, Violinist, Scholar

This portrait of Jan Hambourg is signed "To my dear friend and disciple Sammy Hersenhoren with my most sincere wishes for his J.S.B. – and the rest! Jan Hambourg, Paris, June 1933." (Courtesy Jeanie Hersenhoren)

back to Toronto a polished young gentleman – and he never lost the polish.[45]

An undated letter Isabelle wrote to Willa Cather from Paris – by then they had moved back to Paris from their villa in Ville d'Avray – refers to Sammy's departure:

> When Jan writes to Sammy, I'll add a word telling him you will be glad to see him if he goes to New York – to either write or telephone you. He will be so pleased. He sailed for Toronto via New York a week ago last Wednesday....
>
> Did I tell you that S. one day at tea looked lovingly at Jan's tea cup – a big one S. remembered from V. d'Avray, so I found one like it and gave it to him. He was *delighted*....
>
> He heard Xavier play some of Xavier's own compositions, also the double Bach with Jan and was thrilled.... He has learned to work, developed his taste a lot, and he has kept what he had. He has many virtues, young Sammy. Where he got 'em I don't know – in the beginning they just were.... He has a voice like a fog horn, a big one – and he still has his nice dimples when he smiles. He said he *longed* to go to Florence. He has kept up his Italian *after a fashion* because there is an Italian restaurant in Toronto....[46]

Soon the Hambourgs moved to an elegant apartment at 46 rue du Bac in an opulent building with a long history. It was built in 1728 by the grandson of Samuel Bernard, a banker to Louis XIV. Later, Paul François Jean Nicolas Barras lived there, the man who arrested Robespierre in 1794 and who introduced his former mistress Josephine de Beauharnais to his chief adjutant, the young Napoleon Bonaparte. After Barras' time the building passed to Louis Veuillot, the editor of the newspaper *L'Univers*. In 1890 the father of Jean Cocteau sold it to the members of the Deyrolle dynasty of naturalists, who still own it. The Deyrolle enterprise, founded in 1831, sells scientific instruments, zoological, entomological and mineralogical collections, and curiosities, books, trophies and stuffed animals from all corners of the world, including – in the spring of 1997 – a stuffed moose from northern Canada. At one time the family owned a copy of *Les Trois Mousquetaires* by Alexandre Dumas *père*, "bound in the tattooed skin of two duelists *en costume Louis XIII*" – let the reader decide what this means.

According to the telephone book, at the time Jan and Isabelle lived there, other apartments were occupied by the Chinchilla Club, the Club of Pedigreed Goats, the Federation of French Aviculture Clubs (aviculture – the breeding and rearing of birds), the Leghorn Club, and a syndicate of breeders of Jersey cows.

The Canadian composer Murray Adaskin met Jan in Paris in the summer of 1929. He was studying there with his friend Philip Clark. "One day," Adaskin recalls, "we went to the Paris branch of the Bank of Montreal to cash some Canadian travellers cheques. Not expecting to see a person we knew, Philip noticed a man reading a newspaper and said he thought he looked like Jan Hambourg, which indeed he was. After a brief conversation he invited us to visit him in his home. Together, he and his wife welcomed us most graciously. They showed us their stunning collection of art. It was the first time I had seen original works by the impressionist painters. It was a memorable visit for us."[47]

The same year Jan and Isabelle had Murray Adaskin's violinist brother Harry and his wife to dinner. As Harry rang the bell he heard "a good violinist" playing the opening bars of the Prelude of Bach's E major Partita. He thought Jan was teaching and apologized for coming early. But no, Jan had not been teaching and Adaskin wasn't early. It was not Jan who was playing. It was his parrot Coco. "This I couldn't believe. I know good fiddle-playing when I hear it, and this was no parrot. However, Jan led me to a room containing a large birdcage, and in it sat an intelligent-looking, big, bright, green parrot. It looked me over with a knowing, baleful eye, and Jan tried to coax it to – I have to say to 'play' – the Bach Prelude. But it wouldn't. We were leaving the room when I heard the same violinist 'play' the opening bars of Kreisler's *Liebeslied*. It was uncanny, and it was Coco."[48]

The Hambourgs' house in Ville d'Avray. On the photo Isabelle wrote to Willa Cather: "The two windows in front and one at side yours." (Courtesy Willa Cather Pioneer Memorial Collection, Nebraska State Historical Society)

The building at 46, rue du Bac in Paris where Jan and Isabelle Hambourg had an apartment. (Photo: Madeline Koch)

Soon the Hambourgs made friends with an even younger violinist than Sammy Hersenhoren, the eleven-year-old Yehudi Menuhin, who was being acclaimed as the greatest child prodigy since Mozart. He soon called Jan "Uncle Jan." Yehudi was in the company of his parents and two sisters, Hephzibah and Yaltah, and was so well looked after that he was never given an opportunity to cross a street unescorted until he was eighteen.

Menuhin described Jan in his autobiography:

> Jan was [a] Russian-Jewish violinist, but of English background. Although he had studied with Ysaÿe and achieved excellence, he neither performed nor taught; he did not need to; his American wife, Isabelle, daughter of Judge McClung of Pittsburgh, was as rich as she was beautiful and distinguished. Their apartment, in a luxurious block not far from the rue de Sèvres, faced onto a *cour* planted with trees, and just as their home looked inward, isolated from the bustle of the public street, so did their lives; and the one and the other were new to me. In the United States everything faces out, the way of life no less than the buildings, and the courtyard, which has travelled from the east as far as Britain, has never taken root there. The Hambourgs loved their life and found in Paris its ideal setting; amid good music, good books and good food, they dwelt in perfect contentment, seeing nothing to strive for and feeling no need to strive. We often visited them.... He knew a good deal about wine and food – indeed he had been elected a member of the *Société Gastronomique* – and often Isabelle and he took us to some noted restaurant, where our knowledge of French cuisine advanced by leaps and bounds. Perhaps because they had no children of their own, Jan and Isabelle took a warmer interest in us three than might be expected of adults of their sophistication; with the result that windows were opened onto their so different lives, revealing to us new worlds in the most natural way possible without anyone's troubling to underline the novelty.[49]

Jan was "a *bon vivant* and an unquenchable enthusiast," the American journalist Robert Magidoff wrote in his biography of Menuhin. He was "forever excited about one thing or another, his enthusiasms as momentarily unyielding as they were quickly passing. But he never wavered in his passion for fine food and his admiration for Yehudi's talent."

In 1931 Jan went house-hunting in Ville d'Avray with the Menuhins. The house they chose was near the Parc St. Cloud. "All in all," wrote Magidoff, "this was probably the [Menuhin] family's happiest period together, the happiest and the most comfortable. The Gallic charm of the house was enhanced by Jan Hambourg's one-time servants, Ferruccio and his wife Bigina, who did the household chores with mirth, devotion and efficiency. Formerly a jockey, Ferruccio was small and wiry, looking somewhat ridiculous alongside his slow, enormous bosomy Bigina. They adored each other and were not in the least embarrassed at being surprised in an embrace by one or another of the children as they cleaned house or prepared the meals."[50]

In his autobiography, Yehudi Menuhin described the house they had chosen.

> There was yet another floor above, where my mother had a sitting room and where lived Bigina and Ferruccio, our cook and handyman, whom we might have inherited from an Italian operetta but who were in fact supplied by the Hambourgs.[51] Ferruccio was suave and small, Bigina was enormous; he had been a runner and was very lithe on his feet; she was a real cook, massive, good-natured, rooted to the kitchen. Sometimes they would make ice cream, a lengthy operation by hand churn, which Ferruccio would turn, singing the while; in those days we called ice cream "Tra-la-la." Bigina and Ferruccio stayed with us until we left France.... I looked them up the first night I reached liberated Paris, before the end of the war, and was delighted, but not overly surprised, to find them safe, sound and as endearing as ever.[52]

One of Jan's unquenchable enthusiasms was Bach's sonatas and partitas for solo violin. Yehudi Menuhin reports: "On more than one occasion I witnessed Uncle Jan's constant ritual: every weekday he attired himself in a wine-red velvet jacket, chose his Amati or his Peter Guarnerius, and played one of Bach's six works for solo violin, beginning the cycle on Monday, completing it on Saturday. Like God, he rested on the seventh day. Some decades ago his edition of the solo sonatas was published."[53]

The edition to which Menuhin referred was published by Oxford University Press in 1934. Clement Hambourg deposited at the National Library in Ottawa a copy bearing Jan's elegantly and meticulously written dedication to "the memory of my master Eugène Ysaÿe." Clement noted that the edition had been "greatly praised by Jascha Heifetz and a great many other violinists."[54] It is no reflection on Jan's achievement that the publisher was not able to capitalize on this praise, nor that the edition was considered to be merely one of many and has, in effect, been forgotten.[55]

Jan made Bach's six magnificent sonatas and partitas for solo violin the centre of his musicianship. (The difference between sonatas and partitas is of interest primarily to musicologists. Both are suites.) They are indeed milestones in the history of western music. The great Bach scholar, theologian, medical doctor and humanist Albert Schweitzer, with whom Jan was in touch, was one of the few who, like him, understood that Bach's inventiveness and spiritual depth had never been surpassed and that these works were compositions of extraordinary perfection and expressiveness. These men were ahead of their time, in the sense that they made an enormous effort to determine the composer's intention in the context of the musical culture of his day, and placed it ahead of all other considerations. This effort was not unlike the aspirations of those who today prefer music to be played with the instruments for which it was composed. It is regrettable that neither Jan nor Schweitzer ever saw the original, very beautiful autograph, which has been published since their time. Recent editors, for example those connected with the *Bärenreiter* edition, who have had the opportunity to study the autograph rather than early editions, attempt to confine their alterations and additions to the minimum.[56]

The sonatas were written for solo violin, but for several voices, not for one voice. They are polyphonic. The logic, beauty and subtlety of their musical architecture require the kind of concentration most easily attainable in the intimate surroundings in which chamber music is best performed. Had it not been for the invention of recordings, their survival might have depended on the relatively small audiences who attend chamber music concerts and on enthusiasts like Jan and others who play them for themselves or, privately, to small audiences in their homes. Today, recordings by (in alphabetical order) Heifetz, Kramer, Menuhin, Milstein, Oistrakh, Szeryng, Szigeti and others have made it possible for millions all over the world to admire and love the sonatas in their homes the way Jan did. As to the cello sonatas, credit for their discovery must go almost entirely to Pablo Casals.

Between the baroque period and this century the violin and cello were not considered appropriate instruments for compositions for more than one voice. The piano and the organ were. Haydn, Mozart, Beethoven did not write for solo stringed instruments. Even Felix Mendelssohn, who inspired the great Bach revival in the nineteenth century, considered Bach's solo sonatas for violin not viable in their original form and composed a piano accompaniment for the famous Chaconne in the D-minor Sonata. Robert Schumann, who also published an edition, composed piano accompaniments for all six. "To us," wrote Albert Schweitzer, "it is incomprehensible that two such great artists could believe that they were thus carrying out Bach's intentions."[57] Prominent violin teachers in the early nineteenth century like Ferdinand David thought the sonatas were useful as student exercises, because of their technical challenges. It was not until the end of the nineteenth century that Joseph Joachim, whose own edition was one of Jan's two basic texts, introduced them into the concert hall. But then they often suffered the fate of being considered mere virtuoso pieces.

Jan described his work in an article for the *Monthly Musical Record*, a British publication, which is reprinted in the Appendix.

This article received a polite review in the same publication: "Careful perusal bears out most of the claims made for it. Undoubtedly there is some difficulty in the playing of Bach's chords when the essential note of the theme happens to be the lowest.... Mr. Hambourg is of great assistance to the conscientious violinist. But only time can show whether his suggestions can be accepted without reservations."[58]

The Musical Times, however, was more critical: "There is something to be said for Mr. Hambourg's theory – but something may also be urged against it. If we play in the old way the essential note which represents the melody is short and less important than the harmonic notes on which the bow comes to rest. In the Hambourg way the bow comes to rest in the right place, but it breaks the continuity of the melody by inserting the harmony between two melodic notes. The result is sometimes quite happy, as in the Chaconne. Elsewhere its use might seem questionable if not altogether objectionable."[59]

There has been a good deal of Bach research since 1934. Scholars now believe that Bach did not intend the performer to play chords together on three or four strings, which Jan and Schweitzer assumed, even if the bows in his time permitted it. We now know he wanted the chords broken like the chords on a lute, not sustained.

Jan could have passed for a Frenchman. As a boy he had studied with Ysaÿe in Belgium – in French. In 1910, when he arrived in Toronto at the age of twenty-eight, his interviewer from the *Canadian Courier* noted that he seemed "particularly fond of the modern French romanciers, Balzac, Flaubert and Zola; he reminds you of a Gaul with his electric energy, his *joie de vivre.*"

Willa Cather, too, had a passion for France. She had spent four semesters at the University of Nebraska reading French literature. In 1902, soon after they met, she and Isabelle McClung travelled to France. Her "letters" on Dieppe and Rouen, on the cemeteries of Paris, on Barbizon, Avignon, Marseilles, Le Lavandou and Arles, were published in the *Courier* and in 1956 collected and issued as a book.[60]

A logical consequence of Willa Cather's and Jan Hambourg's love of France was their love of French cooking. After the First World War, while they were living in Greenwich Village, Cather and her friend Edith Lewis had a French cook, Josephine. Edith Lewis wrote in her memoir:

> Josephine's father had kept a well-known restaurant near Pau, and she herself was a splendid cook, so that at 5 Bank Street we were able to give a great many dinner parties. She was an important figure in our lives at that time – high-spirited, warm-hearted, impulsive, brimming over with vitality, and intelligent, as the French are; with great humour, very quick perceptions about people, a rather merciless philosophy of life. She would never speak English, and we were forced to speak our very lame French with her. Her personality was so pervasive and uncompromising that she created a sort of French household atmosphere around us: and I think there is no question that this contributed, to a certain extent, to such novels as *Death Comes for the Archbishop* and *Shadow on the Rock*.[61]

The Hambourgs were spending part of the summer of 1919 in a rented house in Scarsdale, New York, on holiday from the Hambourg Conservatory in Toronto. Cather was living across the street and was able to lend them Josephine for a time. In return, Cather could listen to Mozart, Beethoven and Schubert quartets every evening, which Jan played with his friends. "The gods on Olympus do not have such music," she wrote in a letter.

The Hambourgs were so enamoured of Josephine and so afraid Cather might take her away, that they would even play request programs for Josephine.[62]

Once the Hambourgs had moved to France and found a house in Ville d'Avray, they invited Willa Cather to stay with them. They even fitted up a study for her, hoping she would write there. But she could not. "I hate to leave France or England when I am there," she told an interviewer, "but I cannot produce my kind of work away from the American idiom." She went on to say she loved life at Ville d'Avray.

"But I was so busy drinking in the beauty of the place that I could not work. I went from there to Paris, hoping to achieve a working state of mind, but again it proved impossible. The Seine absorbed my thoughts. I could look at it for hours as it reflected every mood of the ever-changing skies, and the colourful life surging around me was utterly distracting as well."[63]

If the beauty if Paris distracted Willa Cather from work, the beauty of Quebec, which she visited for the first time in 1928, did the very opposite; it propelled her into a period of intensive creativity. For beauty to stimulate creation it has to strike a chord in the innermost recesses of an artist's psyche – in Willa Cather's case a profoundly American psyche – at the right psychological moment. Quebec was French, but it was French *in America,* the Old World in the New World. Since her beginnings in Nebraska – she had taken Latin and Greek at the University of Nebraska and read Pindar, Herodotus, Homer and the Greek dramatists before she studied French – the Old World was part of her.

Death Comes for the Archbishop, her most remembered novel, had been published in 1927. The location was New Mexico, the time the nineteenth century, the subject religious heroism, the landscape picturesque, the main characters wise and sophisticated, and the plot full of action. Now, having seen Quebec, she decided to do for Quebec in the late seventeenth and early eighteenth centuries what she had done for New Mexico in the nineteenth. The new subject had the added advantage over the Southwest that it allowed her to deal with her lifelong association with French civilization. *Shadow on the Rock* became, for a time, the most widely read novel in America.[64]

"From the first moment," wrote Edith Lewis, "that she looked down from the windows of the Château Frontenac on the pointed roofs and Norman outlines of the town of Quebec, Willa Cather was not merely stirred and charmed – she was overwhelmed by the flood of memory, recognition, surmise it called up; by the sense of its extraordinary French character, isolated and kept intact through hundreds of years, as if by a miracle, on this great un-French continent."[65]

As the title suggests, the novel is full of fog and twilight. She was not concerned with the pioneering beginnings of French Canada in the early seventeenth century, but with colonists who had had time to put down roots. The main characters are the apothecary Euclide Auclair, his twelve-year-old daughter Cécile and her friend Pierre Charron, a *coureur de bois*. Pierre ultimately marries Cécile. Auclair is medical advisor to Count Frontenac, who had brought him from France with him. The novel is episodic in character, and the story, which opens in October with the last ships sailing down the St. Lawrence, leaving the Rock cut off from France for the winter, is less important than the domestic arrangements of the Auclair house, and less important than the quarrels between Governor Frontenac, who was, according to the historian Francis Parkman (Cather's main source), "the most remarkable man who ever represented the crown in the New World," and Bishop Laval. There is little of the robust, sardonic tone of *Death Comes for the Archbishop*. Instead there is a muffled, luminous haze.

In 1930 Willa Cather celebrated the New Year in Quebec City, to experience it in the dead of winter. In May she sailed for Paris, to visit the Hambourgs. She had not seen Isabelle for seven years. By now Isabelle had been seriously ill for two years with chronic nephritis, for which at the time there was no cure other than nursing. She was to live for another eight years.

> I remember our stay there as a happy one [wrote Willa Cather's companion, Edith Lewis], in spite of the anxieties that shadowed it.... For two months Willa Cather followed the trail of Count Frontenac in Paris. She used to walk often along the Quai des Célestins and about Frontenac's old quarter; she visited the church of St. Paul, and Saint Nicholas-des-Champs, where Frontenac's heart was buried, and spent many mornings at the Musée Carnavalet, looking up things she wanted to know. With Jan and Isabelle Hambourg she made a short trip to St. Malo. There had been a tremendous storm the night before, the greatest for twenty years along that coast, and the sea was flinging great waves over the sea-wall. Weather was always a very positive

element in Willa Cather's consciousness. She had a poet's attitude towards weather, to her it was one of the rich contributive constituents of life. It is interesting to note how much weather plays a part in the Quebec story.[66]

Soon after, Cather had an amazing Old-World-New-World adventure. She and Edith Lewis spent a few days in Aix-les Bains. They liked the old-fashioned watering-place, with its opera house and formal squares. They did not like modern luxury hotels – they could have stayed, if they had wanted to, at the Splendide, with King Alfonso of Spain and the Aga Khan, who happened to be registered there, as fellow guests. But they preferred the plain, old-fashioned Grand Hotel.

Every evening, in the dining-room, they observed a distinguished old lady, well over eighty. In the morning they saw her get into her car and drive off with her chauffeur, taking paints and canvas and a camp-stool with her. At last they became acquainted – the old lady spoke excellent English. Turgenev's name came up. "I knew him well at one time," the old lady said. Cather was astonished. Her mother, the old lady explained, had died at her birth. She was brought up in her uncle's home. "My uncle also was a man of letters, Gustave Flaubert, you may perhaps know him."

So the old lady was "Caro" of Flaubert's *Lettres à sa nièce Caroline* – Caro, who had sat like a mouse in her uncle's study when she was a little girl, and who later become his literary executor.

"The room was absolutely quiet," Cather described the scene later. "There was nothing to say to this disclosure. It was like being suddenly brought up against a mountain of memories."[67] The old lady was delighted in turn to meet someone who knew her uncle's works intimately and was passionately fond of them. The meeting between the two seemed to have been planned, Elizabeth Sergeant recalls, "in Willa's heaven."[68]

Another encounter was to follow, with more lasting consequences. On Cather's return to Paris, Jan introduced her to Yehudi Menuhin. By now Yehudi was fourteen, his younger sisters Hephzibah seven and Yaltah five.

> They were endlessly captivating, amusing and endearing, the most gifted children Willa Cather had ever known, with that wonderful aura of imaginative charm, prescience, inspiration that even the most gifted lose after they grow up. They were also extremely lovable, affectionate, and unspoiled – in some ways funnily naive, in others sensitive and discerning far beyond their years. They had an immense capacity for admiration and hero-worship, and Willa Cather became, I think, their greatest hero.[69]

When they met again the next year on the West Coast, Willa Cather wanted to dedicate *Shadow on the Rock* to them. She changed her mind only when she was told the Menuhin parents were very much opposed to the lionizing of their children.

Menuhin understood very well what his family gave Cather. "We, who had found our American author, gave [her] her European family."[70] When Isabelle died in 1938, Menuhin went to see Willa Cather to comfort her. The friendship lasted until the end of her life. He called her "a rock of strength and sweetness."

Edith Lewis remembered

> the Menuhin family's winter visits to New York, in the years that followed, as a sort of continuous festival, full of concerts and gay parties; orange trees and great baskets of flowers for Willa Cather arriving in the midst of snow-storms; birthday luncheons with Russian caviar and champagne; excursions to the opera, where she took Yaltah and Hephzibah to hear *Parsifal* for the first time; long walks around the reservoir in Central Park, where the three children all wanted to walk beside her, and had to take turn-about. They discussed very abstract subjects together – art, religion, philosophy, life. If Willa Cather had been writing *War and Peace* I am sure she would have abandoned it to take these walks.[71]

In March 1947 Yehudi and Hephzibah visited Willa Cather with their children a few hours before sailing for Europe. They had often "filled her apartment on Park Avenue "with the voices of youth."

She thought the beauty in the natures of the Menuhin children transcended mere "giftedness," and she confided to one correspondent that she would rather have left any other chapter of her life left out than the Menuhin chapter, which had brought her so much happiness. At the end of that morning the Menuhins quietly slipped on their things, the appointed cabs were waiting, and they drove away.

That was the last time they saw Willa Cather.[72]

The Canadian musician from Hamilton, Clarence Lucas, who became Mark's composition teacher in London in the 1890s, and who has just been "rediscovered," also was a friend of Jan's. Lucas moved to France in 1923 and Jan found him a house in Sèvres in which Lucas's daughter Jessica still lives. In 1933 Lucas moved to London, where he died in 1947 at the age of eighty-one. To the very end of his life he was active as a composer, arranger, lyricist and translator.

In his last year – and presumably before – he had business dealings with Jan, who by then also lived in London. Lucas described these last dealings in letters to his wife in Canada.

> March 24, 1947
> I am glad that the money has been paid.... I am not going to risk the endless worry of dealing with Jan Hambourg again. He does not care how much trouble he causes others.

> March 28, 1947
> I hope Jessica will yet receive the ... money I paid Hambourg on December 10. I have no time to bother with that old Jew. He is not as dishonest as he is unintelligent. He lost an enormous amount of money trying to win the Derby horse race. Imagine a fool and an amateur trying to win from those professional sharks.[73]

Jan had moved to London after Isabelle's death. He and Luba shared an apartment near the Queen's Hall. Jan kept busy – he was founder and director of the Parnassus Sunday Concerts, with an office on Berkeley Square.

Jan had made his will before the war.[74] He appointed his sister Galia and his stockbroker Vincent Poore executors.[75] These were the main bequests:

> a) To Willa Cather in memory of her wonderful and loving friendship with my late wife Isabelle my violin Isabella by Nicolo Amati dated 1665.[76]
> b) To my sister Luba my picture by Murillo and all my other pictures not otherwise bequeathed by this my Will or any codicils thereto.
> c) To my said sister Galia all my red wine.
> d) To my brother Mark all my white wine.
> e) To my brother Boris all my music.

On September 29, 1947, Jan died, in a train near Tours, France. Willa Cather did not live to receive his Amati violin. She had died five months before him, on April 24, 1947, in New York City.

Boris Hambourg

THE TOTAL MUSICIAN

Mark, however genial, was a prodigy, a virtuoso, an arresting, charismatic, dominating personality. Boris was not.[1] He was instead "dark and jaunty, airy, whimsical and gay," an intuitive, accomplished, natural chamber musician.[2] Elie Spivak said of him in his final tribute in 1954, "To him, living and making music were synonymous."[3] The accompanist Gerald Moore described him as a "man of a particularly sweet and gentle nature."[4]

Boris had thick black hair, later grey, usually wore glasses, and was a fastidious dresser. At home he enjoyed wearing a maroon smoking jacket, and in the summer he sported a white, Italian suit. He often wore an artist's neck-cloth, not a neck-tie. He had a friendly, warm, gentle, urbane smile and enjoyed speaking French. He had joined the Arts and Letters Club in Toronto with his father in 1911 and remained an active member for the rest of his life.

When Boris was a little boy the great Joachim heard him play and predicted a brilliant future for him. Naturally, his father saw to it that his training would be the best available. In London he had cello lessons from Herbert Walenn. At fourteen he left for Frankfurt to study cello with Hugo Becker and composition with Ivan Knorr at the Hoch Konservatorium. Becker had played the first cello in the opera orchestra and was appointed director of the chamber-music class at the Konservatorium. Boris also studied in Berlin and in Godinne-sur-Meuse with Ysaÿe, who coached him in chamber music.

After his début in Bad Pyrmont in 1903 at the age of nineteen, he gave a series of recitals in London and on the continent and played with Mark and Jan in 1905 in the first of various Hambourg Trios and with Jan, John Robinson and Eric Coates in the Hambourg String Quartet.

(There was a succession of violin-cello-piano Hambourg Trios. In 1910 a Hambourg Trio consisting of Jan, Richard Tatersall (piano) and Paul Hahn (cello) gave a number of concerts in Toronto. In 1915 Mark, Jan and Boris performed together in a Tchaikovsky concert at Massey Hall, and in the same hall twenty years later played the Beethoven Triple Concerto, after which they toured briefly. Later members of Hambourg Trios were Alberto Guerrero, Reginald Stewart, Géza de Kresz, Harry Adaskin, Elie Spivak, Vino Harisay – and Clement Hambourg. The de Kresz Hambourg Trio, consisting of Géza de Kresz, his wife Norah Drewett and Boris, performed from 1948 to 1952 in Toronto and also made a tour in the U.S.)

In 1909 Boris toured with Mark and Jan in South Africa. By the time he was twenty-six and came to Canada to visit his family after a concert tour in the United States, at Christmas 1910, he had already given forty-five concerts in South Africa and seventy-five in New Zealand and Australia earlier that year.[5] At first he did not intend to stay in Toronto but he liked what he saw and changed his mind. Six years later, after the death of his father, he became director of the Hambourg Conservatory of Music and, beginning in 1923, for twenty-two years, the cellist in the Hart House String Quartet, the only member who remained with the quartet from beginning to end. He composed six preludes and six Russian dances for cello and was editor and arranger of eighteenth-century masterpieces. He gave cello recitals in 1911, 1920, 1925, 1930, sometimes arranging his programs in cycles covering specific periods. Boris was one of the first musicians in his era to take an interest in works by early composers, and his series of historical recitals in the Aeolian Hall in London was well researched and presented.[6] In 1934 he was the first Canadian instrumentalist to appear on television, on the BBC.[7]

Many remember him as a devoted, generous teacher. The violinist Morry Kernerman – "a little Heifetz," his parents thought – describes him as his saviour.[8] His family did not have the means to pay for his lessons. Who knows what would have happened to him, he wonders, if Boris had not given him a scholarship at the Hambourg Conservatory when he was five or six. Generally, a young person who could

The young cellist – Boris Hambourg in his twenties.

not pay did not have to pay. Even food and residence, when necessary, were provided. Boris "was an angel of mercy to many young and needy students who came from all parts of Canada," Elie Spivak said of him.

Marcus Adeney, who had a long and distinguished career as a cellist in Toronto, was fourteen and living in Paris, Ontario, when he heard the Hambourg Trio perform in nearby Brantford.[9] He was so thrilled that he asked his mother, herself a violin and piano teacher, to introduce him to the cellist, hoping to study with him. Boris duly took him on and from then on the boy came to Toronto by train regularly every Saturday for his lessons. Adeney praises Boris's generosity with the same affection, admiration and gratitude as Kernerman.

In 1928 Boris, by then the cellist of the Hart House String Quartet, confessed to Adeney that he did not really like teaching and asked him to take over many of his students. Adeney did enjoy teaching and says this was "of enormous importance" to him at the time. The conductor, composer and cellist Glen Morley studied with both Boris *and* Adeney in 1928-1929. Boris continued to play with gifted conservatory students in public.

All the Hambourgs, at various times and in various degrees, suffered from acute shortages of money, but only Boris was often described as distinctly parsimonious. In fact, his parsimony had a certain style and was the cause of much amused comment. Paul Scherman[10] went so far as to use the German and Yiddish word *Schnorrer,* cadger, to describe him. In his travels with the Hart House Quartet Boris was said to make a practice of vanishing from sight the moment a taxi-driver or porter had to be tipped.

Thanks to Mark's global celebrity, the Hambourgs were regarded as a royal family in the world of music when they arrived in Canada in 1910. They skillfully used it to advance their fortunes. As Ed Hausmann wrote in the *Star Weekly*: "From the beginning the Hambourgs made it clear that they were assuming the role of musical authorities and benevolent celebrities. They exuded the best of continental manners and mannerisms and they were accepted on their own terms."[11]

There were few concert musicians they had not met in Europe as fellow performers, at parties, in the foyers of concert halls, in agents' waiting-rooms and, in early life, in the best conservatories. Just as big-name performers were free to boast they knew the Hambourgs, the Hambourgs were free to boast they knew *them,* it being clearly understood that it was wise, and in everyone's interest, to keep the concept of *knowing* conveniently vague. Of all the Hambourgs, it was Boris who was the most cunning in the game of networking. It was said he sometimes considered an invitation to a potentially useful social gathering an unnecessary formality.

Mark had been right to advise his father to choose Toronto.[12] In his teens he had often performed in English provincial cities like Birmingham and Manchester, and he could sense that Toronto had many things in common with them. But what Birmingham and Manchester lacked was Toronto's vast, underdeveloped hinterland with its potential riches, unimaginable in the Old World. It gave Toronto its optimistic self-confidence.

As a small Russian boy when the family went to England, Mark had benefited from his restless father's spirit of adventure. Now, in his second emigration, Professor Hambourg's instinct once again proved sound. Unlike any city in the United States he might have chosen, Toronto was emphatically and agreeably British. The British in London, after all, had responded well to his personality and to his ideas on musical education, and in Toronto as in London the benefits to be derived from English freedom and tolerance would be immeasurable.

Mark was by no means the first Russian-born pianist to play in Toronto. His – and Beethoven's – look-alike, Anton Rubinstein, had given a concert there in 1872, as had other great names, from Jenny Lind to Hans von Bülow. Whenever foreign stars came to visit they sold out. The building in which they usually appeared, Massey Hall, was built in 1894 and owed its existence to the manufacturers of agricultural machinery whose president, Vincent Massey, after Professor

Hambourg's death, was to play a major role in Boris's life. (Massey went on to shape the cultural life of Canada after the Second World War as chairman of the Massey Commission, and later became Canada's first native-born governor-general.)

Toronto was not London, but Mark was right – it was a good place for a new school of music. It was already the choral capital of North America. There was the Mendelssohn Choir, established in 1894, and a multitude of church choirs. Also, Toronto had a tradition of patronage by its wealthy merchant families – not only the Masseys but also the Gooderhams and the Eatons and others. The city offered just the right soil in which a cosmopolitan school of performers might to take root and sprout.

The *Star Weekly* recounted: "The time was right for the arrival of a family of famous Europeans, and Toronto was proud, even smug, when Professor Michael Hambourg, the internationally known pedagogue, chose this city as a new home for himself and his family. He filled everyone's idea of what such a person should be: a magnificent patriarch, complete with a shoulder-length mane of gray hair and a noticeable Russian accent."[13]

Was there a need for a new conservatory? After all, the Toronto Conservatory of Music, which was affiliated with the University of Toronto for the purpose of preparing candidates for university degree examinations, was already there. Sixty shareholders had come together to found it in 1886 and it had become the most prominent music-training institution in Canada and one of the most important in the British Empire.[14] However, until Ernest MacMillan became principal in 1926 and introduced a number of reforms, it was essentially a conglomeration of private studios. There were no real courses, like those given in music schools in the United States and abroad, but it did have an effective national examination system modelled on Britain's. (Annual music examinations had not caught on in the United States.) And there were no public subsidies or endowments. To cover operating costs, the school depended entirely on commissions extracted from teachers and revenues from examinations. Money and education lived together in an uneasy partnership.[15]

The Toronto Conservatory of Music (today the Royal Conservatory of Music) offered instruction in practical and theoretical music, as well as elocution, foreign languages, public school music, acoustics, piano tuning, vocal anatomy and hygiene. There were two departments: the Academic, for young students and amateurs, and the Collegiate, which offered programs in professional training for performers and teachers. It had started an orchestra which evolved into the Toronto Symphony Orchestra, phase one (1906-1918). Its headquarters, built in 1897, was at the southwest corner of College Street and University Avenue, where the glass-and-cement Ontario Hydro Building now stands.

There were also several private academies, among them the Toronto College of Music, founded in 1888 by F.H. Torrington, and the Metropolitan School of Music, started in 1893 by W.O. Forsyth and absorbed in 1912 by the Canadian Academy of Music, at 10 Spadina Road. The latter was founded by the soldier, financier and music-lover Colonel Albert Gooderham "for the purpose of keeping gifted students in Toronto and bringing outstanding teachers from Europe." The Academy "had a warm and delightful aura," Harry Adaskin remembered, "which without doubt reflected the amiable and affectionate qualities of its founders, Sir Albert and Lady Gooderham."[16] It was merged with the Toronto Conservatory in 1924 when Gooderham became chairman of the board of the latter.

Colonel Sir Albert Gooderham was a benevolent presence in the background of much of Toronto's musical activity. The foundation of his family's fortune was the Gooderham and Worts distillery, of which he was vice-president, but his interests as soldier, philanthropist and soldier were broader. He had joined the Tenth Royal Grenadiers in 1885 at the age of twenty-four when the regiment was involved in its final skirmish with Louis Riel. The services of the young officer were not required. Later he became lieutenant-colonel of the regiment. Among his other achievements was his role in financing the Connaught Laboratories. Sir Albert was in his seventy-fifth year when he died in 1935, a few months after being knighted for his philanthropic work.

The glittering star of Colonel Albert Gooderham's Canadian Academy of Music was the violinist, composer and conductor Luigi von Kunits, who arrived in Toronto a year after the Hambourgs, and with whom Mark had once played the Kreutzer Sonata in Pittsburgh on one of his first American tours.[17] Soon he became the chief competitor of the Hambourg Conservatory's violin department. Von Kunits was the predecessor of Sir Ernest MacMillan as conductor of the Toronto Symphony Orchestra in its second phase (1922-1931), and the man whose personality and musicianship shaped a whole generation of violinists, some of them alive today.

In his obituary in 1931 in the *Toronto Star,* the critic Augustus Bridle recalled: "On stormy days, with a big muffler and a slouch hat, we saw him hurrying to rehearsals. On Sunday mornings, with his violin case under his arm this cultured graduate of the University of Vienna and the Vienna Conservatory, born within sight of the classic spire of St. Stephen, a master of philosophy, languages and law, went to the little Unitarian Church on Jarvis Street to play some simple big thing by a great master."[18]

"He had a golden disposition," Lou Taub recalls. "He never said an unkind word to any pupil. All he could do, he said, was to teach you the fundamentals of violin playing. What you did after that, was your own business."[19] Lou Taub's father was not well and delivered bread at night by horse and wagon. He earned about eight dollars a week. Lou's violin lessons cost four dollars. It was a good thing that he got lessons free in exchange for teaching von Kunits' son Latin. Later, Taub solved his financial problems while at the University of Toronto and Osgoode Hall law school by playing the violin in the silent movie houses.

For Frank Fusco,[20] von Kunits was the reason he came to Toronto from Ohio. "When he died," he says, "I was lost."

Maurice Solway, who later became a teacher at the Hambourg Conservatory, was another of von Kunits' students.

> Dr. von Kunits was a remarkable man in so many respects it is difficult to know how to begin a description.... He often corre-

sponded in Latin and Greek; his children had Greek names. He was a composer who often used his own Violin Concerto in E-minor as a vehicle in concert performances. His String Quartet was performed by the Academy String Quartet (the house ensemble of the Academy of Music which, during the war, [the First World War] presented works as recent and challenging as the first two String Quartets by Arnold Schönberg).

Von Kunits made his mark on Toronto during the second decade of the century not merely as a pedagogue. He led weekly string rehearsals – sessions which gave his students the unprecedented thrill of playing works from the standard orchestra repertoire.[21]

Harry Adaskin, remembered another aspect of von Kunits: "His general personality was one of amiable detachment, which however didn't go as far as to obviate the pleasure of kissing his attractive girl pupils on the lips when they came for their lessons – in a fatherly way, of course."[22]

Like Jan, von Kunits had studied with Ottakar Ševčík in Prague. But no Hambourg had ever studied composition, as von Kunits had, with Anton Bruckner. And no Hambourg had studied music history, as von Kunits had, with Eduard Hanslick, the model of Beckmesser in Wagner's *Meistersinger*. And no Hambourg had been asked by Brahms to play the second violin, as von Kunits had, *at the age of eleven*, in the composer's three string quartets (Brahms knew his father). A musician who at the age of twenty-one had played his own Violin Concerto with the Vienna Philharmonic was indeed a worthy competitor of the Hambourgs.

Before coming to Toronto in 1912, von Kunits had been concertmaster and assistant conductor in Pittsburgh, for a time under, of all people, Victor Herbert. On his doctor's advice, because of a mild heart condition, he declined the position of conductor of the Philadelphia Orchestra and took the less strenuous position on the staff of the Canadian Academy of Music in Toronto. The Philadelphia job went to the second choice, Leopold Stokowski.

Von Kunits founded the *Canadian Journal of Music* (1914-1919) and wrote articles for various music publications. He had a Central European sense of humour. Many of his musical reviews carried the byline A.L. (All Lies). After the First World War his name came up in a different connection. When a chair of music was proposed for the University of Toronto, an anonymous letter appeared in the press urging that only a pure Britisher, born of Empire stock, be given that important position. This was a veiled attack not on von Kunits, as one might have expected, but on Augustus Vogt, the principal of the Toronto Conservatory, who was born in Canada *of Swiss-German parentage.* In 1919 Vogt became dean of the Faculty of Music, when the conservatory and the faculty merged in the same building. No one challenged the anonymous letter-writer's position publicly, not surprisingly considering the hatred the Germans had aroused during the war just ended. In an ironic letter to his wife, the twenty-six-year-old Ernest MacMillan, just back from a German POW camp, mentioned von Kunits, among others, as a suitable candidate, adding, not pejoratively because he must have deplored the letter's jingoism, that, however, von Kunits was "an out-and-out Hun." One can imagine the expression of amusement and longing on his face as he concluded, "Shouldn't mind the position myself."[23]

There was no need for him to worry. The chair of music was never created and MacMillan was appointed principal of the Toronto Conservatory in September 1926, after Vogt's death, and four months later dean of the Faculty of Music. In 1975 the Orford Quartet revived Luigi von Kunits' String Quartet. A bronze bust of him can be seen in the lobby of Roy Thomson Hall, where the Toronto Symphony Orchestra plays today.

Professor Michael Hambourg, his wife, Catherine, his sons Jan (aged twenty-eight) and Clement (ten, old enough to spend the ocean voyage playing chess with the ship's captain) and teen-age daughters Luba and Manya arrived in Toronto in August 1910. Boris was on a concert tour. Mark and the oldest daughter, Galia, had stayed behind in London. By this time she was married to Reginald

Grey Coke, the second son of Thomas William Coke, Earl of Leicester of Holkham, a lieutenant in the Scots Guards who had been wounded in the Boer War. Coke was much older than Galia and the marriage was not a happy one.

For a short time after arriving in Toronto Michael Hambourg taught at the Yonge Street studios of Heintzman, the piano makers, possibly as a result of a gentlemen's agreement concluded previously in London. Donald D. Sinclair wrote in the *Canadian Courier:* "If the Hambourgs are successful in their aspiration to instruct Canadians in the higher branches of music, it may mean that other European masters will migrate to Canada. Then, parents will be saved the expense of maintaining their daughters [sic] in Europe for advanced study. Canada will be the centre of musical art. Indeed it may come about that present conditions will be reversed; the post-graduate trek will no longer lead from Canada to Europe, but Canadawards."[24]

On a visit to Toronto in 1913, Mark played Beethoven's C-minor Piano Concerto in Massey Hall "with a *transforming* eloquence," Harry Adaskin, who was twelve at the time, remembered, "an eloquence I've rarely heard since – it became one of the highlights of my life."[25] On the occasion of that visit, Mark's father established the Hambourg Conservatory of Music in his rented home at 100 Gloucester Street. He took an advertisement in the Might City Directory announcing "The Hambourg Conservatory of Music / Director: Professor Michael Hambourg / A Distinguished School with a Distinguished Faculty, which includes Professor Michael Hambourg, Jan Hambourg, Boris Hambourg, Senor Paul Morenzo, David Ross, George Dixon and others. Music in all its Branches. Year Book from Secretary. / Phone North 2341. 100 Gloucester Street."

In that same year, 1913, the fourteen-year-old Gerald Moore, who was to become one of the great accompanists of his generation, arrived in Toronto from England with his mother. They went to Heintzman's on Yonge Street to buy a new piano. As Moore described it in his memoirs, "The salesman was electrified when the small boy cascaded up and down the keyboard and played his party pieces; he must take me that evening to play to Michael Hambourg who would give me a scholarship. This seemed the most exciting thing that had ever happened to me."[26]

Michael Hambourg, that "dear old gentleman, a picturesque personality with his big benevolent presence, his white mustache and imperial," took the boy under his wing and gave him a scholarship, under conditions Gerald Moore described as "extraordinary generous." He undertook to pay back the professor ten per cent of his first two years' earnings when he became a professional. No doubt he did so.

Later that year, the Professor transferred his conservatory to 194 Wellesley Street, at the northeast corner of Wellesley and Sherbourne streets, a gracious and spacious Victorian villa belonging to the eminent surgeon Dr. J.F.W. Ross, whose wife, it seems, was a member of the Gooderham family. Within a short walk were five other buildings designed for or inhabited by members of the Gooderham family.

No licence or charter was required from the city or the province to start this new conservatory. It was not designed as a formal institution, with curricula and degrees, though for a time it did have exams. Association with the Hambourg name, it was assumed, would have magical powers in the professional musical world beyond the reaches of any educational bureaucracy and would be far more potent than any academic parchment. From the beginning, the conservatory was conceived as a performance-teaching establishment which would also give space on a rental basis to teachers and students. Most of the students were to be youngsters who also attended elementary or high schools. Others would be of university age, or even older. A big house was essential. With whose help Michael Hambourg managed to acquire this mansion remains a mystery, but the choice of the location testifies to his spectacular skill in managing upward mobility.

To the east was Cabbagetown, inhabited by working-class English and Irish immigrants living in cottages and terraced row housing built between 1860 and 1880, and who grew vegetables in small lots. Jewish immigrants had established themselves on Spadina Avenue and its side-streets some ten blocks west.

The Hambourgs, in contrast, moved to a street synonymous with wealth and power, only a short distance east of the baronial Gothic

Boris Hambourg ~ The Complete Musician

(Left) Luigi von Kunits was the pre-eminent violin teacher in Toronto – and thus a rival of the Hambourgs.

(Below) Advertisement for the Hambourg Conservatory in the Might City Directory, 1920. Jan had not yet departed for Europe, and the famous piano teacher Alberto Guerrero had just arrived from Chile at Boris's invitation.

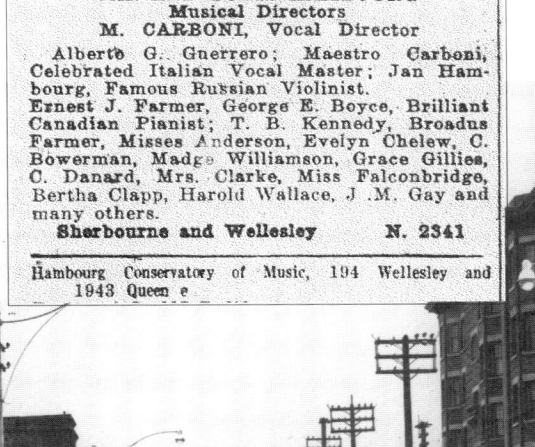

THE HAMBOURG FAMOUS CONSERVATORY
JAN AND BORIS HAMBOURG
Musical Directors
M. CARBONI, Vocal Director

Alberto G. Guerrero; Maestro Carboni, Celebrated Italian Vocal Master; Jan Hambourg, Famous Russian Violinist. Ernest J. Farmer, George E. Boyce, Brilliant Canadian Pianist; T. B. Kennedy, Broadus Farmer, Misses Anderson, Evelyn Chelew, C. Bowerman, Madge Williamson, Grace Gillies, C. Danard, Mrs. Clarke, Miss Falconbridge, Bertha Clapp, Harold Wallace, J. M. Gay and many others.

Sherbourne and Wellesley   N. 2341

Hambourg Conservatory of Music, 194 Wellesley and 1943 Queen e

Looking eastward along Wellesley Street from Sherbourne Street, before the widening of Wellesley. The Hambourg Conservatory is the building on the corner at the left. Sherbourne Street, though in decline by the 1940s, was considerably more stately. (City of Toronto Archives)

125

Euclid Hall at 515 Jarvis Street, the home of the Masseys, at the northeast corner of Wellesley and Jarvis streets. The houses along Sherbourne and Jarvis streets, wrote Toronto historians William Dendy and William Kilbourn "were built from the late 1850s on in a multitude of different styles, both picturesque and plain. Among the later apartment buildings and parking lots a surprising number of these mansions still stand. Very few of them are now private houses, but a succession of towers, gables, high dormed roofs and decorated façades still proclaim the magnificent past of Sherbourne and Jarvis."[27]

"Society" did not move from the Sherbourne-Jarvis area to Rosedale and Forest Hill until the 1920s, and later to Bayview. Among the Gooderham buildings was 592 Sherbourne Street, now the Selby Hotel. In it Ernest Hemingway and his wife lived for a short time in 1920 when he was working for the *Toronto Star*. His view of Canada differed somewhat from the Hambourgs'. He called Canada "a busted boom country ... pretty much gone to hell." The Hemingways did not stay long.

Opposite the Hemingways' residence was another mansion, 559 Sherbourne Street, which from 1882 to 1913 had been the home of the fabulous tycoon Sir Henry Pellatt, the builder of Casa Loma, Toronto's "castle." Sir Henry's former home had been converted into the Tudor Hotel. It was sadly run-down by the time, thirty years after the Hambourgs arrived, Wyndham Lewis and his wife spent the first three years of the Second World War there in self-imposed exile. Lewis, one of England's most original, versatile and prolific avant-garde modernists, was "that rare combination, a painter and writer both, who sustained and developed these talents in parallel."[28] In 1914, at the age of thirty-two, he had shaken the world of art and writing by launching the bulky and spectacular magazine *Blast*. The Tudor Hotel, torn down when the St. James Town apartment development was built, became the location of Lewis's scathing novel *Self-Condemned*.[29]

The contrast between the Hambourgs' and the Lewises' dispositions – and between their respective perceptions of Toronto and Canada –

could not be more striking. The Hambourgs, who had the advantage of peace and prosperity when they arrived before the First World War, were entrepreneurs, upbeat and determined to make the best of things. What they considered their unique opportunity Lewis deplored as dreary backwardness. He saw Canada as "the most parochial nationette on earth" and "Toronto the Good" as "a sanctimonious ice-box," the "bush metropolis of the Orange Lodges."[30] He also thought that it was better "to live as a shoeblack in London than be a Bank President in these parts."[31] To his future friend Marshall McLuhan he called Toronto "that disgusting spot" and to an English correspondent he observed that "the only intelligent people here – like the painter [A.Y.] Jackson – regard a marriage with the States as the best bet, and I think the same."[32]

Self-condemned appeared in 1954.

> Momaco [Toronto, a play on Mimico, a nearby village] was so ugly, and so devoid of all character as of any trace of charm, that it was disagreeable to walk about in. It was as if the elegance and charm of Montreal had been attributed to the seductions of the Fiend by the puritan founders of Momaco: as if they had said to themselves that at least in Momaco the god-fearing citizen, going about his lawful occasions, should do so without the danger of being seduced by way of his senses.[33]

There is no record of Boris Hambourg ever visiting the run-down Hotel Tudor, so close by. And it is unlikely that he ever met Wyndham Lewis.

Lewis reflected, in his stinging prose, the face Toronto showed to the less inquisitive visitor, and to many of its natives as well. Morley Callaghan, after all, moved to Paris to escape his suffocating and provincial hometown. At the same time, though, unlike the bland industrial towns in Britain that the city seemed to resemble, Toronto was a haven for large groups of immigrants, who tended to settle in concentrations near the centre of the city, bringing their cultural interests and aspirations with them. The Jewish community, for example, virtually staffed the strings section of the Toronto Symphony Orchestra.

Toronto's complacent philistinism, its prudish laws about liquor and Sunday concerts, its preoccupation with commerce, its colonial pretentiousness, these were all things the Hambourgs learned to deal with. Had Wyndham Lewis been endowed with a more open frame of mind, he might have observed the undercurrents of change already on the move that would lead to a very different, more cosmopolitan city.

The Hambourg's mansion on Wellesley Street had more "atmosphere" than the prosaic Anglo-Saxon Toronto Conservatory at the corner of University Avenue and College Street. The institutions represented two different worlds. The Toronto Conservatory made money from examinations; the Hambourg Conservatory (at first) prided itself in not having them.

On the ground floor there were two large studios on each side of the hallway. A majestic stairway, heavily carpeted, led to the second floor, where there were four more large studios and four smaller ones. A wing containing three more studios faced Sherbourne Street.

Harry Adaskin writes: "On the second floor there was a small corridor that led to a beautiful large room and a huge tiled bathroom. It was obviously originally what real estate people today would call a master-bedroom-en suite. The corridor was like a private entrance to this suite, and, as living where I had to rehearse every day appealed to me, I suggested to Boris that he rent us this set-up. Boris, who always appreciated some extra income, cheerfully agreed, and we moved in at once."[34]

The Hambourg family lived on the third floor. A large attic had been converted into a recital hall, which was stifling in the summer and cold in the winter in spite of a coal-burning stove. The fire department considered the stove a hazard and did not allow it to be used.

For a year Harry Adaskin and his wife had "a delightful apartment" in the building. "Our rent was, if I remember rightly, $35 a month, and we would have been glad to live there forever."[35] The violinist Paul Scherman, who was not on the staff, also lived happily at the conservatory for a while. His friend Hyman Goodman recalled that Boris turned up occasionally to borrow sugar.[36]

Elderly alumni vividly remember the fifty or sixty framed pictures on the walls of the foyer. Most of them were photographs of musical celebrities with flattering dedications to one or more of the Hambourgs. But there were also letters, posters, caricatures, concert programs, reviews and other mementos. There could be no doubt that the Hambourgs had a direct pipeline to everybody who mattered. A beautiful photograph showed the teenage Yehudi Menuhin, not playing the violin but studying a score. Next to it hung a framed letter by him written to Boris in French. Morry Kernerman, then seven or eight, remembers that Boris told him Menuhin spoke several languages and had a different tutor every day, according to the language of the day. The letter was evidently written on the French day. There were autographed photographs from Ignace Paderewski, Eugène Ysaÿe, Theodor Leschetizky, Fritz Kreisler, Harold Bauer, Myra Hess, Pablo Casals and Mischa Elman. In every room of the house there were busts and reproductions of musical icons.

By 1914 the faculty comprised twenty teachers of piano, eleven of voice, eight of violin, four of theory, two each of cello, organ, flute, mandolin/banjo and composition, and one each of drama, French, German and dancing. Pupil enrollment was nearly five hundred.[37] Beginning in 1918 branches of the conservatory flourished throughout Toronto, and during the 1930s some of the teachers taught at their pupils' homes.

Among the teachers over the years were, in various degrees of involvement, Marcus Adeney, Boris Berlin,[38] Helmut Blume, George Boyce, Giuseppe Carboni,[39] Rachel Cavalho,[40] Henri Czaplinski, Norah Drewett,[41] Ernest Farmer,[42] Broadus Farmer,[43] Eduardo Ferrari-Fontana,[44] Emil Gartner,[45] Géza de Kresz, Eleanor Griffith, Alberto Guerrero,[46] Clement Hambourg, Redferne Hollinshead,[47] James Campbell McInnes,[48] Yasha Paii,[49] Bernard Preston, Marcel Ray,[50] Fanny Silverman, Maurice Solway, Reginald Stewart.[51] Some of the teachers (including some not discovered by the author) were too unorthodox to be acceptable at the Toronto Conservatory. William Krehm recalls them as "iridescent birds."[52]

The story of the legendary, handsome, red-haired, free-spirited violinist John Langley is worth recalling. His only recorded connection with the Hambourgs was that in May 1928, when Géza was in Europe, he played second violin in the Hart House String Quartet at the second CPR Festival in Quebec City while Harry Adaskin played first. But that is not what makes him memorable. If it is true that he had as much natural talent for playing the violin as for making love, an activity in which he was rumoured to display rare inventiveness and originality, he must have been a tremendous violinist. One of his girl friends was Moo-Moo. He was making $125 a week playing the violin in Rex Battle's orchestra at the Royal York Hotel.[53] To preserve his income whatever happened, he had his hands insured. He then had a "hunting accident" and lost one finger on his left hand. He attempted to collect from the insurance company, which took the view that it wasn't an accident at all and refused to pay. Langley sued. The insurance company lawyer asked the court, "Why can't he play the violin with three fingers?" The court was unmoved and made the insurance company pay John Langley $125 a week for life. He went to Jamaica with Moo-Moo, bought a plantation and took up painting. It is not known whether the insurance company ever found out that apparently John Langley actually did learn to play the violin again with three fingers. But not in public.[54]

Harry Adaskin's younger brother, the composer Murray Adaskin (born 1909), met Professor Michael Hambourg only once, at a late evening party at the Hambourg Conservatory.

> It was after a recital in Massey Hall by Mischa Elman who was often a guest artist in Toronto. There was much animated conversation among the guests, when Michael, a quite distinguished elderly gentleman, offered a toast to the guest of honour, saying, "Well, Mischa, I suppose there are no two violinists like you and my son Jan. To you both."

Elman immediately replied, "No, Professor, you can't count Jan in with me."

Dead silence – Elman's accompanist looked embarrassed and the general conversation commenced once again.[55]

In his memoir of the Arts and Letters Club, the critic Augustus Bridle told another story linking the Hambourgs with Mischa Elman. He must have referred to an earlier visit since in 1913 Murray Adaskin was only four. Elman was twenty-two.

> One day about 1913 the boy wonder, Mischa Elman, came for lunch with his accompanist, manager and conductor Frank Welsman of the Toronto Symphony, with whom that night he was to play the Tchaikovsky Concerto. Three Hambourgs were there to greet their fellow-Russian, with a grand company of other musicians. Problem: would this volcanic youth play – for the Club?
>
> Flaherty's fiddle was in the library – in one of those lockers that we built to rent at a dollar a year for tobacco, lotion bottles, etc. The fiddle lacked two strings. I hustled out to Nordheimer's to buy them…. "No," spluttered Elman, when somebody hinted about his playing. "Imagine me playing any old pick-up violin… No thanks!" Then Professor Hambourg said to the young Muscovite, "Mischa, these men are all artists. You are a young great artist. You – must – play!"
>
> Silence for a moment. Then Elman barked at his manager, "Go get my violin at the hotel!"
>
> After all but eighteen members had gone, the youth stood on the corner dais with his accompanist and played a Handel sonata, to the smallest audience he had ever looked at.
>
> Recently, a bald-headed visitor to the Club recalled this episode. The man was Elman.[56]

Since his arrival in Toronto in 1910 Michael Hambourg had made friends with prominent people of all kinds, not only musicians. Some were close to the world of labour. This was in keeping with the

Professor's social concerns and those of the friends he had left behind in Bloomsbury, Chiswick and Chelsea. As Michael Piva writes: "Under the glitter of such ostentatious displays of wealth as Henry M. Pellatt's Casa Loma lay the squalid underbelly of the industrial city. Despite some minor improvements the mass of Toronto's labouring men and women continued to toil in grimy, unsanitary, poorly lighted and ventilated shops and factories, with little or no security for the future."[57]

On May 1, 1914, at a Grand Concert in the Association Hall at Yonge and McGill streets, Michael Hambourg, faithful to the spirit of Kropotkin and Volkhovsky – this was three years *before* the 1917 Revolution – personally supervised the musical part of the celebration of May Day, "the international working class holiday of the awakened and intelligent section of the working class." The musical part included the "Internationale" and "Red Flag" sung by the choir of the Young Peoples' Socialist League (Jewish). The concert was organized by a joint committee representing a large number of socialist and labour organizations of Toronto.[58]

Michael Hambourg did not live to welcome the February Revolution. He died of a heart attack on June 18, 1916, shortly after giving Gerald Moore a lesson. The Toronto *Globe* published a lengthy obituary:

> The sudden death from heart failure of Professor Michael Hambourg late Sunday evening has removed from the artistic life of Toronto a picturesque figure which for the past six years had been like a connecting link between this city of the new world and the famous music masters of the old world such as Rubinstein and Tchaikovsky....
>
> Professor Hambourg, who since his coming to Toronto had founded and firmly established the Hambourg Conservatory of music on Sherbourne Street, was born in 1855 on the banks of the Volga in the district of Jaroslaw in Russia, and at an early age commenced the study of the piano. He received his musical training in Moscow and St. Petersburg, now Petrograd, at Con-

servatories of Music under the two Rubinsteins, Tchaikovsky, and other eminent masters of the day.… His most brilliant pupil was his own son Mark.

The initial tour of Mark Hambourg finally was the means of taking father and family to London in 1890. From that time until 1910 when he came to Canada Michael Hambourg was prominent in London and had been a professor at the London Academy and the Guildhall School of Music. He also was a director of the Hambourg Conservatory in London. When he came to Canada he brought with him recommendations from such eminent masters of the piano as Rosenthal, Paderewski and Professor Leschetizky.…

Rheumatic trouble contracted in London never entirely left the late Professor Hambourg. He suffered from it continuously during his residence in Toronto and it finally reached his heart with fatal results.

The deceased is survived by his wife and seven children. Messrs Mark, Jan and Boris, an elder daughter married in England, Misses Luba and Manya, and master Clement.…

Professor Hambourg's life in Toronto established a wide circle of friends. His manner was most gracious and he had an unusual memory for faces and names. Professor and Mrs. Hambourg frequently entertained when their home circle became the charming scene of spontaneous and rapturous music from the family artists and others who might be present.

Professor Hambourg, besides being a piano teacher of remarkable talent, was a pianist whose emotional characteristics never failed to arouse enthusiasm. He early became a member of the Arts and Letters Club where his singular ability was quickly recognized and where he was frequently called upon to contribute to the program of a musical night.[59]

Jan and Boris were in New York when their father died and hastened home for the funeral. The *Globe* carried another report:

A lasting tribute to the memory of Professor Michael Hambourg, founder of the Hambourg Conservatory of Music, was the conspicuous presence at his funeral yesterday afternoon of so many children, those whom he had taught to love music. Amongst the eloquent and beautiful array of floral offerings which covered the casket was a humble bunch of wild flowers to which was attached a card bearing in a childish hand the words "I loved him."

There were present also to pay respect to his memory the foremost musicians of the city, including Dr. Vogt, W.O. Forsyth, Luigi von Kunits, Signor Carboni, Signor Morenzo, Paul Wells, Edward Himmelberg, Rechab Tandy, and the entire staff of the Hambourg Conservatory of Music. The funeral service, which was held in the Hambourg Conservatory of Music on Sherbourne Street, was conducted by the Rev. R.E. Hutchison of Meadville Theological School, a former pastor of the Unitarian Church, Toronto, and the Rev. Hodgins, its present pastor. Interment took place at Mount Pleasant Cemetery, and the pallbearers were Professor James Mavor, Archibald Brown, R.D. Tiffreys, Harry Wimperley, Augustus Bridle, David Rose, E.H. Farmer, and Redferne Hollinshead.

The many floral tributes included a beautiful design formed like a broken harp and made of roses, carnations and orchids, the contributions of the staff and pupils of the Hambourg Conservatory.

The Arts and Letters Club, of which the late Professor Hambourg was an honoured member, sent a beautiful lyre formed in carnations and lilies.[60]

After the Professor's death Boris became the director of the Hambourg Conservatory. His mother, Catherine, continued to live there. Though she did not hold an official position, her presence was felt everywhere. Harry Adaskin remembered her as a lively lady and an excellent hostess.[61] Paul Scherman and Lou Taub described her as a handsome, intelligent and dignified lady who inspired respect – "a woman," Lou Taub said, "of strength and feeling."

One day, Mrs. Hambourg came in while the fourteen-year-old Lou was having a violin lesson and asked him to play for her. When he finished she put her hand on his head and said in German, *"Aber das ist ja wunderbar."* (But that is really wonderful.) He remembers very clearly that she said it in German, not in Yiddish. "The Hambourgs often spoke German to each other," Taub recalls. It was not unusual among educated Russian Jews to speak German or French on occasions when they did not want to speak Russian or Yiddish.

Six years after her husband's death, on September 11, 1922, at the age of sixty, Catherine Hambourg committed suicide. The reasons may be known to members of the family, but not to those outside. The death certificate stated that the cause of death was "inhalation of illuminating gas." The word "accidental" was added because it was the practice in Ontario until 1963 to conceal suicide "for the family's sake" unless there was a suicide note.[62] There was no announcement of her death in the newspapers. Boris's sisters Luba and Manya had played no role in running the conservatory and returned to England after their mother's death.

Catherine Hambourg was buried next to her husband in the non-sectarian Mount Pleasant Cemetery. Their grave is marked only by a small, square, unadorned footstone with the words Michael Hambourg on it, nothing else.[63] The only evidence that Catherine Hambourg was buried there is in the cemetery's records. These also include the information that Ivan Hambourg, aged forty-three, was buried there as well, on April 20, 1918, two years after Michael's death. It must be assumed that he was the son of one of Michael's two brothers, both of whom were pianists. There is no mention of him in Mark's published writings. According to the Death Registration in the Archives of Canada, Ivan was born in Russia in 1875 and was a musician. He was married. No relative is named. The cause of death was encarditis. There was no death notice in any of the three Toronto papers.

In his autobiography, Mark described his mother only once, in connection with her sudden appearance in New York in 1907 on unexpected – and unexplained – family business. He wrote she was a "thrifty Russian woman with the selflessness of the best kind of simplicity." In 1916, she must have had a say in the burial arrangements for her husband. An expensive, more than minimal gravestone may have seemed wicked to her.

But there may have been another factor. Paul Scherman said his father, who had come from Poland, had, with great admiration, called her *Zydowka,* the Jewish one, in contrast, by implication, to the other members of the Hambourg family. Could it be that she was not looking forward to her husband and herself spending eternity in a non-Jewish cemetery?

Other factors are equally plausible. One possible reason for Catherine Hambourg's suicide was that one of the "iridescent birds" among the staff of the conservatory, the superb violinist Henri Czaplinski, had seriously endangered the institution's reputation. It is true that none of what Paul Scherman called "shenanigans , nefarious dealings" going on in the period immediately preceding Mrs. Hambourg's death had ever leaked into the press. But she may have been afraid that a public scandal caused by Czaplinski might bring about the collapse of her husband's creation like a house of cards.

Henri Czaplinski was the man chosen to lure violin students away from Luigi von Kunits. He was a good-looking, well-dressed, tall, courtly Pole, about thirty years old who always carried a cane, like a Parisian *boulevardier.* No one knew where he lived. It was rumoured he would rent rooms only in houses where the landlady was attractive or had an attractive daughter. If both were attractive, he would sleep with both, though not simultaneously.[64] He caused one divorce and had affairs with several faculty wives. Among these was the equally promiscuous Eva, a gorgeous woman who ultimately ran away with a dashing Hungarian gypsy violinist with a mellifluous but fake Italian name. All this must have distressed Mrs. Hambourg acutely. Years later, Eva's husband, a member of the faculty she had abandoned, was seen walking the streets. He had taken to drink and was a broken man.

One teacher, Bernard Preston, was particularly concerned that the turmoil caused by Czaplinski and Eva, and by Boris's loose management style, might upset the revered Mrs. Hambourg's peace of mind. Paul Scherman called him "an esoteric gentleman who adored the Hambourgs, especially the old lady." At one time there was even a threat of a teachers' revolt against Boris, which Preston managed to defuse.

Czaplinski's English was rudimentary. One day, waiting outside the studio door for his turn, Paul Scherman heard him scream at a boy named Nathan Green, "Damn you rotter, you haven't done your lesson!" The fifteen-year-old Scherman was not merely afraid of him, he said, he was terrified. "Because, you see," he explained, "Czaplinski was *diabolical*. He was a *monster*." At the same time Scherman was proud to walk with him in the street, his teacher elegantly swinging his cane. Czaplinski could be sarcastic. He asked Maurice Solway to play Bach's Chaconne for him, fifteen minutes without interruption. After Solway was finished Czaplinski commented, "*Ten tawson notes, not vun in tuen.*"[65]

Harry Adaskin's younger brother, the composer Murray Adaskin, who remembers Czaplinski well, firmly rejects Paul Scherman's view that he was formidable and crooked. "I don't know that I would describe him as crooked," he said, "but formidable, yes. He turned the coterie of violinists in Toronto upside down during his brief stay in Toronto. I was one of his students and got along with him without the stress so many experienced. He could bring out the best talent in students in a very brief period of time."[66]

Harry Adaskin had the greatest respect for his teaching approach: "He worked on the principle that if you tried to fulfil the demands of the music you're playing – really tried, no half measures, for transcendental rapture in the Delius Concerto, for demonic fire in Paganini – your body would be forced to produce results. Your body would find the way because of the implacable demands of your higher nature."[67]

What a contrast to the more traditional von Kunits! Von Kunits merely tried to develop the musical instincts of his students, and to serve as an inspiration. Czaplinski, an incomparably better violinist, acted as a model. He knew all the tricks and demonstrated them himself. He assigned work far beyond his students' capacities and showed them how to practise. If he had made recordings, he would be remembered as a virtuoso in Jascha Heifetz's class. One of his stunts was to put on Heifetz's recording of Bazzini's *La Ronde des lutins,* one of the most dazzling pieces ever written for the violin, and to play it along with the record. He had an extraordinary musical memory and a wide repertoire.

Harry Adaskin, about twenty at the time, had been a student of von Kunits. He admired him greatly and had no intention of leaving him. But then he met Czaplinski, who had devised an infallible method of wooing him. It happened that Czaplinski was not only a teacher but also a dealer in precious violins. His inventory included a Giuseppe Guarneri, which he was prepared to sell to Adaskin for a mere $1,500. (Jan Hambourg's violin by the same maker was worth, Jan said, $3,500.) But fifteen hundred dollars might as well have been fifteen million. Adaskin went to see the kindly and generous president of the Academy, Colonel Albert Gooderham, von Kunits' employer. Gooderham received him in the sumptuous headquarters of his liquor empire, Gooderham and Worts. Adaskin asked for help. The Colonel was full of understanding. He gave the young man a cheque for $1,500 to buy the violin, with the verbal understanding that it would belong to him, Gooderham, until Adaskin had paid it off in $100 instalments.

Adaskin had trouble with his bow-arm. Von Kunits had not been able to help him. Perhaps Czaplinski, the miracle worker, could, especially after having sold him the Guarneri. After hesitating for a long time, Adaskin at last did what Czaplinski had counted on: he crossed the floor. Adaskin had been the only adult in von Kunits' class of fifteen. All the youngsters followed him. For Czaplinski it was a tremendous coup. Von Kunits was left studentless.

Fortunately, von Kunits soon after became conductor of the Toronto Symphony Orchestra, where many of his disloyal ex-students later found employment, for five dollars a concert, usually scheduled for five o'clock in the afternoon, in time for them still to play dinner music for Rex Battle at the Royal York Hotel, for Luigi Romanelli at the King Edward Hotel, for Bob Cornfield in Simpson's Arcadian Room or, most important, for evening performances in diverse orchestras in silent movie cinemas.

When von Kunits died nine years later, in 1931, Milton Blackstone, the violist in the Hart House String Quartet, who had studied with him, wrote a column about him for the *Jewish Standard*.

> As I entered for my lesson one day, he was engrossed in a Hebrew pamphlet. For some time I had a vague suspicion that he was a Jew – a suspicion which was shared by many. He read to me several Hebrew paragraphs and translated them. I may say that I was his first scholarship pupil in Toronto and shared many of his confidences which he denied to pupils in later years. He was born into the Catholic faith and complying with the wish of his family, members of the Austrian nobility, he entered a seminary to become a priest. At the age of nineteen he arrived at other conclusions, and decided upon a musical career.
>
> Many Jewish children who had the talent, but not the monetary means, were protégés of his, and received instruction gratis. There is not an orchestra in Toronto which does not contain at least one of his pupils and both Adaskin and myself owe much to him.[68]

Adaskin did not see von Kunits again until he, and two other members of the Hart House String Quartet, played farewell music for him in front of his open coffin in October 1931.

Back to 1922: Adaskin went to see Gooderham to pay his first instalment on the violin he had bought from Czaplinski, Gooderham declined to accept it. Adaskin had not yet had his first lesson with Czaplinski and had no reason to believe Gooderham knew anything about his defection. "Put it in the bank," Gooderham said. "Some day you'll want to go to Europe to study, and if you save up enough you'll be able to go." Adaskin had the feeling that Gooderham took this position because he wanted total control over his violin. He would have preferred him to accept the money. His instinct turned out to be sound. When in due course the Colonel discovered the defection, he wrote a note to Adaskin asking for his violin back. With a heavy heart, Adaskin returned it.

When Adaskin had his first lesson with Czaplinski, he brought his old violin. Czaplinski asked, "Where's the Guarneri?" Adaskin explained that he had had to return it to the Colonel.

> Czaplinski went to the studio door and locked it. Then he took me to the far corner of the room and in a conspiratorial voice whispered: "You must promise me navvair to tell what I now say. Promise!"
>
> There wasn't a thing I could do but dazedly mumble "I promise."
>
> "O.K.," he said. "Do not feel bad about the violin. It's not a Guarneri. It's a fake."
>
> My face must have betrayed the shock I felt. The thought of my having bilked a decent, honest and kindly man out of $1,500 almost gave me a stroke....
>
> "If you my pupil, I navvair sell you such a fake. Navvair! But you then not my pupil. And if not my pupil I have no *responsibilité*."

Many decades later, Adaskin heard Mischa Mischakoff play a Mozart concerto in Toronto. The sound was marvellous. In the intermission, he asked his friend Albert Pratz if he knew what kind of fiddle Mischakoff had. "Oh yes," he said. "I know it very well. It's a Giuseppe Guarneri, and he bought it from the Gooderham family."

A light was switched on in Adaskin's brain. So – when Czaplinski had told Adaskin it was a fake, he merely wanted to make him feel better!

A man with such an unusual code of ethics was bound to be difficult to handle. After Mrs. Hambourg's death, there were whispers about shady financial dealings with students and others and stories about a possible connection between her suicide and Czaplinski's activities, but such whispers never became widespread. Between-the-wars Toronto was not the Berlin of Marlene Dietrich. *La vie de Bohème* at Wellesley and Sherbourne was not interesting to the readers of the daily newspapers.

Boris appeared with Czaplinski in public six months after Mrs. Hambourg's death. He conducted the Conservatory Orchestra in Massey Hall on Sunday, March 10, 1923, the second recital by the Hambourg Conservatory's Violin Master-School, with Henri Czaplinski as soloist.

One day Czaplinski asked Adaskin during a lesson whether he had saved up any money. Adaskin said he had only two hundred dollars. *"I moss go avay for two weeks,"* Czaplinski continued. *"Vould you land me your two hundred dollars? I geev you back as soon as I retorn."*[69]

Czaplinski went to Philadelphia. Neither of the Adaskin brothers ever saw him again. But some time later Harry found out his address and wrote him a long, careful letter, telling him how much he had loved his lessons with him and how very much his playing had improved under his guidance. His deepest sorrow was that a great master seemed to be willing to destroy a friendship for a mere two hundred dollars.

Many of Czaplinski's other students had also been asked to lend him money, but Adaskin was the only one to receive a letter from him, enclosing a cheque for two hundred dollars, expressing regret that he had been unable to return it sooner.

From the *Philadelphia Evening Ledger*, July 14, 1941:

> An announcement by Germany of the release from prison of "Heinrich Schablinsky, former violinist of the Philadelphia Orchestra" on June 26th, led veteran members of the association today to believe the released prisoner was Henri Czaplinski, who played here between 1924 and 1927.
>
> Gerhard Starcke, reporter for DNB, the German official news

agency, said "Schablinsky" (probably the Germanized version of the Polish spelling of Czaplinski) said he was arrested by the Soviet secret police in 1939 while teaching at Lwow (Lemberg), Poland, and since had been imprisoned at Bialistok and Minsk....

[In September 1939, after the Nazi attack on Poland, the Soviets occupied Poland's eastern provinces, including Lwow, in accordance with the terms of the Ribbentrop-Molotov Pact concluded in August.]

The reporter said several of the musician's teeth had been knocked out and he was in tatters. The violinist told Starcke a story of being released from prison at Minsk during a Nazi air raid, marching 60 miles under Russian guard and escaping during another aerial attack after many of his fellow prisoners had been killed by the OGPU.

The freed violinist further related to the German reporter that he was a member of the Philadelphia Orchestra for several years and played under the direction of Leopold Stokowski. He also added that he taught music at Princeton University. However, a check of the Princeton records failed to reveal any former member of the faculty under either spelling of the name....

Yasha Kayaloff, a veteran member of the Philadelphia Orchestra and concert master of the Robin Hood Dell Orchestra, declared at his home in Chestnut Hill today that the man Germany said was loosed from prison was undoubtedly Czaplinski.

"I remember Czaplinski as a brilliant member of the orchestra's first-string violin group along about 1925," said Kayaloff. "He was with the orchestra for several years and gave many concerts in the Academy of Music foyer. He was Polish and went back to his native country several years ago. I haven't heard from him and I don't know of any other orchestra member who has."

Records of the Philadelphia Orchestra Association show Czaplinski was a member from 1924 to 1927, prior to which time he was concert master at the Fox Theater under Erno Rapee....

He was born in Warsaw in 1890. He listed himself as married. He studied at the Leipzig Conservatory of Music and the Masters' School of Violin Playing at Vienna, Dresden, Berlin, Leipzig, Mannheim and Brussels and gave many concerts in Finland. For two years he was a teacher at the Hambourg Conservatory at Toronto.

Czaplinski was not a United States citizen at the time he was member of the Philadelphia Orchestra.

In 1923 Boris, at the age of nearly forty and after his mother's death, married Maria Beauchope, a witty, dignified, self-confident lady ten years older than Boris and endowed with a diploma as a piano teacher. Maria had heard Boris play during one of his tours but had not met him then, nor later in London, where she had gone to finishing school. She came from a Scottish military family, her brother was a colonel in the Scots Guards, she had been presented to the Prince of Wales and had been brought up in New Zealand, where – this is not entirely certain – she had been a friend of the short story writer Katherine Mansfield. Jan's obituary pointed out that Mark, Jan and Boris had all chosen wives of Scottish descent.[70]

Soon after 1919, when she arrived in Toronto, she and Boris at last met. Their backgrounds could hardly have been more disparate, but their marriage, like that of Mark and Dolly, was to be exemplary. He adored her and she adored him.

For the wedding Mark came over from England: "At the reception I was obliged to shake hands with some six hundred guests, repeating each one's name as I did so in true American style, 'How-de-do, Mr. Jonathan. How-de-do, Mrs. Kanak,' until my head reeled, unsustained as I was by anything more potent than ginger pop, for prohibition was at its zenith in Canada and officially every entertainment was bone-dry, just as unofficially one was almost drowned in the inevitable reaction."[71]

After their wedding, Maria, as *châtelaine* and, as it were, successor to Catherine Hambourg, quickly took charge of the conservatory. She was excellent about money, of which there was never enough. In fact, for the next thirty years, until Boris's death in 1954, much of her creative energy was invested in making the institution appear to be

THE BROTHERS HAMBOURG

(Above) Reginald Stewart, Henri Czaplinski and Boris Hambourg. (Courtesy Murray Adaskin)

Boris and Maria "Borina" Hambourg.

solvent, which it rarely was. (It was a characteristic of all four Brothers Hambourg, and their father, that they often, perhaps usually, lived beyond their means. An exception was Jan during his marriage to Isabelle, who supplied the means.) Borina, as Maria came to be nicknamed, never expected Boris to support her, and he never did. She herself taught at the conservatory. Feeling socially superior to most of the people she dealt with, many of whom had no money either, she thought there was nothing demeaning about scrounging. It was said to be amusing watching her pass a grocery store on Wellesley Street and ask the owner, an onion in her hand, "I need only the one – is that all right?"

On the other hand, she was by no means amused – she was horrified – when some penniless White Russian refugees, some of them taxi-drivers, who were inhabiting the conservatory's basement, procured a scruffy swan from Grenadier Pond in High Park. It was required for their Russian Easter dinner. The deed was done by jumping over the fence, seizing the swan, strangling it and driving off before anybody could take down the licence-plate number. It was roasted without feathers and skin. These had to be attached to it again before it could be served on a silver plate, according to ritual. They must have made a colossal mess in the kitchen.

As to Maria's managerial talents, no detail escaped her. Henceforth – the strictest economy, especially when it came to generous scholarships for gifted students. When Maria discovered how much money the Toronto Conservatory was making from exams, she persuaded Boris to introduce them too. They lasted at least for a year or two. Marcus Adeney liked Maria but remembers her as a "damn nuisance." The *Toronto Star* wrote she "was very conscious of class distinctions and bore herself with a regal mien."[72]

Evidently, Maria turned out to be the perfect complement to Boris's already well-developed networking skills. If the poor Jewish students at the conservatory thought she was haughty or, more to the point, anti-Semitic – and some did – it was because she saw no point in wasting time on a group of people who were in no position, as yet, to help the conservatory survive. To call her a snob, which many did, was off the point. She was a person of natural dignity, entirely secure within herself, and had nothing to prove to anybody

Maria's world was the world of music-lovers, who had their own society which overlapped with other societies. For Maria, the rich were commodities, rather than people to envy, emulate or look up to. Their value lay entirely in their potential usefulness as patrons and sponsors. She and Boris became skilful at involving them in schemes to raise money, such as forming satellite companies like the Hambourg Concert Society, a concert booking agency.

Since the musical world was inhabited by many Jews, the question whether Maria herself was anti-Semitic was off the point. She was married to Boris Hambourg, and that was that. Her job was to help the conservatory survive in profoundly anti-Semitic Toronto. However, she must have soon found out that Toronto was by no means consistently anti-Semitic. A few particularly able Jews in the world of business, such as Sir Sigmund Samuel, were able to achieve considerable recognition.[73]

To woo and win the artistic, university and business communities, Maria gave regular Sunday evening "At Homes," especially when distinguished foreign artists were in town. They were sometimes financed on an ingenious barter principle since cash was always in short supply.

As the *Star* recounted: "Local musicians and music teachers mingled with society matrons and their daughters, while a string trio or quartet played in the background. There were always a great number of people, and there was often a great fuss being made over a European artist who might be passing through Toronto.... The foreign musicians were easily identified by their shoulder-length hair and their intense conversation and gestures."[74]

When the Flonzaley Quartet or big stars like Ethel Barrymore or prima ballerina Anna Pavlova were in town, the parties were lavish. The party for Pavlova began after her performance at Massey Hall and lasted into the night. The food table included roast suckling pig, cold Restigouche salmon and cut glass bowls of punch.[75]

The Toronto journalist Miriam Bassin Chinsky was a little girl when she had to play at a piano recital at the Hambourg Conservatory with other students of Eleanor Griffith. The time was the mid-thirties: "When we arrived at the conservatory there was a lively buzz in the corridor outside the concert hall, in contrast to the tense atmosphere which usually preceded any student recital. We discovered that two special guests would be in attendance. They were the Honourable Mrs. [Galia] Reginald Coke and her daughter The Lady Sylvia, visiting from England." (Galia had two daughters, Sylvia and Stella.)

Miriam's mother had taught violin at the Hambourg Conservatory before she was married and knew Galia. She invited her and Sylvia to dinner at their modest apartment on Yonge Street near Keewatin, over her husband Sam's tailor shop.

Miriam remembers:

> Galia and Sylvia, with little fingers elegantly extended, devoured the full-bodied chicken soup, gefilte fish with beet red horseradish, roast beef, potato pudding – crisp on the outside, fluffy on the inside – vegetable and apple cinnamon pie. There was also a bottle of home-made port wine in a crystal decanter.
>
> A few days later when Daddy was glancing through the *Toronto Star*, he paused and handed the women's page to Mama. There, in the column which I think was called "Society Highlights" was a photo of the patrician Lady Sylvia in a full-length silver-spangled sheathe with an ostrich boa. Accompanying the picture was a list of the élite that had entertained The Lady Sylvia and her mother....
>
> Included in that list were Mr. and Mrs. Samuel Bassin and their daughter Miriam.[76]

At around the same time, the impoverished young Graham McInnes, the older son of the great bass-baritone James Campbell McInnes, was visiting Toronto. He had met Mark and Dolly Hambourg in Chicago and wanted to give a party for his father, who taught at the conservatory.

I approached brother Boris who turned me over to his wife Borina who clearly controlled the purse strings. Yes, they would be glad to let me give a party for my father in the main salon. She had known my father long and favourably. She was delighted at this development. Musicians should stick together. A distinguished cellist like her husband, a distinguished singer like my father. I was doing the right thing. Of course there would unavoidably be a bit of a mess to clear up afterwards and, well, in short: ten bucks. I gulped a bit and paid it out; then went on to outlay at least four times that amount in drink.[77]

In the twenties, two or three hundred sophisticated, sometimes well-travelled, often native-born Torontonians were genuinely devoted to the arts and prepared to work hard for them. They sat on the boards of Massey Hall, the Toronto Symphony Orchestra in its various phases, the Art Gallery, the Royal Ontario Museum and several foundations, and formed a loyal public, keen to assist the city's slow, hesitant emergence, after the First World War, as a centre of creativity of some originality, preparing the way to the flowering of the arts after the Second World War.

Boris had to heal the wounds caused by the shenanigans and scandals at his conservatory. He could only do that with the active support of that community, many of whose members were regular guests at his Sunday evening *soirées*, worldly people who chose their restaurants not according to the menus they offered, but according to the *live* music played. Just as Mark had cultivated many friends outside the world of music, just as Jan was far more than a violinist, so Boris always made a point of associating with non-musicians. He was never seen reading a book, but he knew that musical institutions could only flourish as integral parts of a wider cultural (and financial) establishment. Poets of the stature of E.J. Pratt, Charles G.D. Roberts and Arthur Stringer were on Maria's guest list and enjoyed the cosmopolitan conversation about the arts at her gatherings.

Michael and his son Mark had been ardent members of the Savage Club in London. Michael and Boris continued this tradition in the Arts and Letters Club in Toronto. Throughout the twenties and thirties many of its members were frequent visitors at functions taking place at the Hambourg Conservatory. The club had been founded as an arts club in 1908, but it was only under Vincent Massey, its tenth president, that it found in 1920 what was to become – and still is – its permanent headquarters, at 14 Elm Street. The club played a crucial but hard to define role in the history of all the arts in English Canada. As Massey wrote:

> Countless members without rest
> Embark upon this fascinating quest
> To find the Arts and Letters spirit,
> Or draw approximately near it,
> It's there, all right,
> But please don't analyse it.[78]

The club was the home of the Group of Seven, the painters who, through their colourful representations of the northern landscape, became quintessentially Canadian artists of great power and originality.

The art historian F.B. Housser put it in perspective:

> Before 1910, a Canadian art movement inspired by the Canadian environment was not thought possible. Canadian art authorities did not believe that our rough landscape was art material.... Our hinterlands were supposed to be ugly as a medium of expression for a painter unless disguised to look like Europe or England. The view held in artistic circles in the Dominion ... was that Canada was a colony of Great Britain and the colonial must needs express himself through methods approved by time and the intelligentsia. To reflect our day and environment would be a vulgar adventure.[79]

Of at least one of the group, Arthur Lismer, it is known that he enjoyed visits to the Hambourg Conservatory. J.E.H. MacDonald, by

Boris Hambourg. (Courtesy George Heinl & Co. Ltd., Toronto)

The "heraldic arms" for Boris Hambourg at the Arts and Letters Club, Toronto, designed by J.E.H. MacDonald. In the centre is his instrument and the four angels represent the Hambourg brothers. (Arts and Letters Club of Toronto) seven years the oldest member of the group, designed a Hambourg "coat of arms" for one of the windows in the dining-room of the Arts and Letters Club – a visual demonstration of the family's prominence in the history of the club, and thus in the arts in Canada.

There were several important instances of a fruitful conjunction of business and the arts. The Eaton Operatic Society was the first musical institution the family that owned Canada's most important department stores endowed after the First World War. It presented light operas from 1919 to 1965, including, beginning in 1931, a large number of Gilbert and Sullivan productions. The Eaton Auditorium, on the seventh floor of their College Street store, was built in 1929, and was one of the two finest small concert halls in Canada. (The other was the small concert hall of the Winnipeg Auditorium.) Rachmaninov and many giants performed there, and in 1945 Glenn Gould made his recital debut in it as an organist. In 1977, the auditorium was to become a victim of the wrecker's hammer, but thanks to the valiant efforts of a number of public-spirited citizens led by Eleanor Koldofsky, who appreciated its beauty and historical significance, it has been declared a heritage site and is untouchable.

A lively and memorable figure, and a potent influence, was Lady Eaton, née Flora McCrea, the daughter of an immigrant from Northern Ireland. Jack Eaton, the son of the founder of the T. Eaton Company, fell in love with her, and she with him, when she was a student nurse of eighteen. Genuinely fond of music, and later a friend of many musicians, among them Edward Johnson, the Canadian tenor and general manager of the Metropolitan Opera in New York, she was herself a singer who performed in Massey Hall.

Outside the world of music – though he was honorary president of the Mendelssohn Choir – by far the greatest philanthropist at the time was Sir Edmund Walker, the president of the Canadian Bank of Commerce. He died in 1924, at the age of seventy-five, having played a pivotal role in the early history of the Royal Ontario Museum. "Sir Edmund Walker was never a rich man…" wrote Lovat Dickson. "Throughout his life all that he could spare was spent on his collections and in supporting, to the extent that he was able, the museum that he had helped to bring into being and the other institutions with which he was involved – the National Gallery of Canada, the Art Museum of Toronto (now the Art Gallery of Ontario) and the Champlain Society, to name a few."[80]

In 1924, the year in which Vincent Massey entered Boris's life, the future governor-general of Canada was thirty-seven. His grandfather Hart Massey, the son of the founder of the Massey Manufacturing Company in Newcastle, Ontario, had merged the company with its rival A. Harris, Son & Company in Brantford, to form Massey-Harris, the gigantic manufacturer of agricultural implements and the source of the family's wealth. In 1910 Vincent Massey joined his father and aunt as a trustee of his grandfather's estate.

Hart Massey's testament was without precedent in Canada. He died in 1896 and left the bulk of his wealth to benefit educational, religious and public causes.[81] Already in his lifetime his philanthropy had included gifts to Victoria College, to Methodist colleges and organizations in Canada and the United States, and of course the building in Toronto in 1894 of Massey Hall, a memorial to Charles, his oldest son, who had died in 1884. Concerts there were to be for all people to enjoy, and the price of a ticket was not to exceed twenty-five cents.[82] The Mendelssohn Choir had been one of Hart Massey's enthusiasms and the new hall was to give it a superb home.

In 1910 it was decided to finance the construction of the unique institution which was to become Hart House, in memory of Hart Massey's public service. Eight years later, after Vincent Massey had served for three years as a staff officer during the First World War, and had married Alice, a daughter of Sir George Parkin, the secretary of the Rhodes Trust, the Massey estate was converted into a foundation. This made it possible to devote moneys to specific charitable and educational purposes. Vincent Massey acted on the advice of his cousin George Vincent, the president of the Rockefeller Foundation.

Hart House was formally presented to the University of Toronto on the first anniversary of the Armistice, on November 11, 1919. Its high purpose was expressed in the Founders' Prayer:

That the members of Hart House may discover within its walls the true education that is to be found in good fellowship, in friendly disputation and debate, in the conversation of wise and earnest men, in music, pictures, and the play, in the casual book, in sports and games and the mastery of the body; and lastly, that just as in the days of war this House was devoted to the training in arms of the young soldier, so, in the time of peace its halls may be dedicated to the task of arming youth with strength and suppleness of limb, with clarity of mind and depth of understanding, and with the spirit of true religion and high endeavour.

From 1919 until 1935, when Vincent Massey moved to London to become Canadian high commissioner, he and his wife took an intense personal interest in Hart House. When they left, in the midst of the Depression, it had become a primary cultural centre for the entire community, a hive of cosmopolitan activity with modern music and the latest plays being performed to knowledgeable audiences. By then a new era was emerging and new centres were springing up, but still Hart House remained faithful to its "final goal, – the creation of a society that did not depend on traditional loyalties, that was bound together by an interest in the arts and in public life."[83]

There were some who mocked the "Oxbridge" pretensions of Hart House, Wyndham Lewis for one. The chapter "I Dine with the Warden" in his book *America, I Presume* is a satirical account of a visit to "Brunswick Hall." But in a letter of November 19, 1940, to Terence W.L. MacDermot, who was then Master of Upper Canada College and later a distinguished diplomat (and also the father of Galt MacDermot, the composer of the musical *Hair*), Lewis confessed, "The more I think of that Hart House burlesque, the more I feel that if the Master (whom I rather highhandedly borrowed to have a little fun with) realized how *impressed* I was – for I can say with my hand on my heart that I do not believe another such educational, or recreative, wonder is to be found anywhere on this earth, and that it is a tremendous feat to have built up that *hive* of collegiate activity – he would not mind the burlesque form my admiration took."[84]

As a serious and bookish student before the First World War, Vincent Massey was passionately interested in the stage. Even after the war he acted in and directed plays in the Hart House Theatre. As president of Massey-Harris he once played the part of a cockney burglar. Later, when he had to give up his personal involvement in the theatre, his "enthusiasm for, and envy of, his successful actor-brother Raymond never waned."[85]

Raymond had been working in the family business when he decided in 1921 to leave Canada and go to England to become an actor. He was twenty-five. First, he had to call on his father, Chester, in the Massey mansion at 515 Jarvis Street:

> He lay on the couch in silence. After about ten minutes he got up and took my arm. He led me into a room called the gallery where most of his pictures were.... We sat down by the fireplace. It was quite a warm day but father asked me to light the fire.
>
> There was another long silence. At last father said, "I think you are quite right to go to England and to go on the stage. I think you will be a very good actor. I think you will be able to serve God as well in the theatre as in the implement business which your grandfather founded.
>
> "There is one promise I want you to make. That is that you will not act or practise on Sunday."
>
> This was a tough situation. I knew of course that I could not and would not keep such a promise. All year I had rehearsed on Sundays. But I had to give that wonderful old man peace of mind. I crossed my fingers and promised.
>
> Then he knelt on one knee, the way he did in family prayers, and made a prayer to God for my success and honesty as an actor.[86]

In 1923, after Henri Czaplinski had escaped to Philadelphia, Boris had to make a determined effort to find a suitable successor as star-violin-teacher quickly. Otherwise the Hambourg Conservatory's violin students would go back to Luigi von Kunits, from whom

Czaplinski had snatched them. Boris mobilized his networks and struck gold.

Géza de Kresz, the musician who was to be an important element in establishing the historic connection with Vincent Massey, was forty-one when he came to Toronto. He had the bearing of an officer in the Austro-Hungarian army – impressive, tall, with an intriguing whiff of distant Mongolian or gypsy ancestors.

"I was born in Budapest, Hungary – all violinists come from Hungary, you know," he said in an interview soon after his arrival in Canada.[87] A doctor's son, he was to study law, he said, but then – he heard Ysaÿe play. "That settled it. No more law. From that time the violin was my life. I studied with Ysaÿe, first in Brussels, then I went with him to Godinne where – this is the first gesture of the finger of fate – I met the Hambourgs, Boris and Jan. We played together, under the direction of Ysaÿe."[88]

Since then he had had a splendid career, as a soloist with many orchestras and as concertmaster of the Vienna Tonkünstler. In Bucharest he also taught at the state conservatory and was first violinist of the court-appointed Carmen Silva String Quartet. The Rumanian queen mother – we have met her before – was the former Prinzessin Elisabeth zu Wied-Neuwied, the student at whom Leschetizky had thrown a book when she played a wrong note in Mendelssohn's G minor Concerto. She commanded the quartet to play to her twice a week. "She usually listened alone, sitting absorbed in the music. Sometimes she joined us in trios, piano quartets and quintets. She was beginning to get old and liked the slow movements best. As a girl she had had a fine technique, but her day was nearly done. Sometimes there were guests, and on gala occasions she would show us off with great pride."[89]

Géza was concertmaster of the Berlin Philharmonic under Arthur Nikisch and also taught at the Stern Conservatorium. In 1918 he married the eminent English pianist Norah Drewett, whose musical career in Canada was to parallel his. "This was a real romance – they met in a salon in Vienna and quite by chance discovered that they both played a sonata that was very little known at that time, though famous now – the one that César Franck, greatest of the modern French composers, wrote as a wedding present for Ysaÿe. They played it and parted, each to go on long and arduous concert tours. Later, they met again and the wedding present sonata had sown a fatal [sic] seed – Norah Drewett became Madame Géza de Kresz."[90]

It happened that Norah had been a friend of Mark's wife when she was still Dolly Mackenzie. They had met in London when Dolly was a violin student, hoping to be accepted by Ysaÿe, and Norah was a young pianist.

> Dolly had a large attic-room in her father's beautiful house facing Green Park in Westminster. There we were able to play till late into the night, and it was so comfortable, and there were such lovely bits of furniture, pictures and collections of Toby jugs which amused me so much, that I loved to go to her. We also went to concerts together.
>
> She was a delightful type – a mixture of aristocrat and bohemian – and when, a few years later, she married the pianist Mark Hambourg, she was able to keep this dual life, her old Scots friends being as fond of her as her new Jewish relations. By coincidence, Géza was also present at her wedding, and we were together (unknown to each other) at the reception. Dolly became a colleague and friend of his at Godinne, Ysaÿe's summer home, where Géza met Mark's younger brother, Boris Hambourg.

In 1919 the de Kresz's first daughter, Mária,[91] was born, the second daughter in 1923. The inflation in Berlin was "staggering," he remembered later. "Before the war a dollar was worth 4.20 gold-marks, by the summer of 1923 one dollar could buy one million marks, and by the end of the year 4.2 billion." On July 1, 1923, a cable arrived from his old friend Boris. "Could you join me in Toronto in September? Three thousand dollars minimum guarantee."

Without hesitation Géza accepted, cancelling a European tour arranged for the following season, and rejecting offers from Berlin, Bremen, Dortmund and Cologne. "The New World," he explained later, "the old friend and our British sympathies were equally strong incentives to do so."

They rented a house near the Hambourg Conservatory, at 88 Huntley Street, large enough to accommodate Norah Drewett's mother, who soon followed them from Berlin, and with space to give music lessons at home. Among Géza's earliest pupils were Murray Adaskin, Adolph Koldofsky and Maurice Solway, whom in 1927 Géza sent to study with Ysaÿe – such a seminal event that Solway added to his name "pupil of Ysaÿe" when he published his autobiography in 1984. The reason Géza sent him to Belgium was that he knew he "did not have the teaching resources or the playing ability of a Czaplinski."

As Solway explained, Géza "seemed to represent a return to the laxness with which Dr. von Kunits could sometimes be charged, and my progress slowed down decidedly. Much to his credit, de Kresz was enough of a musician to see this for himself, and convinced Mr. [Boris] Hambourg that it was time for me to study with a great European master. Without such a teacher my chances of starting a solo career were slim. Mr. de Kresz, who was truly selfless and considerate about the whole business, thought I should study with the great Belgian virtuoso who had been his own teacher."[92]

Harry Adaskin was twenty-two, seven years older than Maurice Solway, when Géza arrived in Toronto. It was the beginning of a difficult relationship lasting fifteen years. There was a marked difference in age, experience and background between the two. Fifty years later, Adaskin was amazed to note that his feelings towards Géza were still ambivalent. The arrival of de Kresz, he wrote, "silently and secretly heralded a turning point in my life."

Adaskin had recently been studying Indian philosophy. "And the turning point was one of enormous importance in *anyone's* life – it was the beginning of awareness.... He was the first person I was able to get close to who was an educated product of nineteenth-century Central European provincialism. I knew all I wanted to know about *un*educated provincialism. I was brought up in it. But de Kresz was a man of the world, well educated, very knowledgeable, spoke four languages fluently. He came from a reasonably well-to-do professional family, was well-connected socially in Hungary and through those connections could make his way everywhere."[93] Géza made him aware, he wrote, that "even stature, education, and good background" could be compartmentalized, and thus prevent one from adding to one's spiritual growth.

Géza and Norah arrived in the late summer of 1923. On October 30 they gave a joint recital in Massey Hall. They played Beethoven's Kreutzer Sonata, the Tchaikovsky Violin Concerto, the Paganini Caprice Number 24 and three Hungarian dances by Brahms.

The next day the *Mail and Empire* was pleased: "He is not a dry and coldly intelligent master of the technique of the instrument. He played with emotional colour, and the compositions that have dramatic possibilities are interpreted by him with fire and abandon."

One of the reasons Géza came to Canada was his hope of forming a string quartet with his old friend Boris as cellist. Géza had met Milton Blackstone, who was the obvious choice for viola. Blackstone was a New Yorker whose grandfather had been head cantor in the Russian city of Grodna. He had come to Toronto at sixteen to play in the Toronto Symphony Orchestra. Music had been his passion all his life. "I was poor," he recalled, "and could not afford money for concerts as well as for lessons, in New York.... And there were many concerts. When I was only ten years old, I used to hang around the stage doors of the concert halls, and I got to know the valets and secretaries of the artists and I would often run errands for them. Then when they would want to pay me I would beg to hear the concerts instead. I heard all the great artists in this way."[94]

Later, Blackstone became the business manager of the Hart House String Quartet. Harry Adaskin recalled: "He was remarkably good at it. He was also very happy doing all this work because it kept him from practising. He loved practising with *us,* or any single *one* of us, but he hated practising alone. How he managed to play as well as he did I'll never know. He had a beautiful tone and always played his best at concerts. Nervousness, or stage-fright in his case, made him play better than ever. Often, through lack of practice, he would play badly at rehearsals. Came the concert, he was at his best. It was a great gift, and we all wished we had it. It was a kind of showman's gift, and Milton was a showman."[95]

Géza, Boris and Blackstone played together in the mornings, two or three times a week. But to form a string quartet, a second violinist was needed. It was Blackstone who suggested Adaskin. Blackstone had played with him in von Kunits' student quartet, and later with Czaplinski. Blackstone was asked to phone him.

Harry Adaskin was uncertain. "I was at that time quite busy, I was doing a lot of practising. I had a large class of pupils and in the evening I played light trio music with a cellist and pianist in a smart new little upstairs restaurant opposite the King Edward Hotel. I made (for me) lots of money. So I put Milton off with a vague promise to drop in some morning for a quartet session."

Blackstone had to call a second, and perhaps a third time. As Adaskin recalled later, when he thought how he almost missed "what turned out to be the great artistic experience of my life, which had the most far-reaching effect on me generally, I almost shudder. My brother Murray has told me that every proposition made to him, which later turned out to be of immense importance in his life and career, he resisted with maniacal force! So perhaps it's a family trait to resist the inevitable."[96]

Harry was hooked. Blackstone reported later, "We played all the pent-up chamber music out of our systems."[97]

Soon they were ready to go public.

Boris had had his first encounter with Vincent and Alice Massey in November 1920, at a nine o'clock recital in Jenkins Galleries. He and Jan and J. Campbell McInnes were the artists. Before the war, Vincent Massey had been primarily interested in the theatre, and he was as well an early champion of the Group of Seven and collected their paintings. While the Massey family's musical interests had been mostly confined to choral music, Vincent began to develop a taste for chamber music after 1918, when small musical soirées became fashionable in cultivated Toronto society. In 1921 he was elected president of the Chamber Music Society, an organization which seems to have

Géza de Kresz and his wife,
English pianist Norah Drewett.

Harry Adaskin, violinist; in later life lecturer, CBC radio personality and writer of two volumes of memoirs.

soon disappeared. The other major benefactors of the arts, Lady Eaton and Sir Edmund Walker, had little interest in chamber music.

On March 10, 1924, Boris went to see Massey "at 4.20 p.m" – according to Massey's diary – "about the formation of a H.H. String Quartette." Massey was interested. At the follow-up meeting, Boris took Géza de Kresz with him. He may have thought this was a good move not only because of Géza's eminence in the musical world of Europe and his charming personality and old-world manners (not to mention his delightful Hungarian accent), but perhaps also because he and Maria assumed that Vincent Massey would be more easily swayed if it was understood from the beginning that the man who would play first violin in the proposed quartet did not have a Jewish background. In the Canada of the twenties there was no reason to believe that Vincent Massey would be any less anti-Semitic than almost all non-Jews outside the world of the arts. Therefore, it may have seemed wise to take this assumed bias into account. As it turned out, these matters were never an issue between the Hart House Quartet and the Masseys. They lived in two different worlds and were therefore completely at ease with one another.

Colonel Frank McFarland, the financial officer of the Hart House Board of Syndics, also attended the meeting, which went well. Vincent Massey proposed the quartet give a concert at his house at 71 Queen's Park Crescent. A small group of prominent music lovers was invited.

The trial concert took place. The four musicians passed the test and Massey thought the event was "most promising." An official launching was announced. The first concert in the Hart House Theatre took place on April 27, before an invited audience of five hundred people. The program consisted of Haydn's Quartet opus 76, no. 2, the slow movement from Beethoven's "Harp" Quartet opus 74, and a complete performance of Beethoven's opus 96.

"The applause was terrific," Adaskin recalled, "and we went out several times to bow. Then we noticed Vincent Massey get up from his seat and begin walking towards the stage. We went off as he went on, and as soon as the applause subsided he began to speak. This was unexpected, and we were very curious as to what he was going to say."[98]

What he said was that he could see the audience had enjoyed the concert as much as he did, but these musicians all had to make a living as teachers or orchestral players or both. "These gentlemen," he declared, "must not be allowed to disband."

"Wild applause broke out at this remark," said Adaskin, "and we, in the wings, looked at each other in astonishment. Vincent Massey then said, as everyone obviously understood, money was needed for this purpose, and would there be people there tonight who would be willing to do something about it."

All Massey wrote in his diary was "I made a short speech introducing the new adventure."

Four thousand dollars were collected that evening and the musicians went home in a daze. But the next morning they took a close look at the money. Four thousand dollars was a huge sum, of course, but not huge enough to enable them to give up their jobs. They called Vincent Massey and told him. "Let me think it over," he said.

A few days later they were once again invited to the Massey house.

> He and Mrs. Massey sat side by side and told us that they had decided the Massey Foundation would undertake to found the quartet as a permanent entity. We were to decide what salary we needed in order to give up all our other activities and devote ourselves entirely to playing string quartets. Any money we earned at concerts would go to the Foundation to cover our salaries, but if we earned more than that it would go to us. The Foundation would pay all deficits so that we would always have our salaries guaranteed.
>
> Need I try to describe our feelings on hearing this news? Rarely since the time of Haydn had this happened anywhere, and certainly never before in Canada.[99]

The four thousand dollars were returned to their owners.

In a chapter in his biography *The Young Vincent Massey* entitled "The Young Maecenas," Claude Bissell wrote: "The Hart House Quartet is the best example of Vincent's skills and power as a patron. The financial support, although not great, was indispensable, and, at the time, could not have come from any other source. More important, he was a unifying force, who dealt sympathetically with a long success of personal crises and administrative obstructions. He was determined that the quartet should gain international recognition and correct the impression of a Canada immersed in wheat, pulp and politics. In this, the quartet succeeded beyond expectation."[100]

Initially the total salary bill was ten thousand dollars a year, divided equally between the four. The sum increased with each new contract. Colonel G. Frank McFarland, K.C., who, as close personal friend of both the Masseys and as lawyer and secretary of the Hart House Board of Syndics, had been present at the initial conversation with Boris on March 10, 1924, was entrusted to be the man in charge of the details. After his elevation to the Supreme Court of Ontario in the early thirties, the members of the quartet continued to be frequent guests at the McFarlands' house on Russell Hill Road in Toronto.

Claude Bissell wrote that McFarland was, "for Massey's purposes, an ideal officer: a tough administrator, with a good-humoured contempt for an actor's or a musician's grasp of a budget, but, with it all, sympathetic to the arts and quick to recognize artistic excellence."[101]

On June 6, 1924, three months after the formation of the quartet, Boris wrote to Vincent Massey appealing to him to clear up a misunderstanding between Blackstone and McFarland about a financial matter. Massey passed the letter on to McFarland. "Mr. Hambourg has entirely misconstrued my attitude," McFarland replied on June 25 and explained why. He was certain, he wrote, the members of the quartet felt he was entirely out of sympathy with the whole idea and was trying "to queer their pitch," but obviously he had to do what he did.[102] Throughout the relationship McFarland played the role of "tough cop."

Vincent Massey did not wish to be called "patron" of the Hart House Quartet. He preferred to be its "friend."[103] Boris addressed him as "Dear Vincent" when he wrote to him, but Milton Blackstone, who as business manager of the ensemble had a more formal relationship, stuck to "Dear Mr. Massey." Moreover, in his attempt to please his benefactor, he gave Vincent Massey a handwritten, undated political report from the Maritimes during the election campaign of 1925.

> Knowing that you will be glad to hear of my enquiries regarding public opinion in connection with the political situation in good old Conservative Nova Scotia, I can tell you that there will be a decided swing toward Liberalism....
>
> Next week I am going off on a booking tour in hopes of adding New Glasgow, Amherst and Sidney to the list of places where we play.
>
> All of us send you our best wishes for a happy summer, and of course this includes the gentleman whose name is Hon. Vincent Massey and last not least Lionel and Hart [the Masseys' two sons].

Such familiarity with the very peak of the Toronto Establishment did not prevent Blackstone from identifying himself publicly as a Jew. A year after the 1925 election he published an essay entitled "The Jew in the Cultural Arts," in which he listed a large number of contributions to Canada by Jews. "The Hart House String Quartet." he wrote, "whose perfection is recognized by the musical world and whose engagements will take them on extensive tours through the United States, Canada and England within the next fifteen months, includes Harry Adaskin and Milton Blackstone, two outstanding Jewish artists, whose achievements are bringing much credit to Canadian Art."[104]

There was no reason for Blackstone to include Boris, who was not a member of the Jewish community. Ten years later, however, during Hitler's rise to power, Boris publicly associated himself with Jewish causes.[105]

For ten years, until November 1935 when Vincent Massey went to London, the quartet gave him and Alice Massey intense joy. He participated in a direct, hands-on way in its management and took immense pride in its growing fame. In 1925 he resigned as president of Massey-Harris and entered Mackenzie King's Liberal cabinet as minister without portfolio. His subsequent defeat in Durham put an end to his career as a politician. In 1927 he became the first Canadian minister in Washington. He returned to Canada in 1930. In 1932 he became chairman of the Dominion Drama Festival and in the same year president of the National Liberal Federation.

For the summers of 1925 and 1926, the Masseys put at the quartet's disposal the old family home in Newcastle east of Toronto, to live and rehearse together. During the final illness of Chester Massey, father of Vincent and Raymond, in 1926, they quartet played for him in his house on Jarvis Street. Later they were often invited to Batterwood, the Masseys' home north of Port Hope. In 1931, when they were there for a day, Vincent Massey made this diary entry: "The H.H. String Quartet and their wives came down.... A feast of music and other feasting. A Haydn quartet in a.m. along with Debussy's afterwards, and in the p.m. a Brahms quartet with Mrs. de Kresz and a quartet by Beethoven afterwards. The servants all came to hear the afternoon concert."[106]

In the same summer the Adaskins rented a cottage on Lake Ontario at Newcastle, where Harry gave violin lessons to the Masseys' son Hart, who by then was thirteen. Hart arrived there every day in "a long, low, yellow, open, chauffeur-driven Cadillac." The Masseys wanted him to charge normal fees, but Adaskin said this was out of the question, considering all the thing the Masseys were doing for the arts in Canada: "Mrs. Massey burst into a flood of tears. Her husband put his arms around her shoulder and tried to soothe her spirit. She couldn't speak at first, she couldn't stop crying. Yet she wanted to say something, so she spoke through her tears. 'No one's ever, ever said anything like that to us, have they, Vincent? Have they? No one's ever said anything like that.' And she continued to cry."[107]

The quartet had to acquire a repertoire quickly, including many contemporary compositions. In the first season alone, they performed twenty-three different works.[108] In the second, the year in which the *Globe* already called them "a national institution," they gave the Canadian première of Bartók's First String Quartet – no doubt thanks to Géza de Kresz's friendship with the composer. Later, they gave premières of the same work in Montreal, Boston and San Francisco, where there were only seven people in the audience. The *Toronto Star's* Augustus Bridle thought the composition was "of more than casual beauty."[109]

Thanks to Géza, the quartet included in their repertoire a quartet by György Kosy that he had written specially for them and which received its première in the Hambourg Conservatory in December 1930. They played it later in New York. In December 1931 they gave the first performance of Kodály's Quartet, opus 2, in the Hart House Theatre. They also performed other works by Hungarian composers which were not well known in Canada.

In the second season, 1925-1926, they gave the first complete performance of Ernest MacMillan's Quartet in C minor. (He provided exemplary program notes on all the quartet's presentations during the early years). In the same year the radio department of the Canadian National Railways – more than a decade before the birth of the CBC – broadcast a number of the quartet's concerts on radio stations across the nation. In the following years they played regularly for the CNR and for several radio stations in the United States. In 1926 they made recordings for the Victor Company.

In the same year they gave their first concert in the Great Hall of Hart House. Until then, they had only played in the smaller Hart House Theatre. "The hall was so full we could get no one else in. The audience sat there spellbound: you could have heard a pin drop. From then on the Hart House String Quartet gave one of the Sunday concerts [in the Great Hall] each year."[110]

They performed in Ottawa, London, Montreal, Halifax, Kingston and in other eastern Canadian cities, as well as going west and playing in many smaller centres, often with Women's Musical Clubs, sometimes presenting mixed programs with choruses. During the first ten years they made eight transcontinental tours.

Milton Blackstone told *Maclean's Magazine* that their first coast-to-coast tour was a wonderful adventure. "The Maritimes seemed a little dazed by our music making – a little bewildered by it. We were not in the least dismayed. We knew that a few more concerts would make many converts, as they have. The East, well, the East felt itself a little blasé. It was the home of Canada's culture and it knew all about string quartets – even if many of the residents had never heard one. But the West! Here was a Canada which hungered for the pure tone of a string quartet, a Canada of British and European immigrants, people who knew what chamber music was and had longed for it. Why, time and again, when we came on the platform with our instruments, the applause was deafening."[111]

The quartet took a special interest in French Canada. In May 1927 and May 1928 they gave recitals at the Canadian Folk Song and Handicraft Festival in the Château Frontenac in Quebec City, which included folk-song arrangements by Ernest MacMillan, Eskimo and Indian melodies arranged by Alfred Laliberté, and Leo Smith's Paraphrases on two *Chansons*. On May 24, 1928, at the CPR Festival in Quebec City, the winning work was a premiere of a work by the Winnipeg composer George Bowles.

In Ontario, to circumvent the provisions of the Lord's Day Act, which forbade commerce on Sundays, and even concerts and sporting events for which admission was charged, they gave recitals on Sunday evenings in the First Unitarian Church. These were organized by the String Quartet Club, a legal ploy to evade the law. The club existed until 1926.

On July 1, 1927, they participated in the Diamond Jubilee of Confederation, broadcast from Ottawa. They played the slow movement from MacMillan's Quartet and folk-song sketches by MacMillan and Leo Smith. They performed in the Parliament Buildings and were invited to Rideau Hall, where they gave a short recital after the reception. The Governor-General, Lord Willingdon, presented them with cufflinks decorated with a W and a little crown on top. Boris gave his pair to Joseph D. Sheard, who is now a judge in the Ontario Court, General Division, and occasionally wears them in court. His father had taken cello lessons from Boris. Later, Joseph Sheard came Clement's (unpaid) lawyer. He believes that, to the quartet's grave disappointment, the cufflinks were their only payment, but he is not sure.

The third season (1926-1927) coincided with the hundredth anniversary of Beethoven's death, which they observed in four concerts of all his quartets and the Great Fugue, three given by the Hart House Quartet and one by the Kilbourn Quartet of Rochester. Walter Sinclair read the text of the Heiligenstadt Testament at the first concert. In 1928 they commemorated the anniversary of Schubert's death by including one of his works in each of their Toronto concerts. In 1932 they celebrated Haydn's, and in 1933 Brahms's birth.

In 1927 they toured the U.S. for the first time, for four and a half weeks, visiting eleven states and giving fifteen concerts. In the next, the fourth season, they toured the United States again, this time for sixteen weeks. They were so successful that they were urged to move their headquarters to New York. This, however, did not "suit the inclinations either of the members of the quartet or its sponsor, and so it will remain Canadian, which of course will not prevent its frequent visits to the United States."[112] They often played at schools and colleges and in February 1927 they gave a concert of popular music in Massey Hall, organized by the *Toronto Telegram*. Each ticket cost twenty-five cents, in line with Hart Massey's original intention.

Sometime in 1927 they received an invitation to play Maurice Ravel's one and only string quartet in New York in the presence of the composer. This was to be his first visit to the United States. For the quartet this was a singular honour. Ravel was one of the most famous composers in the world, but, at fifty-three, though he was much influenced by jazz, he had never been to America.

Mark had met him a year or two earlier. "Well, *Maître*," he enquired in French because Ravel did not speak English, "have you nothing new coming out for the piano?"

"I am just writing a piano concerto," Ravel replied. "But I have not quite finished it."

"I hope I shall have the pleasure of playing it," Mark observed.

"Not until after six months. I cannot allow anybody to play the concerto till I have played it several times myself. Otherwise if my

The Hart House String Quartet in 1925. From the left, Géza de Kresz, Milton Blackstone, Boris Hambourg and Harry Adaskin. (University of Toronto Archives)

The quartet seeks bookings for its first transcontinental tour.

THE
Hart House String Quartet

First Transcontinental Tour
Now Booking --- Season 1925-1926

In the first year of its organization, the Hart House String Quartet has played to capacity audiences in Montreal, Kingston, Hespeler, Hamilton, London, Sackville, N.B., Napanee, Peterboro, Ottawa, Halifax, etc., and

14 "SOLD OUT" CONCERTS IN TORONTO

Application for Dates and Further Information to .. Secretary, Hart House String Quartet, Hart House, Toronto

London and Paris Acclaim

HART HOUSE
STRING QUARTET

"An Admirable Body, Worthy to Rank With the Most Serious Organizations." —Morning Post, London.

ERNEST NEWMAN—
(Sunday Times)

We shall all be glad to hear these people play again, for their tone steals agreeably upon the ear, and they have a firm musical grasp upon whatever they undertake.

HERBERT HUGHES—
(Daily Telegraph)

Such a debut as this is indeed probably unique . . . This most admirable group of players . . . at once acclaimed as an ensemble of the first rank . . . In all they did, there was the liveliest sense of rhythm and unanimity of mind.

FOX-STRANGWAYS—
(Sunday Observer)

The Hart House String Quartet have gone far in the art of quartet playing. Their intonation is as good as one could wish to hear, octaves and unisons quite exceptionally good; and they have a real swing . . . We seldom hear our contemporaries presented so intelligently.

DAILY EXPRESS—
FAULTLESS PLAYING BY HART HOUSE QUARTET

. . . As there are only a handful of string quartets in the whole wide world, it is pleasant to record that the Hart House group at Wigmore Hall last night proved to be first rate.

GEZA DE KRESZ
HARRY ADASKIN
MILTON BLACKSTONE
BORIS HAMBOURG

JOURNAL des DEBATS—
Maurice Imbert, Paris.

They can be favorably compared with the most reputed ensembles that we know of.

MONDE MUSICAL—

They immediately established themselves as one of the best quartets in the world.

PARIS DAILY MAIL—

The quartet's tone is beautiful in every degree of intensity, from a truly ethereal delicacy, to a sonority of astounding volume.

MAURICE RAVEL— *writes*

"I was sorry not to be able to come and hear, and shake the hands of, the remarkable artists who interpreted my work with so much musicianship last year . . ."

EUGENE YSAYE— *says*

" . . . in many ways, the finest interpretation of the Franck quartet that I have ever heard. Most perfect quartet playing."

SECOND EUROPEAN TOUR
SEPTEMBER—DECEMBER 1930
NOW BOOKING U. S. A.
JANUARY—APRIL 1931

And Now
THREE NEW YORK RECITALS

FEBRUARY 14	FEBRUARY 17	FEBRUARY 21
FRANCK .... Quartet E. MACMILLAN ...... Two Sketches *(Based on French-Canadian Folk Songs)* DEBUSSY .... Quartet	DELIUS .... Quartet JOHN BEACH .... Poeme DOHNANYI, Quartet, A Minor, Op. 33	BEETHOVEN .. E Flat Major, Op. 74 HAYDN ...... G Minor, Op. 20, No. 3 SCHUBERT .... D Minor, Op. Posth. *(Death and the Maiden)*

Regarding Tickets for Recitals or Open Dates Apply RECITAL MANAGEMENT ARTHUR JUDSON, New York City

Poster for three concerts in New York in 1930.

Gentleman and players – Vincent and Mrs. Massey with the Hart House String Quartet at the Legation in Washington, 1929. The players are, from left, Harry Adaskin, Milton Blackstone, Boris Hambourg and Géza de Kresz. (University of Toronto Archives)

An outline of the programs for the 1932-1933 season.

ON OCTOBER 29th, the Hart House String Quartet will inaugurate its ninth season of subscription concerts in Hart House Theatre. It is interesting to note that the first concert of this series marks the Quartet's four hundred and tenth public appearance, eighty one of which have been made before Toronto audiences.

⁌ The inclusion at each concert of one work by Brahms, whose birth centenary is being commemorated this season of 1932-1933, brings to mind the Quartet's participation, in the past, in world-wide commemorations of Beethoven, Schubert and Haydn.

⁌ Leading in interest will be Brahms' three string quartets, the quintet with piano, and the string sextet in G major. Rudolph Reuter, eminent Chicago pianist, will appear in the quintet, and Leo Smith, cellist, with Thomas Brennand, viola, will assist in the Sextet.

⁌ Of new works, there will be a striking quartet by Villa-Lobos, brilliant composer from Brazil, and an English work by Vaughan Williams. Other novelties will be some four-part fugues by Bach, and an exquisite Mozart quartet, written when the composer was twelve years of age. For the past century and a half this latter work was considered lost, but recently unearthed in Vienna, and will add an unusual touch to the programmes.

⁌ The Invitation Concert of Modern Music (for subscribers only) will include quartets by Honegger, La Violette and Ernest Bloch.

⁌ Subscribers are urged to make early application.

THE PROGRAMMES
(Subject to slight change)

October 29th
Brahms, Quartet in A minor.
Bach, Fugues for string quartet.
Beethoven, Quartet in B flat major, Op. 130.
(Played in memory of Dr. Luigi von Kunits.)

November 19th
Villa-Lobos, 2nd Quartet, Opus 56.
*Mozart, Quartet in A major.
Brahms, Quartet in B flat major.

December 3rd
Brahms, Sextet in G major, for two violins, two violas and two celli.
Bach, Fugue for two violins and two celli.
Beethoven, Fugue for two violins, two violas and cello.
Franck, Quartet in D major.

January 7th
Beethoven, Quartet in D major, Op. 18, No. 3.
*Mozart, Quartet in B flat major.
Brahms, Quinted in F minor, Opus 34, for piano and string quartet.

April 8th
Vaughan Williams, String Quartet.
Mendelssohn, Quartet in D major.
Brahms, Quartet in C minor.

*Recently discovered, and written at the age of twelve.

performance is heard after some other pianist's, the public will find out what a terrible player I am."[113]

Ravel's first visit to America was to give audiences, in the words of the *New York Sun*, "an opportunity to study his prematurely gray hair and his charmingly bland smile."[114]

A few days before the concert Ravel was in Toronto, informally. The main purpose of the visit seems to have been to enable the quartet to receive his blessing. He stayed at the King Edward Hotel. Soon after his arrival all four members paid him a visit in his room, taking their instruments. He greeted them politely and with gravity. He invited them to play. They put up their stands and began. At one point "he leaped up as though he had been shot" and said, *"Pas de retard"* – no *ritardando*. When they had finished he thought for a moment and said, "This is not how I conceived the quartet." They were mortified. Géza asked him how he would like them to play it? But Ravel replied, no, no no. They played with such conviction, any change would be unwise. He was perfectly relaxed about the whole thing and offered them drinks. Then he took them down to the dining room where they had a marvellous meal prepared by the chef, a friend, it so happened, from France.[115]

The New York concert took place on January 15, 1928. On the program was also Ravel's Introduction and Allegro, with the string section played by the Hart House String Quartet. Joseph Szigeti performed the Violin Sonata with the composer, who also played some of his piano pieces, including the *Pavane pour une infante défunte*. This is usually interpreted as a slow, stately dance, but the composer played it at a brisk andante.

The world of music and high society honoured Ravel after the concert at a glamorous party on Madison Avenue, attended by, among others, George Gershwin, Fritz Kreisler, Jascha Heifetz, Bela Bartók, Feodor Chaliapin and Edgard Varèse. Harry Adaskin was there but he had to wait until 1970, thirty-three years after the composer's death, to discover, while reading his biography, all the famous names he might have talked to if he had known they were there and had had the courage to talk to them.

Ravel came to Toronto again to give a concert on the evening of March 22 with the American soprano Lisa Roma, Ravel playing his *Sonatine* and other piano pieces. Among the songs Lisa Roma chose were his *Chansons grècques*. Once again, the quartet played his string quartet.

The concert was given under the auspices of the T. Eaton Company and carried by radio station CFCA. It was the first time Ravel played on radio in North America. The concert was sponsored by the *Toronto Star* and the Hambourg Concert Society. This time the French consul, Ernest MacMillan, the four members of the quartet, and others welcomed the famous man at Union Station.

The morning after the concert the director of the Hambourg Conservatory's Radio Department, Clement Hambourg, aged twenty-eight, commented to the *Star*:

> Ravel has quite taken the place of Debussy and Saint-Saëns as dean of contemporary French music. While it is impossible to appraise accurately the relative rank of any living artist, because the perspective of time is necessary, Ravel is today the most fully equipped artist whom we can put in the scale against Stravinsky and Schönberg.
>
> Maurice Ravel, deeply absorbed in the problems of creative work and little concerned with self-exploitation, has appeared rarely as pianist and conductor in recent years and his visit to this continent is of singular significance to himself as well as of epochal importance to his admirers in this country.
>
> In the works last night, one noticed indubitable traces of the influence of four composers with whom he came in contract during his formative years – Gabriel Fauré, Emmanuel Chabrier, Eric Satie, and Claude Debussy. From each in turn he can be said to have derived clarity, genial romanticism, ironic humour, and impressionism.[116]

Augustus Bridle of the *Toronto Star* interviewed Ravel:

Mons. Ravel is about the height of Napoleon. In a fawn hat and bulgy overcoat to match, a negligée striped shirt and tie en suite and straight iron-gray hair, he twinkles like a morning star, defiant of time, fatigue or place, or anything but the immediate business of seeing and hearing what life is every moment he is awake. Seated at a rotunda table, not caring who heard him talk French about music and life, he spoke through Boris Hambourg, excellent interpreter. He talked volubly and vividly. His eyes snapped with *joie de vivre*. He twiddled all his fingers as he spoke, as though playing on a harp. Tuesday he would be motoring to Niagara Falls – to get a new theme for a composition. Ah! Splendid....[117]

After his visit to Niagara Falls Ravel told reporters: "I am affected always by everything there is as I see it and hear it and feel it. It may be more colour or mass, or motion or sound. It is all one. We moderns take it all in. We never know what may catch us next. A cloud or a foghorn or a pretty face or a crowd or a fire. All is life – for music just as it is for painting or literature."[118]

According to Eugène Lapierre, the biographer of Calixa Lavallée, the composer of "O Canada," Ravel exclaimed on seeing Niagara Falls, "*Quel majestueux si bémol!*" (How majestically B flat!). But, Lapierre wrote, Ravel was *not* inspired by the falls to use them as a motif in any of his compositions, in contrast to Lavallé, who used in "O Canada" a particular motif he heard in the waterfall in the Yamaska River near Saint-Hyacinthe.

In a learned article, the Montreal critic Gilles Potvin dismissed Lapierre's Ravel story as undocumented.[119]

During the 1928-29 season the Hart House String Quartet gave sixty concerts in forty-four cities in Canada and the United States, in five months. Their appearance in Washington early in 1929 was memorable: "The Canadian Minister and Mrs. Massey were hosts to some two hundred persons distinguished in this city's ambassadorial and congressional circles at a concert here on February 15 at the Canadian Legation. The artists of the evening were the Hart

House Quartet of Toronto, which thus made its third annual appearance as representatives of Canada's musical world. Among the notables who attended the concert were: The British Ambassador and Lady Isabella Howard; Alistair MacDonald, the son of Britain's premier; Mrs. Woodrow Wilson; Speaker and Mrs. Nicholas Longworth, Attorney-General and Mrs. Mitchell; Mr. and Mrs. Gifford Pinchot; Alanson Houghton, former ambassador to Great Britain, with Mrs. Houghton."[120]

During the sixth season (1929-1930) they made their European debut with a concert in London on October 8, 1929, in Wigmore Hall, where they played Bartók, Beethoven and Debussy. "There are only two kinds of string quartets," reported the *Daily Express*, "the very good ones and the just bad; and as there are only a handful of string quartets in the whole wide world, it is pleasant to record that the Hart House group at the Wigmore Hall last night proved to be first rate."[121] While in London, they also played twice on the BBC, and they presented the Prince of Wales with their two records.

The *Morning Post* wrote:

> Imperial sentiment has been used so often to cover a multitude of musical sins that it is a double pleasure to welcome these excellent musicians from Toronto. The Hart House Quartet is an admirable body worthy to rank on purely musical grounds with the most serious organizations of this kind. They must be reckoned among the most welcome musical visitors the British Empire has ever sent to the Mother Country....
>
> After the performance the artists' room was thronged with enthusiasts including Mark Hambourg, brother of the cellist, all anxious to congratulate the players.

"We are overwhelmed by so cordial a reception in the heart of the British Empire," Boris Hambourg told the *Telegram*. "The audience was quick to sympathize with our music and generous with their applause. They were as fine if not finer than any audience we have encountered even in Canada."[122]

On October 25, 1929, Vincent Massey wrote a thank-you letter to Mark Hambourg: "This is just a line to thank you most sincerely for all that you and your wife have done to contribute to the success of the visit of our Quartet. They have already given us glowing accounts of your many kindnesses and we are most grateful. The Quartet seems to have achieved a very real success, but much of this has been due to the efforts which their friends have made to give them a good introduction."

While in England, Boris had an adventure at a train station. The quartet was leaving for somewhere. The officer at the gate let the others through but demanded from Boris that he buy a second ticket for his cello. Boris explained that he had been touring in England for six weeks and that this was the first time he had been asked for such a ticket.

"Are you alone?" asked the man.

"No, I am with a string quartet."

"Oh, I see, you are with a band. All right, go ahead."

Before leaving London, Boris gave a cello recital at his sister Galia's home in Chelsea. He played de Falla's *Suite Espagnole*, John Ireland's *Holy Boy* and Hamilton Harty's *Butterflies*. Among those present were Maria Hambourg, Mark and Dorothy Hambourg, Beverley Baxter[123] and his wife, the brothers Maurice (the sculptor) and Constant (the composer) Lambert, Mrs. R.Y. Eaton of Toronto (a cousin of Lady Eaton's husband Jack) and Ashley Dukes, "whose adaptation" (according to the society columns) "of *Jew Süss* has just been produced at the Duke of York's Theatre."

On October 24 the quartet gave a concert in Paris. Then they went to Brussels, where they played for Eugène Ysaÿe, a few months before his death and state funeral. They stopped off expressly, he wrote for *L'Action musicale* in Brussels, "to give me the joy again to hear the quartets by Franck and Debussy (two pillars of my faith) to which these artists added the fifteenth quartet by Beethoven."

"It became an evening of enchantment for me," said Ysaÿe, "and I will never forget the profound sensation I experienced in listening to these works played with an incomparable mastery, an ensemble of an almost unique perfection, which one would have to go back to the time of Joachim's original quartet to equal.… I do not cite these impressions for the sake of advertising these superb artists.… I do it because the spirit of Beethoven, Franck and Debussy was there, and to speak about *them,* evoking and exalting their genius, which does me good and consoles me in my old age."[124]

On May 28, 1931, Colonel McFarland wrote to Vincent Massey, who happened to be in London, that Boris had just come to see him with a proposition "which sounds a bit fantastic to me, but might possibly have an element of business sagacity."

> The Rudolph Wurlitzer Company of New York have a famous 'cello called the Servais Guarneri built by Andrea Guarneri in 1692, and guaranteed by W.E. Hill & Sons of 140 New Bond Street, London. Boris states that it is one of the very finest 'cellos in the world today, and I enclose for your information letter and certificate of W.E. Hill & Sons on the subject. Boris has had the 'cello here for a month and is exceedingly anxious to keep it. The price quoted first of all was $15,000, but after some hammering they have gotten it down to $8,500. His idea was not to buy the 'cello himself because he is quite unable to do that nor to have it bought for him, but that it should be bought for the Quartet and remain the property of yourself, or the Massey Foundation, or whatever individual or group of individuals would be willing to purchase it. He states that there is no doubt that its value will double in the next ten years. All he cares is to have the 'cello to play for the rest of his life and any arrangement which achieves that object would be satisfactory to him.… He mentioned, by the way, that de Kresz plays a Guarneri violin.

Vincent Massey must have given an encouraging reply to McFarland's letter. In September 1932, a year and a half after the original letter, an agreement was drawn up between Ernest

MacMillan, principal of the Toronto Conservatory of Music, Frank McFarland, honorary treasurer of the Syndics of Hart House, and Boris. After Boris's death, the instrument was to pass on to a competent artist to be selected in accordance with a certain procedure. The purpose in acquiring it was to make "a permanent donation to musical education in the Dominion of Canada." There is some doubt whether the agreement was ever executed (only a draft is in the Vincent Massey papers and there is no record at Hart House or the Royal Conservatory) but the project did progress to the fundraising stage: Boris thanked Vincent Massey in writing for his contribution of a thousand dollars and the Arts and Letters Club also contributed.

Frank, the son of George Heinl, Boris's instrument dealer, remembers – he was only a child at the time – that Boris played a cello made by Giovanni Floreno Guidente, not a Guarneri. According to another expert, Monsieur Yann, an employee of Le Canu-Millant in the rue de Rome in Paris, who had his training in Cremona, the home town of the Guarneri family, Andrea Guarneri (1626-1698), the oldest Guarneri, never made any cellos at all – the reference books notwithstanding – only violins and a few violas. Clearly, this is one of the more intriguing mysteries in our story.[125]

Three years later Harry Adaskin heard about a Guarneri violin that had come on the market. He and Vincent Massey were on such good terms that Massey wrote an Epithalamium, a nuptial ode, for the eighth anniversary of the Adaskins' marriage, which was celebrated at Batterwood on August 7, 1934. Shortly afterwards Adaskin asked Massey for advice on the "sponsorship for a loan to purchase a Giuseppe Guarneri violin" which had been reduced from $6,000 to $4,000. Claude Bissell wrote that Adaskin "had been turned down by a bank which would not consider keeping a violin as a security. Vincent did not reply by letter, but, shortly afterwards, he sent a note directing the Massey Foundation to pay $3,500 for a violin to be bought by Harry Adaskin on terms to be arranged with an officer of the National Trust Company."[126]

As Harry Adaskin had feared, there were sharp tensions within the quartet from the beginning, with Géza on one side, Adaskin and Blackstone on the other. Throughout, Boris remained discreetly neutral, "content to play his cello with untroubled perfection."[127] Adaskin and Blackstone were critical of the quality of Géza's tone. Adaskin thought another flaw in Géza's playing was "rhythmical unsteadiness." Moreover, they felt, in the later stages, that his absences from Canada during the summers were too long, that his career as a soloist was in conflict with the interests of the quartet, and that his general orientation had remained too cosmopolitan, too European. In 1929 Géza said in a lecture at the Rotary Club in Budapest, "When I cross the ocean eastwards, I feel I am coming home, and when I return westwards, I feel I am coming home again."[128] Adaskin and Blackstone had trouble with such ambivalence about Canada. Norah Drewett de Kresz had another explanation for their criticism. In her opinion they were simply jealous of her husband since, in contrast to him and Boris, they had little experience as soloists.

On November 8, 1928, Frank McFarland wrote to Vincent Massey, who was Canadian minister in Washington:

> The matter of the First Violin is not yet settled. Apparently certain minor differences such as the making up of programmes, etc., have been smoothed out, but the fundamental question of tone is still exercising Blackstone and Adaskin.... In this connection, Blackstone when he was in New York had several interviews with [James] Levey who, as you know, was until recently the First Violin of the London String Quartet and is now teaching in New York. Blackstone took it upon himself to sound Levey out as to his willingness to play the First Violin with the Hart House Quartet and is convinced that Levey would be quite willing to do it on the same terms as de Kresz. It seems to me that our friend Blackstone exhibited a colossal nerve in carrying on these negotiations, but the possibilities of the situation are intriguing.

On November 10 Vincent Massey replied: "I quite agree with you that Blackstone exhibited preposterous cheek in his discussion with Levey, but I imagine no harm was done and it is interesting to know of the substitute in the background in case our first violin doesn't stay."

On November 18 Milton Blackstone wrote to Vincent Massey:

> I have learned to speak with Col. McFarland of our plans and "troubles" as though I were talking to you, for I know that he reports these discussions to you. There are some things which it is difficult for me to put down on paper. Some phrases sound so cold on paper, but can be warmed up by the human voice to sound less cruel. I refer to Mr. de Kresz. As an artist he has many qualities which are admirable, and there is no gainsaying his great contribution towards the establishment of the quartet's success. Like most mortals, especially musicians, he has his weaknesses which absolutely prevent us from attempting in the large cities a great majority of the works by Haydn, Mozart and early Beethoven. It is essential that these works be included in our repertoire to make the great impression, but we have tried several times to do so without success. I wish you could read this part of my letter and forget about it. But what is really important is our success, and what must be worked out is this. THE QUARTET MUST BE ALL BRITISH AND ALL CANADIAN. Every member's thoughts should be for the advancement of the quartet for the good of Canadian prestige. Our personal benefits and satisfaction can come only if this fact is placed foremost. With de Kresz I feel that his heart is in Europe. At any moment he may receive a commission from the Hungarian or Viennese government to take an official post at their conservatory. Should this occur I am certain he will feel inclined to accept it. He has (with the assistance of his wife) formed a group like that of Fontainebleau, France. This is in Vienna, and is to attract American and Canadian music students to come there to study music and the other arts. It is a very fine thing, but my contention is that his interests

are too divided to bring the greatest benefit to the quartet. After all, I speak in this way because my greatest interest in life, outside of my family, is the quartet.

Equipped with this – and McFarland's – information, Vincent Massey took decisive steps to tie Géza de Kresz firmly to the quartet for the next three years.

> My dear de Kresz,
> This is just a line to confirm our conversation of the other day. You will receive in addition to your $3,000, as a member of the Hart House String Quartet, the additional sum of $1,000 as its first violin for the season 1928-29, the same arrangement to apply to the next three years, making a total annual guarantee from the Hart House String Quartet for this period of $4,000.
> In addition to your salary from the Hart House String Quartet I will be responsible for your receiving for the next three years the sum of $2,000 per annum as your remuneration for certain educational work, the nature of which will be decided between us on your return from Europe.
> I think this accurately covers our understanding. I need not say that my wife and are both very happy that the Quartet is going on. I feel that the next three years will see its establishment on a very secure and permanent basis. As I said to you, I shall tell the other three members of the Quartet of the decision to give the first violin an extra $1,000. The other matter, however, having no relation to the Quartet or its work, need not be mentioned....[129]

From the beginning Vincent Massey had encouraged Géza's ambition to achieve renown for the quartet on the international stage, rather than merely in provincial Canada. Success at home was not enough to achieve Vincent Massey's high objective. He knew that Blackstone, who was having trouble making bookings, was not far from the truth when he complained to him, on June 10, 1929, "Ontario, that is between Kingston and Windsor, is very hard territory.

They are very unmusical and not the least bit cultured, nor have they any desire to be so."

Soon after the Géza settlement Alice Massey wrote a confidential memo to Boris, to which he replied on April 6, 1929, agreeing with her that "in order to preserve the morale and *esprit de corps* of the Quartet (so essential to its proper development and success)" personal conflicts had to be avoided at all costs, and assuring her that he would be happy to cooperate in every possible way by giving her any further information within his power that may be desired. "I am at your disposal," he wrote, "between one and three this afternoon, or at any time after five thirty."

Beginning in 1932, the Hart House String Quartet gave an annual concert of contemporary music in Toronto, performing works, among others, by Bloch, de Falla, Goossens, Hindemith, Honegger, Kreisler, Malipiero, Respighi, Schönberg, Shostakovich and Villa-Lobos. Among compositions by Canadian composers were works by Healey Willan and Amice Calverley.

In the fall of 1932 Géza's involvement in a new project called the Little Symphony raised the Masseys' eyebrows. It was a small orchestra made up mainly of young musicians, many of whom were also members of the Toronto Symphony Orchestra. Harry Adaskin was also a member. Vincent Massey had difficulties with this enterprise: Géza seemed to be trying to compete with the Toronto Symphony, of which Massey had just accepted the presidency, and was not concentrating enough on the quartet. To the latter point Géza replied on October 21, 1932: "Mrs. Massey and you will, I know, understand that nothing is more conducive to better production in one field than activities in parallel directions. It is really necessary for my artistry to seek everlastingly to enlarge my musical horizon, and, far from being detrimental to the quartet, I find this minor occupation a stimulant which benefits my musicality, my leadership, and through that, the quartet." As the ultimate boss of the quartet, Massey imposed the condition on Géza that the Little Symphony give no more than three concerts a year in Toronto and none outside the city. The Little Symphony gave a handful of concerts in 1932, 1933 and 1934 at Eaton Auditorium.

At the Christmas party at the Hambourg Conservatory in 1933 the quartet played the Debussy String Quartet to observe the fortieth anniversary of its first performance in Paris by the Ysaÿe Quartet on December 28, 1893. Maria Hambourg wrote the Masseys: "We enjoyed so much your Christmas card with the cows. I seem to remember those very cows down by the river when Boris and I had a glorious walk there. Thank you so much! The Quartet's Christmas Party was a great success – 175 people. The Quartet played divinely. Boris said afterwards he could swear Ysaÿe stood beside them. They were undoubtedly inspired!"

For the Toronto centenary in 1934 they gave a concert with the pianist Ossip Gabrilowitsch – Mark Twain's son-in-law and old friend of Mark's – in Massey Hall. Towards the end of his time with the quartet, Géza de Kresz gave an interview to *Strad*.

> He pointed out that when the Quartet was founded, his idea was to restrict their programs entirely to the classics of chamber music, but it was found that three complete quartets in an afternoon or evening were rather more than the average audience could digest, so in order to lighten the programs it is now their practice to include an arrangement for string quartet as the second item such as Alfred Pochon's arrangement of *Drink to Me only with Thine Eyes,* Percy Grainger's *Molly on the Shore.* Boccherini's *Minuet* and Julius Harrison's Humoresque on the Devonshire song *Widdicome Fair.* It must not be overlooked that in the early days of the Quartet they played to audiences that had never heard chamber music in any form, let alone the quartets by Beethoven, Haydn and other masters, and the Quartet's early years were spent mainly on pioneer work.[130]

By 1935 the internal difficulties had become insurmountable. Boris could no longer remain on the sidelines and had to take sides against Géza de Kresz. Fortunately, thanks to Blackstone's "preposterous cheek" in 1928, James Levey was standing by in the wings.

Ultimately, Vincent Massey had no choice but to fire Géza, who was in Salzburg teaching at the Mozarteum. He did so in great style in a letter of August 12, 1935:

Dear de Kresz,

A cable from Harry Adaskin will have told you already of the decision which my wife and I have most reluctantly arrived at as a result of several long conversations we have had with the three members of the Quartet who are in Canada, in which we have discussed its affairs and its future very thoroughly.

My wife and I had hoped that the group who first performed in 1924 could have gone on together for many years on an ascending scale of performance and before a constantly widening audience. The last two or three years, however, have been frankly disappointing. The difficulty of finding engagements has not been entirely due to the depression and the critical tone in important press comments suggests that there is another cause.

The matter has been brought to a head by conversations which were initiated by members of the Quartet themselves and in a long talk a few days ago with the three members, in which they were in substantial agreement, my wife and I have discovered a state of mind which is very distressing to us both. The Quartet has in fact lost its essential unity, which, you will agree, is almost as important as the musicianship of its members. Without going into unnecessary details in this letter, I may say that we were forced to the conclusion that if the Quartet attempts to carry on, as organized at present, not only will it decline in prestige, but before this has gone very far, it will probably break up.

We find it very difficult to come to what is quite clearly the basic difficulty. The Quartet, in former years, owes so much to your leadership and musicianship and experience that I am most reluctant to have to say what we have agreed is inevitable. When three members of a body so intimate in their work and in their lives as a String Quartet must be, have decided that they can no longer work happily and successfully under their leader, there is only one course for them to pursue and that is to recommend a change of leadership. It would not be fair to the three members or to the first violin, himself, that they should be asked to continue in these circumstances.

I want to make it very clear that Hambourg, Blackstone and Adaskin are fully aware of the contribution which you made to the Quartet in earlier years, and it is unnecessary to speak of their personal friendship nor indeed of that of my wife and myself, but the three must insist quite honestly and impartially that having regard strictly to the Quartet as a successful organization, your leadership should not continue.

The purpose of this letter, therefore, is to let you know as soon as possible that the recommendation of the three members of the Quartet has been accepted and that your work with the Quartet will have to come to an end. I should naturally have preferred to deal with this matter in conversation rather than in a letter, but in the interests of yourself and all concerned, once the decision was arrived at, no time was to be lost.

Vincent Massey then spelled out the terms of severance, which Géza accepted two weeks later in a telegram from Salzburg.

August 29
Received letter. Accepting proposed solution but in mutual interest must insist that rupture publicly regarded as by mutual agreement. Letter will explain.

In November Géza was appointed professor of violin at the National Conservatory at Budapest and conductor of its orchestra, thereby becoming a colleague of Bartók, Kodály and Dohnányi. (Already in 1906, when Géza was twenty-four, he had written to his mother that he considered Bartók "one of Hungary's greatest composers and pianists."[131]) Though a naturalized Canadian citizen, he stayed in Budapest during the war, teaching at the Liszt Academy of Music. No doubt his conduct was honorable throughout, as indicated by his intervention to save the life of the great German-Hungarian violinist and pedagogue Carl Flesch, a Jew who had lived and taught in Berlin.

Flesch made the mistake of moving to Holland at the outbreak of war, understandably since his wife was Dutch. Like many others, including the highest circles of the Dutch government, Flesch expected Holland to be able to remain neutral, as it had in the First World War. After the German invasion, Flesch obtained a visa to enter the United States, which was still neutral, but he could not get a German exit visa. In August 1941 he was offered a position at the Lucerne Conservatory, at the suggestion of Ernest Ansermet. But by then he had been deprived of his Hungarian nationality, for purely technical reasons, and was in constant danger of deportation. He was arrested twice. Thanks to the intervention of four men, Géza, Ernst von Dohnányi, Ernest Ansermet and Wilhelm Furtwängler, Flesch's Hungarian citizenship was restored and he could, after a waiting period of three months, proceed to Switzerland.[132]

In 1947 Géza de Kresz and his wife returned to Toronto, where he taught at the Royal Conservatory and continued to perform. At the conservatory one of his most eminent students was Betty Jean Hagen, who studied with him on a scholarship from 1949 to 1951. Géza died in Toronto in 1959. Norah Drewett de Kresz returned to Budapest and died there a year later.

Géza's departure in 1935, which coincided with Vincent Massey's move to London to take up the post of High Commissioner, meant that the greatest period of the quartet was over. Géza had been a vital element in Massey's attachment to the quartet and his interest now waned.

On January 13, 1936, the *Edmonton Bulletin* reported: "When Mr. de Kresz retired they decided they must have a topnotcher. Mr. Adaskin set out to obtain Mr. Levey who had retired from the concert field eight years before and was not anxious to re-enter. He was content to devote his time exclusively to teaching and lecturing. Ardent persuasion by Adaskin brought him over to the idea of leading the great HHQ on the understanding that Mrs. L. should make the final decision. She was at that time in New York and Milton Blackstone flew in in a specially chartered plane from Toronto to New York and persuaded her to cable her consent to her husband who on one day's notice hurried to this county. He has been greeted with warm ovations wherever he appeared."

After James Levey, the former first violin of the London String Quartet, joined the Hart House Quartet in 1935 they added to their repertoire quartets by the English composers Edward Elgar, Frank Bridge, Frederick Delius, Arnold Bax and Ralph Vaughan Williams.

On December 17, 1934, Boris had written a letter to the Masseys, who were enjoying a winter holiday in Bermuda.

> Dear Vincent and Mrs. Massey,
>
> In order to celebrate my forthcoming "double" Jubilee – *half a century* – next birthday – *quarter of a century* in Canada. (This peculiar coincidence can of course happen only once in my lifetime.) Mark and Jan have kindly offered to come over to join me in a short trans-Canada tour next Spring as the *original* Hambourg Trio.
>
> May I ask you to grant me the great favour of the necessary leave of absence from Good Friday, April 19th till Empire Day, May 24th, 1935, and your permission for the tour to take place?

Permission was granted. The tour took place.

On April 27, a balmy day before the funeral of Sir Albert Gooderham, to whom the audience in Massey Hall paid their respects "in standing silence," they gave the first Toronto performance of Beethoven's Triple Concerto, with Sir Ernest MacMillan conducting. The *Toronto Star* ran an enthusiastic review:

> On a carnival scale they brought back the glowing energy of early Hambourg programs before the war, when this family of great musicians first broke the cold conventional lines of concert in Toronto [sic]….
>
> When the trio came on after a superb performance of Beethoven's Coriolanus Overture, Boris took the dais with his cello, Jan from Paris beside him with his violin, Mark from London at the Canadian-built piano. The burly dean of the family and veteran of the keyboard looked not a day older than when he

last played a recital on that stage, though two years ago he had an almost fatal illness after a tour in India.

Jan made his re-debut as a violinist in the trio's glorious Romances of Beethoven which Ysaÿe of Belgium, the Hambourgs' old associate, always played together. [The two Romances were written for solo violin and orchestra. This must be a reference to Ysaÿe having accompanied Jan in the past, as conductor of his orchestra.]

Boris did his part of the jubilee in a superb performance of Variations on a Theme by Tchaikovsky, with orchestra.

As expected, the complete crisis came when Mark came prodigiously on for the dazzling B flat minor Concerto by Tchaikovsky. Not for years had this great maestro been heard in almost his native city. Sitting on the bench, he crisply announced that as the conductor had to catch a 10:50 train to Lethbridge, Alta., he would begin with the second Andante.[133]

The concert of the three brothers in Massey Hall was to be the family's greatest single triumph – it was recognized as such at the time. Boris never forgot the enthusiasm with which the concert was received. His staff gave him a gold watch.

This was a short moment of relief for the Hambourg Conservatory. It was suffering deeply from the Depression. Without a substantial share of Boris's salary from the Hart House Quartet to make up the deficit, it could not have survived. One of its teachers decided to go through the phone book systematically, starting with the letter A, to ask if anybody wanted to take piano lessons at a very favourable rate. After six weeks he gave up, without having found a single student. The west wing of the building was rented out as one apartment unit. In another wing rooms that had been used for lessons were made available to teachers and students to live in. A basement studio where once classical ballet had been taught was used for tap dancing lessons.

In June 1935 the quartet was in London for the Jubilee celebrations of King George V and Queen Mary. At a "brilliant soirée" at High

Jan, Mark and Boris Hambourg on the 1935 Trans-Canada Jubilee Tour of the original Hambourg Trio. (Courtesy Remenyi House of Music, Toronto)

The Hart House String Quartet in the late thirties. From the left, Milton Blackstone, Adolph Koldofsky, Boris Hambourg, James Levey. (University of Toronto Archives)

Commissioner Vincent Massey's residence in Hyde Park Gardens the quartet played Mozart, Borodin and Frank Bridge. In the audience were, according to the society columns, the actress Dame Marie Tempest, the conductors Sir Adrian Boult and Sir Malcolm Sargent, the author Sir Philip Guedalla, Mrs. Raymond Massey, Mr. and Mrs. Mark Hambourg, the Canadian soprano Madame Jeanne Dusseau, Miss Ishbel MacDonald, the Countess of Oxford and Asquith, President of the Royal Academy Sir William Llewellyn, the Earl and Countess of Lytton, A. F. Lascelles of the Royal Household and the Hon. Mrs. Lascelles.[134]

In the winter of 1936-1937 they undertook their most extensive tour yet, of the United States, Mexico and Cuba. In January the press carried a story about the quartet giving thirty concerts and covering about nine thousand miles before returning to Toronto.[135] The spring and summer of 1937 they spent in Europe. In April, eleven month's before Hitler's annexation of Austria, they gave three concerts in Vienna. The reviews were mixed. "Their Mozart [the Quartet in D minor] lacks detachment, the hovering-above, the essential transcendental quality. It is like a Botticelli angel with his wings cut off and turned into a good little baby."[136] Another paper praised "the magnificent sound" of their Beethoven Quartet opus 132, but was also critical of their Mozart.[137]

They spent part of the summer of 1937 in England, on the estate adjacent to that of Lady Maud Warrender, a generous patron of music, near Rye, in Sussex. They rehearsed in a disused chapel. In London they spent some time at the Savage Club, of which, thanks to Mark, they were associate members. The building "adjoins Marlborough House, the Queen Mother's residence. From the windows of the club it was possible to see the royal gardens and in them the royal princesses playing."[138]

Later they were booked for concerts in Rome, Pisa and Milan. It was the heyday of Mussolini. On their way by train into Italy, in the border town of Udine, Boris discovered that he was carrying not his but his wife's passport. This discrepancy had not been noticed before during the long journey across many borders.

"Who is this lady?" the Fascist officer was curious to know.

Boris told him.

The man asked for *his* passport.

It was in Canada, Boris replied.

The officer decided some dire plot was afoot. Perhaps Boris had killed his wife and stuffed her body in his cello. On the photo she didn't look like a big woman.

Boris had to sleep two nights sitting up on a wooden bench at the station, while the others mobilized Jan. He and Isabelle were living in Sorrento. Jan rushed to Rome and went to see the British ambassador, who immediately instructed his staff to dispatch a provisional passport to Boris. The story ended happily with the brothers meeting in Rome just in time for the concert.[139]

In September Maria *did* arrive for a brief holiday. In Rome Jan and Isabelle joined them and they stayed at the old Jesuit Monastery Hotel where the Duke of Wellington and Shelley had once registered. A sixteenth-century Jesuit chapel next to the hotel was placed at their disposal and there the two brothers made music together, mainly Bach. Then they went to Sorrento and toured Naples, Pompei, Amalfi and Rapallo. It was a year before Isabelle's death.

When the quartet performed again in Toronto in June 1938 they had been away more than two years. A tour to celebrate their fifteenth anniversary season (1938-1939) had to be cancelled because of the deteriorating political situation.

At the end of the 1937 season, after much agonizing, Harry Adaskin resigned. He had reached a stage when he found quartet life too confining. Vincent Massey at first refused to accept the resignation. "We want the Quartet to go on," he wrote in his own hand from London, and – underlined – "*we want you to be in it.*"[40] But in the end he had to relent.

Harry Adaskin spoke on the CBC: "I have been with the Hart House Quartet for fifteen years (since its beginning in fact) and have had the unusual privilege of seeing the musical life of Canada grow considerably in that time. There are many towns in Canada where until our annual visits began a string quartet had never before been seen or heard. Strange as it may seem, the people there were just as delightful as in any other town, so I quickly came to the conclusion that the function of a string quartet was not so much to be a means for civilizing Canadians as it was for providing an excellent opportunity to the musicians to meet them."[141]

In March 1938 there was a meeting in Toronto of the Canadian Friends of the Hebrew University in Jerusalem. Music was provided by Adolph Koldofsky (who had replaced Adaskin), Boris and Clement Hambourg. Frederick Banting introduced the guest speaker, Edward M.N. Warburg.

"Four million Jews are in terror in Europe today and do not know where they will find physical security," Warburg declared. "There is an insanity rising over Europe today and the lives of thousands of Jews are in danger. Our people are in dire distress."[142]

Adolph Koldofsky was the former leader of the Ševčík String Quartet. In Toronto, before going to study in Europe, he had studied with Luigi von Kunits and, strangely enough, with Harry Adaskin, whom he replaced. For four years, from 1925 to 1929, Koldofsky had studied with Ysaÿe. In 1930 he declined the position of leader of the Warsaw String Quartet and returned to Canada. In 1942 he resigned from the Hart House Quartet. He remained in the public eye as concertmaster of the Vancouver Symphony Orchestra.

In the late thirties Koldofsky discovered a number of unpublished keyboard concerti by Carl Philip Emmanuel Bach in the attic of the Salvation Army's building near the Eaton's Annex, just opposite the old Toronto City Hall. No one knows where they had been before they were donated to the Salvation Army. It took him six years of ceaseless and exhausting effort to authenticate the manuscripts, a notable feat of scholarship. In March and April 1943, on seven CBC radio broadcasts, he directed the performance of five of these concerti by the celebrated harpsichordist Wanda Landowska, an event which attracted the attention of music lovers all over the world. In 1945 Koldofsky moved to Los Angeles, and gave the première of Schönberg's two last works, the String Trio opus 45 and the Fantasy opus 47, which was written for him. Koldofsky died in 1951.

On May 14, 1940, four days after the Nazi invasion of Holland, which seemed to make an invasion of England probable, the quartet was criticized for playing German music. The *Globe and Mail* published a letter which posed the question "Do we need a German music festival?" The attack on Poland the previous September and the Soviet-Finnish war during the winter had not directly threatened England.

> In recent months we have seen the Toronto Symphony Orchestra giving all-Finnish programming in honour of the outraged Finns. We have also a very great Polish singer among us to give a concert in honour – and in aid of – the outraged Poles. Do we all quietly sit by and see our own Hart House Quartet giving a festival of German music – in honour of whom, pray? Germany? I think not. Surely public opinion will prevent such perfidy.
>
> Doubtless, a crowd of well-meaning innocents will raise their hands in defence of pure art, but it is high time that people of our own persuasion looked to the bolstering of our own traditions; high time that we as a community stop this sickly pandering to cultures foreign to us. Why in Heaven's name are we averse from taking a tip from the pre-eminently successful methods of the dictators much as we abhor their tyrannies? We see a simple man, a paperhanger, rise to dominate a continent. But in his nefarious path does he ever make the cardinal mistake of ignoring his own national culture? Not once. If he did he never would have succeeded to the point of foisting that culture willy-nilly on everybody else. And still, how does he hope to succeed? Why, by the apathy of our democracies who teem with innocents spoon-fed to accepting the art of others.
>
> It is a public shame that a prominent musical organization cannot better employ its time than to continue the worship of German gods when it should be alive to the necessities of the times. British music has suffered untold damage in past centuries by this blind ac-

cepting spirit. It should be remembered that the golden age of British music was the time of Elizabeth when British nationalism was at its peak, unweakened by this forever straining after the foreign. We are fighting a death battle for our own traditions. Let us urge our musicians to help by more timely artistic effort.

W. Topham.

Saturday Night responded to Mr. Topham in an editorial on May 25, 1940. The program to which he had taken exception contained a work by Beethoven:

> The writer was unaware that, though born in Bonn, Beethoven as his name proves was of pure Dutch descent, that his life was mainly spent in Vienna, that he was a great admirer of England and fierce in his hatred of dictators. He was the type of irascible gentleman who would have roared with rage against Hitler and would, like most eminent Viennese musicians of the present day, have moved to some democratic country if anything resembling a totalitarian state had been attempted in the Austria of his day.

During the war the quartet performed frequently on army and air force bases and at Red Cross and other fundraising functions.

In 1941 the quartet received another blow – Milton Blackstone resigned. On November 12, Prime Minister Mackenzie King wrote a letter to Boris:

> I understand that on Saturday night the friends of Mr. Milton Blackstone are tendering him a complimentary banquet at the Arts and Letters Club. I am very sorry to hear that Mr. Blackstone's health has necessitated his retirement from the Hart House String Quartet. I send him my best wishes for his early recovery and would like to join with you and his other friends in a tribute not only to his national service in the cause of good music but also to the eminent qualities which have brought him the high regard of all those who know him.[143]

Milton Blackstone's place was taken by Dutch violist Allard de Ridder. He had been conductor of the Vancouver Symphony for the previous eight years and violist in the Vancouver String Quartet. His wife, Pauline, was a grand-niece of Felix Mendelssohn-Bartholdi. Later he became the conductor of the Ottawa Philharmonic Orchestra.

The composer and teacher Godfrey Ridout had this comment about the closing years of the Hart House Quartet: "Later in the 1930s the personnel of the Quartet began to change, and, although performance standards in chamber music were rising generally, those of the Hart House Quartet did not, and in the 1940s it finally sank into oblivion."[144]

The last regular concerts took place at Hart House on June 12, 13 and 15, 1945, a month after the end of the war in Europe. The following April, the quartet gave three farewell concerts which were carried nationally by the CBC. During the last concert Boris spoke.

> His words brought lumps to the throats of the specially invited audience in Hart House Theatre. He had only words of gratitude to all who assisted the Quartet, and of appreciation for the happiness of serving for twenty-two unbroken years in an organization which had contributed so much to Canadian life at home and Canadian stature abroad. "Nothing goes on forever," Mr. Hambourg said, with a brave show of reconciliation to the facts of life; but his listeners heard in these words an echo of their own sadness at the loss of something which had perhaps been taken for granted but which will now be greatly missed.[145]

Dudley Dell wrote a long and eloquent tribute in the June 1946 issue of *Mayfair*:

> When the Canadian Broadcasting Corporation put the Hart House String Quartet on a nation-wide hookup three times during April it was not because of millions of letters from Canadian listeners clamoring for chamber music. No, it was because the moguls of the CBC recognized that the dissolution of this fa-

mous ensemble would be noted with sadness by its admirers in the principal cities of the world, including Canada of course. Canadian wheat, salmon and apples have filled bellies under many alien flags. Canadian asbestos and nickel go everywhere. Canadian gold sleeps in the best and deepest vaults the world over. Canadian men and Canadian machinery made their mark in every theatre of war. Stephen Leacock made a lot of people laugh, including the Scandinavians. And the Group of Seven was sympathetically received in Paris and in Budapest, if not in Toronto. But when the Hart House String Quartet went barnstorming about the world something new and important was added. Even to foreigners who don't like chamber music the visit of a front-rank quartet from Toronto proclaimed that in this fair Dominion, this raw Dominion, there had grown up a civilization which could export a commodity out of which nobody made any money.

The great days of the Hambourg Conservatory were over when Boris engaged the concert pianist Helmut Blume as head of the piano department in the fall of 1942. The title was not very meaningful since Blume had only two students during the year he was on staff. He is understandably under the impression that "business did not seem to be very good at the time." The engagement began shortly after Blume was released from an internment camp, where he had been held with hundreds of other refugees from Nazi Germany. They had been shipped to Canada two months after their arrest as "enemy aliens" in England in the spring of 1940.[146]

There were still some good moments in Boris's musical life. On Saturday afternoon, May 14, 1949, Mark, Boris and James Levey gave a concert in Eaton Auditorium. As already mentioned, Mark played two Beethoven sonatas. But that was not all.

Ronald Hambleton reviewed the concert:

> There was the feeling that here were three musicians who had been asked to sit down and play something, and by a strange co-

incidence they happened to have the music of Beethoven's *Ghost Trio* with them, so they played that....

When they had finished the two brothers, Boris and Mark Hambourg noticed that they had the Beethoven Variations on a theme by Mozart with them, a work for cello and piano. So they played that. The audience discovered that these variations (on a theme from *The Magic Flute)* were charming and humorous. The two Hambourgs appeared to enjoy playing them, and the result was entertaining chamber music.[147]

Two years later, in 1951, Boris dissolved the Hambourg Conservatory and sold 194 Wellesley Street. He died in November 1954 at the age of sixty-nine. He had suffered a coronary thrombosis in May but remained active until his death, preparing for the farewell season of the Music Lovers' Club he had founded some years before, so that, in the words of Elie Spivak in his tribute at the Arts and Letters Club, "his beloved chamber music might exist, and also, that, as a musician, he could play and give to those who wanted it, chamber music in the best of traditions."[148]

At the same occasion Sir Ernest MacMillan spoke extemporaneously: "Boris had a loving character, was kind and charitable, and never gave unkind judgments of other musicians. If he had to disagree sometimes, he did it with a smile.... During the forty years of his membership in the Arts and Letters Club, whenever he was asked to participate in anything he made it appear that he was receiving a favour rather than giving one."

Elie Spivak summed up Boris's essence perfectly. Boris, he said, was a true musician and an artist whose ideals never wavered: "There was always that extraordinary inner urge to bring great music to his audiences. He was not a man who happened to play the cello."[149]

Maria Hambourg had a serene and comfortable old age, though she became crippled with arthritis. Thanks to a modest annuity from the sum Boris had left her, she no longer had any serious financial worries. Generous to her many friends, she was particularly fond of Jessie Macpherson, the former dean of women at the University of Toronto, who died a year before her after her eyesight had been failing. Occasionally, the two old ladies travelled together to Atlantic City for a holiday.

Maria – Borina – Hambourg died in 1966 at the age of ninety-four.

Clement Hambourg

THE BLACK SHEEP

In 1910, soon after the Hambourg family arrived in Toronto, Clement, aged ten, was in bed when the reporter Donald Sinclair arrived to interview Professor Michael Hambourg.[1]

"Canadian boys take lots of sleep," said Professor Michael. "Clement is to be a Canadian. I am going to send him to the Toronto public schools."
"Another budding musician?" I asked.
"Oh no, he has but one ambition – guess – to be a detective!"[2]

Already, as his father could not help but notice, Clement was not an ordinary Hambourg. After a rocky start as pianist and *enfant terrible* – a start that lasted more than half his lifetime of seventy-three years – Clement at last came into his own after 1945 as an Eccentric Character, a promoter and beloved father figure to a generation of jazz musicians.

Nobody remembers him reminiscing about his early years in London, nor did he ever talk about his mother. He was ten when he arrived in Toronto and sixteen when his father died. When he was in his late teens, he performed with Jan and Boris in one of many versions of the Hambourg Trio. He was twenty when Jan and Isabelle left for Europe. For his remaining fifty-three years he stayed in Toronto. Only once, when he was in his early twenties, did he leave for a short time to study with Mark in London. He made his début in Massey Hall in 1925. The critics conceded he had aptitude but unfortunately he wasn't another Mark Hambourg. Through all these years he lived at the Hambourg Conservatory or in various apartments in the vicinity.

Once he began teaching, it was without much enthusiasm, though his students enjoyed his personality. One of them was Pierre Salinger, then six years old, later President Kennedy's press secretary.[3] Salinger's father was a mining engineer who, together with his family, lived for a few years in Toronto. Salinger thinks of Clement as a wonderful person who coached him magnificently for his one and only public concert at the Canadian National Exhibition in 1931.[4] In 1963, Clayton Fritchey, special assistant to Ambassador Adlai Stevenson, wrote to Clement on stationery of the United States Mission to the United Nations, presumably in reply to a letter from Clement: "After watching the distinguished performance of our friend, Pierre, since he went to the White House, it seems to me a pity that more of our public servants could not begin their careers with a lesson or two from you."

Relations with the *châtelaine* of the Conservatory, his sister-in-law Maria Hambourg, were, to put it delicately, difficult. In 1928 Clement married Katherine Fitzgerald, the secretary of the Conservatory, and they had a son.[5] This *mésalliance* – Hambourgs were supposed to marry the daughters of lords, not secretaries – formally confirmed his status as a second-class Hambourg. The young couple lived in the basement.

Rumours persist to this day in musical circles about Clement's parentage, that he was perhaps only a half-brother of Mark, Jan, Boris, Galia, Luba and Manya. Whatever the gossip, the U.K. Registry Office records show the parents of Clement Hambourg, born on July 31, 1900, to be Michael and Catherine Hambourg.[6] All Clement ever said about the past was that, while he revered his father and his brothers, he had always been the black sheep of the family.

In 1929 Clement made an important discovery.

> The house was nearly empty. Clement saw a figure in the shadows and ran outside, shouting that there was a burglar on the loose. He described the incident so vividly that it became a news-

paper story. Clement learned a lesson he would never forget. He was good copy.[7]

Good copy or not, he continued his conventional performer's career as a pianist and gave frequent recitals in and out of town, some under the auspices of the Women's Musical Clubs. If there were any indications that he was on the way to becoming an *enfant terrible*, it has not been recorded.

It did not take him long to catch the attention of the press again. In his capacity as director of the radio department of the Hambourg Conservatory, he submitted a brief to the Radio Committee of the House of Commons, which was discussing the report of the Royal Commission chaired by Sir John Aird, the president of the Canadian Bank of Commerce. In 1929, the commission laid the foundation for public broadcasting in Canada. In his brief, Clement complained about the misuse of Canadian talent by broadcasters.

On the Hambourg Conservatory's stationery it was stated that the radio department was under the direction of Clement Hambourg, "broadcasting exclusively over Station CFCA, the Toronto Star." The *Star* wholeheartedly supported the Aird Commission's recommendation. On April 1, 1930, the newspaper declared that if it were a matter of its own interests, it would favour private ownership, but radio broadcasting was a natural monopoly that should be under the public ownership of the nation.[8]

The *Toronto Star* had owned CFCA since 1922, which was early in the history of broadcasting – in the U.S. only four commercial stations were broadcasting regularly at the time. (CFCA was the radio station which carried the Ravel concert when he was in Toronto in 1928.) The function of Clement's radio department at the Hambourg Conservatory was to train students in microphone technique and to obtain engagements for them to perform on the air. No doubt it was at CFCA that Clement first developed his interest in recording music, which later in his career was to be for a few years his main source of income.

In the early thirties Clement followed up this new and enjoyable role as upholder of the public interest and promoter of ill-treated Canadian artists when he accused Ernest MacMillan, Healey Willan, H.A. Fricker[9] and Leo Smith,[10] the pillars of Toronto's musical establishment, of driving talent "into the backwoods of musical obscurity." As the *Toronto Star* explained, "By now Clement's relations with high society were just about nil, and those with his sister-in-law very much strained."[11]

But he wasn't a mere gadfly. He thought deeply about important things. On March 9, 1935, Clement published a powerful article in *Saturday Night* under the heading "Whither Modern Music?" It placed his ideas about art and society in a wider context and revealed a well-informed and independent mind. In an introductory note the editors found it necessary to point out that they were not convinced the present state and future destiny of music were really "as deplorable as Mr. Hambourg maintained," but that they found his "contentions extremely interesting and so, we hope, do our readers." One assumes few of them remembered his observations about Ravel written seven years earlier and reflecting a more amiable point of view.

> The trend of modern life has been one bad wrench after another from the old standards of morality, with its inclusive bolstering of such ancient virtues as honesty, love, loyalty, decency, courtesy, charm and friendship. To me, modern music is a psychopathic expression of the twentieth century.
>
> Modern life demands of a man that he assassinate his associates as soon as convenient, that he torpedo his non-lucrative relationships in any event, and that aesthetic and ethical relationships be damned. How could it be otherwise than that modern music is the most cacophonous, grotesque combination of sounds possible of human conception, compared to which the vocal emanations of a first-class zoo sound musical and appealing.

Clement then proceeded to discuss Paul Hindemith, whose "postwar Germany was afflicted with incurable putrescence":

The vortex of German industrialization has spun his mind around at incredible speed, and the *Furor Teutonicus* has whipped him up to a rhythm which makes his music symbolical of murder and all its passions. Ten years before the advent of Hitler and his gorillas, Hindemith knew what it was all about.... [The article was written only two years after Hitler had come to power.]

Frankly, I see no future for modern music. Mozart is the distillation of the sentiment of music. His architecture is simpler, and thus greater than that of Bach. The greatest music died with Mozart. The mechanization of music has fairly killed its more sensitive possibilities....

The public has become absolutely tone-deaf and its musical mentality has become atrophied.... Artists with a message can hardly get an audience together. Why listen to serious interpretations in concert halls when cheese factories and undertakers' establishments will cram your ears full of something that'll do for music? Until the radio works itself out of the public mind, heaven help music of any sort....

The moderns have attempted a great service in providing a mental and emotional catharsis, a sort of release from the almost unbearable conditions of the twentieth century, but have they succeeded?

Clement joined the army when war broke out in 1939, but he had poor eyesight, was given a minor clerical job and was released in 1942. (Until the end of the war he sought occasions to play the piano for the troops.) When he left the army he did not return to the Hambourg Conservatory but rented the basement of 1184 Bay Street, on the west side between Bloor and Charles streets in Toronto, and converted it into a recording studio.

The studio was at the northern fringe of the Gerrard Street Village, Toronto's "Left Bank," centred along Bay Street between College and Dundas streets. The painter Harold Town described the Village as the only real Bohemia Toronto had ever known. "It helped us get through the Wasp, work ethic dominated days of Toronto before the influx of immigrants after the Second World War shoved us into the twentieth century." He described the studio of Albert Franck, "a magnet for young painters":

> There was an Oriental whorehouse around the corner on Elizabeth Street. "Why worry, see Madam Alice" lived next door and read tea leaves or cockroaches, whichever fell into your cup first. Anneke [the painter's daughter] continually tried to show Jack and Nancy Pollock's pet skunk Lavender to her friends from Central Tech art course, but it was always under the couch. She sold her first drawing to a steel baron from Hamilton for a dollar – it was of a naked lady who ran past their door one day and later told the judge she was invisible. The Dennys lived across the road. Father played Bulldog Drummond on the CBC, mother made a career of dying her hair and Pilgrim, their son, wore open-toed sandals for all seasons and confided loudly to anyone that his parents weren't married. He went back to England and, rumour had it, married a girl called Goat and became a Druid. The great Ken Dawson, whose patrician face belonged to the court of the Medicis, was the Village mayor and historian. His dry wit made the Sahara seem a watering hole.[12]

Clement's recording studio nearby was the germ of the future House of Hambourg. Having passed his mid-life crisis in the army, he was beginning his love affair not so much with jazz but with young jazz musicians. The world of jazz became a refuge for him after he recognized there was no future for him as a classical musician. He became a promoter, a showman. His love of jazz, which he occasionally proclaimed, always contained an element of opportunism and a certain lack of sincerity. But his belief in the talent of his young jazz musicians, and in their importance to the future of the world of music, could not have been more deeply felt. He himself never played jazz and did not know very much about it. After all, it was not so long before that, whenever somebody at the Hambourg Conservatory was playing jazz with the window open, Clement would shout down, "Stop the noise or shut the window!" (expletives deleted).

His place on Bay Street did not as yet have the magic that made the House of Hambourg so famous in the fifties that "Clement's name was mentioned in Paris, New York, London or Los Angeles, wherever touring jazz companies gathered."[13] But it set the stage. The basement consisted of boxlike, imperfectly soundproofed recording and rehearsal studios. Young jazz musicians, some of them students from the university a few blocks west, came with their instruments (unless they were pianists) to have recordings made.

Soon they began to have jam sessions – throughout the night – *without* Clement recording them. One of the young musicians was Norm Amadio, who became a close friend. He was born in 1928 in Timmins in northern Ontario of Italian parents and studied the piano with the Grey Nuns in Timmins and briefly with Boris Berlin at the Royal Conservatory. Playing bebop under the influence of Lennie Tristano, Bud Powell and others, he subsequently became one of Toronto's leading jazz musicians.

In the summer of 1949 the twenty-one-year-old trumpeter Gordon Delamont also opened a studio in the building. Born in Moose Jaw, Saskatchewan, and raised in Vancouver, he had studied briefly in New York and soon became a major figure in the Toronto jazz world, mainly as a teacher and mentor of a whole generation of musicians who were only slightly younger, Moe Koffman[14] and Hagood Hardy among them. Two of Delamont's most talented students were the composers Ron Collier[15] and Norman Symonds.[16] Delamont's composition *Collage No. 3* was recorded in 1970 by the Ron Collier orchestra, with Duke Ellington as soloist.

Word of Clement's place got around among visiting American big-name musicians who played at the Colonial or the Town Tavern. After closing, they began dropping in for jam sessions, just for the fun of it. They mostly played bebop – the new, progressive jazz.

People came to listen.

Early in 1945, his first marriage having come to an end, Clement married Ruth Nadine, known as Ruthie, the total bohemian, eight years younger than he. They were made for each other. She was a creative, imaginative person, businesslike – which Clement, most definitely, was not – and an extremely hard worker. An accomplished musician and teacher herself, she had moved to Toronto in 1920.

When Clement married Ruthie she sold "custom jewelry, fringe products and custom luxuries" and ran a "school of voice production for singers and speakers, and of microphone technique."[17] Norman Symonds recalls that Ruthie was a great friend of Lorne Greene, the wartime CBC announcer nicknamed the "Voice of Doom." Their common interest must have been elocution. After the war Greene ran the Academy of Radio Arts on Jarvis Street until he went to Hollywood in 1953 and television fame in *Bonanza*.

Ruthie made dolls. She taught physical culture. She was interested in the occult. In her looks she never changed. She was pale and paid no attention to her clothes. No one remembers her as particularly interesting physically. She always wore her light reddish-brown hair pulled back in a bun at the nape of her neck. Some described her as *petite*. One of her cats was called Takatak. Ruthie hated daylight. Madeline and Ed Bickert's favourite mental picture of her "will always be Ruthie with a mouthful of nails, while she completed some carpentry task, while Clement stood by nodding approvingly and muttering 'Very good, Ruthie, very good.'"[18]

Ruthie's manner of speaking was theatrical, as though she were always on stage. When she wasn't making things or coaching she was cooking. Many guests still remember her small, deep quiche-like "pizza-pies" filled with a red meat sauce, her lasagne, barbecued spare ribs always simmering on the stove, pot roast sandwiches (opinions on these admittedly vary), chocolate cake soaked in rum, and apple pie "to die for." "I never studied this business of cooking," she said, "and I don't have much variety but what I make I want to be good."[19]

Clement's sister Luba welcomed Ruthie into the family. She wrote to Clement and Ruth from the London apartment she shared with Jan:

She sounds as if she belonged to me too – a designer of beautiful things – how divine! I just know that Ruth would love this setting, this charming house with its detail and finish and now I am doing some specialized work, too – lovely cushions of old velvets, gold braids and laces, etc., antique pieces – as well as of course always furnishings. I didn't want to mention all this so soon as I really want to talk about you. Clement has always been my baby brother, you know, and I have always wished something special for him and now it has happened. I am so happy for both.... I do wish we could all be together here. – How splendid that you are playing so much for the troops.[20]

Clement and Ruthie had a stormy, dramatic marriage. There is a play about them, *Boom, Baby, Boom* by Banuta Rubess, with music by her husband, Nic Gotham.[21] The jazz play was "a study of how people confront a painful past and ominous future." Banuta Rubess and Nic Gotham had discovered that the story of the House of Hambourg was ready-made for the musical stage. There was hardly any need to fictionalize. The play takes place in 1959. "The world has lost Lester Young," Rubess wrote in the printed introduction, "and is about to lose Billie Holiday. The Cuban missile crisis is down the road. Nixon is visiting Khruschev. The papers are full of news about fallout shelters and heroin addiction." Clem, "a patron saint of the Toronto jazz scene," appears on stage as an oddball who "ambled through life with a bowler on his head, a cigar between his teeth and a Chihuahua on his elbow." He is considered a "profligate black sheep by the old society of pre-war Toronto." Ruthie "slaved in the kitchen, sewed costumes for the Victory Burlesque for extra income and belonged to a mystical order which communed with the spirits of the dead. Their apartment was overrun by eighteen cats. Ruthie conducted fierce quarrels with Clem." The story begins when a Latvian immigrant, a "spunky yet haunted aspiring beatnik," who had arrived in Canada as a refugee at the age of six, climbs in through a window of the club. The play ends with a coda, after the demise of the club, with Ruthie addressing the audience directly.

Welcome, welcome, welcome. I remember you – you were so hungry all the time. And you – you lived in that nice house on Bridle Path. And you – you were dating that lovely girl from Settlement House. And you. You'd just come here from Newfoundland. You proposed to your girlfriend in the parking lot. And you. You're driving cab now. And you. And you. Who the hell was born in Toronto anyway except Vincent Massey....

Ruthie was usually smiling but she could be fierce. Clement made the major decisions, she enforced them. He was even-tempered, talkative, idiosyncratic, chuckled a lot and was full of stories and anecdotes, some involving big names ("My father hated Stravinsky"). Don Francks remembers Clement showing him a 1912 edition of the *Illustrated London News,* on the departure of the *Titanic.*[22] He used to say on occasions like this, in the manner of an English schoolmaster, "My dear Francks, you must read this." Once Clement presented him with a cake of soap allegedly from the *Titanic* – "the only thing that floated."

Ruthie was unpredictable, capricious and superstitious, which did not prevent many people, including Clement, from adoring her. When she told him off, he would shake his finger at her and say, "Now, now Ruthie...." On one occasion she rushed out of the kitchen and took a swing at him – fortunately she was not armed with any lethal kitchen utensils – and he stood on her feet in self-defence. But Clement always deferred to her, something she never abused.

The jazz scene in Montreal was far ahead of Toronto's. It had the Café St. Michel, the Alberta Lounge (the home of Oscar Peterson) and Rockhead's Paradise, supported largely by the black population of St. Henri. In Toronto no clear lines could be drawn on the basis of colour. If any line could be drawn at all, it would be between those jazz musicians who worked for the CBC – these were the days of radio – and those who did not. Jazz journalist Mark Miller noted: "The distinction would hold for the better part of the next twenty-five years. Eventually the CBC gigs – the jazz shows among the more common 'variety' work – took their place with all the other studio assignments that were available once the city became the centre of the English Canadian entertainment industry with the advent in 1952 of television."[23]

Jazz at the Philharmonic was an annual event at Massey Hall, presenting mainstream, swing-oriented jazz. On May 15, 1953, however, in a seminal event for Toronto jazz lovers the five greatest figures in the world of the new jazz – Charlie ("Bird") Parker, Dizzy Gillespie, Charlie Mingus, Bud Powell and Max Roach – gave a concert in Massey Hall.

"When we opened our recording studio after the war," Clement recalled, "we were thrown into the midst of jazz musicians and my outlook was broadened. I've been steeped in music all my life and I was not going to be chained to a particular kind."[24]

In her book about the poet Gwendolyn MacEwen, Rosemary Sullivan wrote: "In the 1950s, Toronto was still a Presbyterian construct, devoted to order and cleanliness, but that veneer had begun to crack as the city grew up and away from its colonial roots.... Eventually Clement's wife began to charge for her coffee and the House of Hambourg was born like a jazz improvisation."[25]

The idea of operating an after-hours establishment had been Ruth's. Born and raised in the southern United States, she was used to the numerous jazz emporiums that spread through that area with the rise of jazz. Ruthie remembered, "We at first charged nothing, because we just liked to have the musicians come to our place. Then, when they [presumably the people who dropped in] insisted on paying, we accepted and I became the cook."[26]

Few young musicians had a chance to perform "progressive" jazz in English Canada until Clement and Ruthie came along. Clement was determined to help change attitudes: "Jazz has always been treated in an off-hand way. I decided I wanted to do something for – as it is said in Russian – 'the ragged orphans.' I wanted to take them out of the class of dead-end kids and bring them into an atmosphere of respectability."[27]

The legendary trumpeter Herb Spanier, with whom many of Clement's young musicians "hung around" when he was in Toronto, declared: "Before I came to Toronto, there was very little happening in jazz. As far as I'm concerned, the jazz era in Toronto started when I got there. I just grabbed all the guys who could play and we played almost every night at Clement Hambourg's."[28]

Clement was exhilarated. For him, it meant escape from the frustrating past. And for his musicians, a new image. "People always seem to associate jazz with lawlessness," he said. "The movies, I guess. It's this idea that I've been fighting for years. Jazz is as respectable as classical music. And I'm sure it's more symbolic of our North American culture than the classics."[29]

In 1926 Clement had been the first Canadian pianist to play, and broadcast, the solo version of Gershwin's *Rhapsody in Blue*, originally written for two pianos in 1924.[30] He could not know that this was, indirectly, his introduction to his new passion. "I was surfeited with the best," he said "I craved a new expression and modern jazz gave it to me"

There was a story about him in *Weekend Magazine*:

> "You see, this is a very educational place," says Clement, his eyes gleaming behind his steel-rimmed spectacles. Looking at his mane of white hair and half-smoked cigar, it is easy to understand when he muses.
>
> "The RCMP asks is this man nuts or has he got a diabolical scheme... a chap with his musical background devoting his life to jazz."
>
> ... Nothing is ordinary at the House. The waitresses are pretty – and work in high heels. The menus are scrawled on odd bits of paper. The food delivered via dumb waiter from the kitchen above is delectable.[31]

Since Clement was born in London he often said "jolly good." "Very nice, very nice" was another of his terms of praise – but he spoke neither Canadian nor English English. He spoke *Hambourg* English, English with a touch of the continental European, though he had never lived on the continent. He always wore the same black rumpled black suit, often with a black turtleneck, unless, in the winter, he sported a Second World War RAF flying suit – fleece-lined leather, with a dangling cord attached. He joked about being "plugged in." He often wore it while collecting admissions in the back archway of the House of Hambourg – a fine sight.

It did not take Clement long to learn a new language. *Cool, man, baby, hep, hip, dig, groovy, hot* – he soon mastered the vocabulary. He often referred to himself in the third person, which gave his speech a special stage effect. "Clement is just breaking even," he said, during the brief periods when he did. "I'm a visionary," he says in Banuta Rubess's play, "not a business man. Just think of it – everyone who wants to play can play. Everyone who needs to listen, can listen. Everyone who wants to dream – can dream."

Clement managed with short snatches of sleep, but Ruthie needed more and could not operate after waking up unless she had had two or three cups of coffee. Once the nocturnal House of Hambourg was a going concern on Cumberland Street people wondered where they slept during the day. (Answer – on the second floor). Clement often had fanciful schemes to make money, for a time it was selling "near-beer."

This is how the journalist Mackenzie Porter described him in a story about Dave Caplan, the "show-biz tailor":

> Clement Hambourg, a man in late middle-age with tawny hair hanging about his shoulders, a rumpled suit, a tie all awry, and the sort of expression you see on absent-minded professors in comic strips, showed Caplan a photograph of a scantily dressed woman with a nubile figure. She was standing in the classic pose of the Greek urn carrier. Hambourg said she was one of his wife's physical culture students and asked Caplan to guess her age. Caplan guessed thirty-five. Hambourg clapped his hands triumphantly and cried "She's ninety! Truly! A veritable Ninon de Lenclos!"[32]

The new jazz required a virtuoso technique as brilliant as that of his brother Mark, but it was based on improvisation and not on the printed page. Clement continued to play the classics, and pop tunes, and, like the masters of jazz, he was an excellent, imaginative improviser. But, as has been mentioned, he never played jazz.

Clement did not think of the move into jazz as a radical break. On the contrary, the glory of the Hambourg name legitimized the new music. To the composer Ron Collier, for one, "Clement's musical background and foresight were invaluable at that time in our lives. As a budding composer 'Hambourgs' was the primary outlet for my jazz quintet to rehearse and perform new pieces. I could always depend on Clement for a subjective critique, which he usually related to a classical composer or style."[33]

In 1965 Clement told Jon Ruddy of the *Toronto Telegram:*

> I've never regretted my love of jazz. Why should I? I feel the classics more deeply because of it. All music is good, beautiful. Folk music – GOOD! Hell, musical prejudice is almost as bad as racial prejudice.
>
> And how could I compete with my family, anyway? My brother Mark would call down from heaven and say 'Don't bask in my shadow!' The people who think I am a subversive, a Guy Fawkes who blew up the honours of my family – permit me to laugh and guffaw!
>
> I got out of my family's way. I looked for something else. I couldn't do it as well. I venerate the memory of my father and my brothers.[34]

Much later, on August 20, 1970, the *Toronto Telegram* carried this letter:

> Illustrious piano
> Further to George Kidd's excellent article on the Heintzman piano, I would point out the following added facts:
> My illustrious brother Mark Hambourg played the Heintz-

man in all his trans-Canada tours, used it in Massey Hall with Luigi von Kunits and the TSO in 1935, with Reginald Stewart and Promenade Symphony Orchestra in 1949.

Clement Hambourg

The second venue of the House of Hambourg, beginning in 1952, was the basement of 142 Bloor Street West, half a block east of Avenue Road, next to the site which was to become, in 1956, Holt Renfrew, before the store moved to its present location. Once again, the place was frequented mainly by musicians who wanted to practise and to jam, any time during the day or night, just as they had on Bay Street. He "gave us a sandbox to play in," as Don Francks put it. Ruthie charged twenty five cents for a cup of coffee and fifty cents for her famous chocolate cake.

Soon the club became one of the two places where musicians could publicly perform progressive jazz, i.e. bebop. The other was the Jazz Artists Club, but it was only open intermittently at a Lithuanian Hall in the west end of the city. Mainstream jazz on the other hand, often performed by big-name American musicians, was played regularly in the Park Plaza Hotel, the Colonial Tavern and the Town Tavern, and also at the Silver Rail, Toronto's first licensed lounge, which had opened in 1948, and at Melody Mill, a large boarding house for jazz and classical musicians – and a club – on the east side of Jarvis Street, south of Carlton. That club lasted for a few years before it ended in the mid-fifties.[35]

The third location of the House of Hambourg, 159 Cumberland, was a fourteen-room Victorian brick house with three storeys and a front porch, one of several residential houses in a row all looking very much alike. It was one of several buildings owned by Paul Gibson Pinder. He did not know what to do with the basement and heard of Clement. He asked him if he could so anything with it. If so, he would "accommodate" him. Clement was delighted and turned the basement into a cellar club that was to become the House of Hambourg for the next five years – the great years. The "accommodation" con-

THE BROTHERS HAMBOURG

(Left) Clement Hambourg. (Photo by Erik Christensen/Globe and Mail)

HOUSE OF HAMBOURG
Rear of 134 Bloor St. W.
(Delectable Cuisine—Free Parking)
FEATURING CANADA'S FOREMOST JAZZ STARS
Fri. after Theatre—
KOFFMAN — BICKERT
Sat. After Theatre—
LANDER — AMADIO
Sun. After Church
COLLIER — TROMBONICUS
Paintings by Award Winner Denis Burton and colleagues
RESERVATIONS — WA. 3-6068

An advertisement, c.1955-56, for the House of Hambourg at its third home.

JAZZ MECCA
The Slumming Earle
Restaurant Revolution

RYERSONIAN
FEBRUARY 24 1956 THE RYERSON CAMPUS NEWSPAPER

Knock Three Times and Whisper Low

By TOM ALDERMAN

These House of Hambourg jam sessions last so long they disturb Sunday morning services. Paris? Chicago? New Orleans? Wrong on all counts. This joint jumps in respectable, blue-law Toronto

Press clippings testify to Clement's flair for organizing publicity for his jazz club. The article by the young Tom Alderman includes photos by Rolf Bjordammen of Ed Bickert (guitar) and Clement and Ruth lighting the wood stove.

Clem and Ruth Hambourg stoke up the 100-year-old stove at the House.

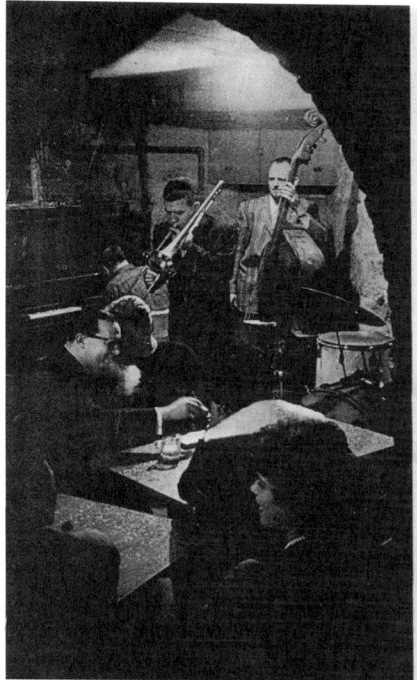

Clement Hambourg ~ The Black Sheep

In "The Jazz-Happy Tailor" (in *Maclean's Magazine*) Mackenzie Porter wrote about Dave Caplan, who haunted the clubs, indulging his love of jazz while trying to sell suits to the performers. Caplan is the man with glasses puffing cigarette smoke in the vaulted cellar of the House of Hambourg.

In "House That Jazz Built" (*Weekend Magazine*) Bert Petlock told how visitors would "go through an ill-kept garden, pass under a faded blue awning and descend into a smoke-filled cellar. They are in the House of Hambourg and the joint is jumping. The large, low-ceilinged cellar is divided by a row of brick arches. The walls are bare brick and are hung with paintings."

sisted of Pinder never pressing him for rent, a pleasantly agreeable arrangement since Clement would normally be in arrears. Pinder was a skilled bricklayer. He built an imposing arch in the back of the house, at the rear of 134 Bloor West, across what was to become Holt Renfrew's parking lot, connecting the left half of the building with the right half, making it a very attractive place. The club opened in February 1954.

Tom Alderman wrote in the *Ryersonian:* "This swinging jazz room in the heart of the city's booming Bay-Bloor district captures the aura of mystery and excitement generally associated with the jazz cellars of 1925 New Orleans, Chicago and New York."[36]

The parking lot behind the club's subterranean, brick-arched basement, which at night was illuminated by orange bulbs and candles, was often muddy and Ruthie had good reason to complain about dirty shoes messing up her floors. Clement would sit at the door over an antique cash register – "enter, man, enter" – and take one dollar admission.

The *Toronto Star* described the club:

> A staircase leads to the shadowy basement from which sweeps swinging music of a modern jazz group. Your coat is checked by a young man sporting a curly orange beard. Other youths are talking quietly and listening to the music through a vent in the floor above the bandstand.
>
> The halls are hung with weird splashes of colour – abstracts, creation of young Canadian painters.
>
> From the kitchen, where Mrs. Ruth Hambourg scurries between her crowded oven and rows of delicacy-crammed shelves, comes the mingled aroma of frogs' legs, shrimp, spaghetti, spare ribs and pizza.
>
> Downstairs, in the brick-arched restaurant, illuminated by a few orange and blue bulbs, are packed close to a hundred customers. They listen to the jazz until the early hours, daring to talk only in whispers. There is no liquor.
>
> Several weeks ago, the Hambourgs decided to use their studio

as a gallery for Canadian paintings. Five young painters, Dodie Sperry, Peter Harris, Dainis Miejasz, Denny Burton and bearded Robert Smith are now displaying their work.[37]

At one time, when the enterprise had expanded to occupy the rest of the building, he had three bands playing – but not for very long – one in the basement and one each on the first and second floors. Dennis Burton, then a fourth-year student at the Ontario College of Art, was not only allowed to hang his pictures – he sold quite a few – but also to act as hat-check boy and coat-hanger.[38] He could keep the tips, an agreeably profitable arrangement. Burton recalls large pictures of celebrities in one of the rooms, no doubt inherited from the Hambourg Conservatory, with personal dedications by men like Stravinsky and G.B. Shaw. On the second floor there was a large room with recording equipment which Ruthie rented out for meetings by groups of believers in flying saucers and the Rosicrucians. "One time I had to hustle the boys out quiet-like," said Clement, "'cause they were disturbing the Sunday morning religious services of some sect I rent the upstairs recording studio to."[39]

Another room was rented at one time to the twenty-year-old tenor saxophonist Don (D.T.) Thompson, who lived there for a year.[40] The guitar-player Ed Bickert, about the same age as Thompson, also had a room on the third floor for a while. It was no bigger than a closet.[41] There was also a room on the same floor to which no one had access where Ruthie kept her sewing things – afghans, mannequins – "in a state of unbelievable chaos." Ruthie designed clothes, and people trying on diaphanous "vaguely Isadora Duncan-like things" with lots of chiffon and flowery patterns were always wandering about, among salons filled with Ruthie-made clothes for sale "by appointment." The rooms were full of new paintings and drawings, and "in the cubicles flutists were practising their flutes." On the third floor there was a large room inhabited at one time by the trombonist Ron Collier, and after him, from January to May 1956, by Dennis Burton and his former wife, the singer Donna Miller who appeared in the CBC's *Showtime*. The washroom was on the second floor, where it could be reached either the normal way, by stairs, or, on special occasions, by an outside fire escape. Ruthie only allowed Burton one bath a week, his lady two. Relations with Ruthie, he reports, were strained. She seemed to think the Burtons were plotting to take over the club. But she was never personally hostile.

Ruthie was by no means a mother-figure, not at all warm and cuddly. Clement's lawyer, Joseph Sheard, who acted for him out of friendship mainly in the area of landlord-tenant relations, found her "unapproachable," a woman who did not trust lawyers and did not, in his judgment, exude "a warm ambience." Some of the eighteen-year-old volunteer waitresses who worked for her – often girl friends of jazz musicians – found her intimidating, and for that matter they found the old man – *very* old to them – a little "weird."

Ed and Madeline Bickert, for good reasons, remember the scene particularly well: "Clement was a great romantic and I think felt partly responsible for us marrying – our courtship having taken place largely under his roof. And so as a wedding gift Clement and Ruthie presented us with a record – it was a recording of Clement accompanying himself on the piano, while he sang 'Let me tell you that I love you' – a song he had written for us, all duly recorded by Ruthie. The record label bears the inscription in Clement's handwriting 'To Madeline and Eddie from Clement and Ruthie – a prognostication of the attainable.'"

Most customers were young couples. As one enthusiast put it, "Man, those musicians just keep playin' an' playin' an' playin' an' they don't stop until they're layin' on the floor, all tuckered out, an' can't get up no more." CBC producers often dropped in, for amusement and talent-scouting. Clement paid his jazz musicians as well as he could – he saw them as victimized. Norm Amadio played for him for seven dollars a night – he could have made a couple of hundred, he said, at the CBC. The low pay was tolerated by the musicians' union. Even today in small jazz places "scale" is paid only rarely.

Years later, Hagood Hardy recalled fondly that he carried his instruments across Avenue Road after performing at the Park Plaza Hotel to continue playing through the night at 159 Cumberland.[42] At least four of Clement's young jazz protégés who fifty years ago he thought of, quite rightly, as belonging to a victimized group have since received the Order of Canada – Hardy, Moe Koffman, Phil Nimmons and Ed Bickert.

The club was open on Friday and Saturdays from 11 p.m. to 3 a.m., and on Sunday nights from 9 p.m. to midnight. Clement continued to make recordings, mainly for young musicians he was going to promote. Jazz celebrities visiting Toronto like Oscar Peterson, Hazel Scott and Sarah Vaughan were allowed to play on a concert grand.[43] On weekends, long line-ups of jazz lovers formed in the parking lot, especially after a photo-story about Clement and Ruthie had appeared in 1957 in *Weekend Magazine* under the title "The House that Jazz Built."[44] Occasionally they had to hire a policeman to control the crowds. For a time a young Hungarian, Charlie, was Clement's right-hand man and bouncer. There was never any trouble with the police about drugs, and there was no smoking of marijuana on the premises. As to liquor, having had one or two bad experiences, Clement and Charlie invariably pounced on guests caught with hidden bottles. (Toronto's "blue" laws of the time made obtaining a licence to serve liquor in such a club next to impossible.)

Tom Alderman wrote in the *Ryersonian*:

> The balding, white-haired proprietor of the House, Clement Hambourg, who bears an amazing resemblance to that old Puritan Oliver Cromwell, both in features and manner of speech, likes to refer to his place as "a Parisian scene under Cromwellian control."
>
> "What I mean is this," Clement explains. "Good jazz is best enjoyed in the proper atmosphere. Like dark cellars with a bit of light, lotsa smoke, after-hour sessions, swinging music. You know what I mean? That's what I mean when I say Parisian atmosphere. But you got to have some restrictions. The cops keep tabs on places like this. So no liquor. None of that stuff. We could be closed down overnight. That's what I mean by under Cromwellian control. Understand?"[45]

A drawing by George Feyer, whose cartoon feature "Feyer Play" appeared regularly in the Toronto *Telegram*. (By permission of Michaela Feyer)

Clement Hambourg in 1959. (City of Toronto Archives)

This policy was so well understood that the police became involved only when neighbours complained about the noise.

Tom Alderman continues:

> "It's the greatest," says Amadio, one of Canada's top pianists. "We play the kind of music we like. And we get paid for it."
>
> Guitarist Bickert likes to play at the House because musicians rarely have to bother with requests.
>
> "No commercial stuff, man... not even 'Lullaby of Birdland.'... We just swing the way we want to," says Bickert. "We get a lot of famous musicians dropping in and it would be great to have them sit in. That's impossible because of the union. They like to come and listen, though. They understand what we are playing, even if most of the audience don't...."
>
> "This is a place I like to bring a date when I'm in Toronto," says John Smith, a salesman in from Vancouver. "It's cosmopolitan, like Paris or London. It has atmosphere."[46]

Clement had sudden enthusiasms about the books he was reading. The writer and comedian Don Cullen remembers references to George Sand – "what a wonderful woman!" – when Clement dropped in on him in his cold-water flat. Later, in the mid-seventies, when Cullen was head writer for Global television's program *Everything Goes,* every musician he worked with was an alumnus of the House of Hambourg. Clement was always upset about the state of the world, not usually a matter of top priority for his artists. Students were more responsive. He railed against the Bomb, McCarthyism, Sputnik, the Cold War. One of his milder terms of abuse was "nogoodniks" – he was good at invective – and, like many second-generation Russians, he was afraid of the Soviets. He called them Bolsheviks. In his place, jazz was the stimulant to get the ideas flowing. There was talk about existentialism and Jack Kerouac. For young thinkers the House of Hambourg performed a function not unlike that of the Café Flore on the Left Bank. There, at the same time, Jean-

Paul Sartre and Simone de Beauvoir were playing Clement and Ruthie!

All this came to an end in 1960 when they had to vacate the premises because the building was to be torn down. It had earned Clement and Ruthie a solid place in the story of Yorkville, Toronto's equivalent of San Francisco's Haight-Ashbury. (Yorkville is the street north of Cumberland, and became the label for the drug-and-youth culture of the sixties). There was something symbolic about the date, 1960, when they had to move.

Ten years later, in 1971, David Lewis Stein remembered the period of transition:

> The gentility was fading from Yorkville but it was still a small town street, lined with trees and secluded from the hurly-burly of Bloor and Avenue Road. It was a place to retreat to after the long nights of talk and beer in the King Cole Room in the basement of the Park Plaza Hotel. It was a good place for young men who were fresh out of university and didn't really have any idea of what they wanted to do with their lives and for the pretty girls who got jobs at the CBC or became high school teachers while they waited for something – just what, nobody knew – to happen to their lives. I met the young woman I eventually married at a party on Bellair Street, in a house between Cumberland and Yorkville.[47]

Very soon, the Beatles, rock and folk-music were in and jazz went into decline. But it never disappeared altogether from the Toronto scene. Nostalgia set in quickly: as early as 1969 Bernadette Andrews wrote in the *Toronto Telegram:*

> If you were in Toronto in the 1950s you'll have heard of the House of Hambourg – that Bloor Street bastion blasting three floors of progressive jazz. It was the first of the coffee houses that still swung post-bartime on Fridays and Saturdays and offered an almost exclusive outlet on Sundays.

Well, Clement Hambourg started it all. It almost finished him, with musicians' union salaries, rental fees and the fact that Clement, always an eccentric, was no businessman.

Between the jazz sets, there would be Clement, through the candle-lit coffee house scene, he'd be playing... Beethoven, Bach, or maybe Chopin.[48]

Other after-hours places were opening up as the sixties unfolded. The First Floor Club, the Minc Club, the Cellar Club and other cosmopolitan late-night entertainments began to compete with Clement. Later, discos arrived on the scene, and rhythm and blues clubs, where you could also dance.

The fourth venue of the House of Hambourg was the dark basement of the Ward Price auction house on Grenville Street. The only way Clement could pay rent was to surrender to the landlord the four or five pianos he had, his only physical assets of any value, which in due course were auctioned off. When the last piano had gone, the arrangement came to an end. Clement and Ruthie took an apartment on Yonge Street.

Ron Collier recalls: "When the House moved to Grenville Street, it lost its charm. It was a theatre with a stage and a much larger seating capacity than the Cumberland Club. The intimacy between the musicians and audience wasn't the same. It seemed as though we were always doing a concert. Something that started in a basement had lost its ambience in this more formal setting. And if you only attracted a small audience, the wrath of Ruthie would be upon you. It was the beginning of the end."[49]

In the first year business was not bad. Clement played the piano more than he had on Cumberland. Phil Nimmons performed one evening a week. But the good times did not last.

One day, the CBC producer Stan Jacobson dropped in. He had some experience producing plays on the stage and in summer stock. Clement showed him a room above the club with a stage, designed for auctions. "Could you do anything with that?" Clement asked. He did not have to ask twice. It soon became the House of Hambourg Theatre. Jacobson had lunch with Nathan Cohen, the theatre critic, who had just come back from New York, where he had seen the off-Broadway production of the experimental anti-drug play *The Connection* by Jack Gelber. Cohen, who had given the play an enthusiastic review in the *Toronto Star,* suggested it for Clement's place. Jacobson bought the rights to put it on. It was the first time the play was shown outside the U.S. The director was George McCowan, and the actors, among the best in town, were, in order of appearance, Arch McDonell, Paul Wayne, Don Francks, George Sperdakos, Sydney A. Forbes, Martin Lavut, Howard Matthews, Gordon Pinsent, Les Rubie, Joyce Spencer and Percy Rodriguez. The play dealt with jazz musicians who were looking for a connection to drug-dealers to provide them with a heroin fix. Don Francks played Leach and the stage was Leach's "pad." Dennis Burton designed the poster.

As the audience walked in and took their seats the actors were lounging around on the stage, talking, practising their instruments. Maury Kaye played the piano, Archie Alleyne the drums,[50] P.J. Perry alto, and Ian Henstridge bass. The actors chatted with the audience, the audience with the actors. Audience participation was a sixties concept in the world of politics, education and theatre. All borders were blurring. In this case, no one could tell when the performance began because the national anthem was played as a jazz improvisation and it was not easy to decide when to rise. On one occasion, after the action had at last unquestionably started, a young woman in the audience, highly agitated, ran up on the stage and tore the needle from an actor's arm as he was injecting himself. She also bit one of the actors in the hand. It turned out her boyfriend had died from a fatal overdose not long before. She had to be sedated.

The play opened on November 29, 1960, and ran for nearly two months. Jacobson says he had never seen a happier man than Clement. Don Francks remembers it as the most exciting theatrical event of his career.

After *The Connection,* Clement presented Ben Hecht's *The Front Page* and other plays.

In 1961, a year after Mark Hambourg had died at the age of eighty-one, Dolly wrote from London:

> It is sad that your theatre venture came to an end. According to Luba's report, you started rather well with a very controversial play which has since been on in London....
>
> I am really delighted to hear that you have started to play the piano seriously and think Ruth is very right to urge you to do so. After all, to propagate the highest class of music is the real Hambourg tradition and now that all our generation alas has gone who is there left to do it but you…?[51]

Evidently, Dolly had forgotten that Clement, who was twenty-one years younger than Mark, was nevertheless of his generation.

One person who did not like Clement, or any form of post-Dixieland jazz, was the *Globe and Mail's* jazz critic Patrick Scott. He enraged Clement so much that Clement asked his lawyer Joseph Sheard to send a formal letter to the managing editor:

> Mr. Hambourg has in the past been referred to by Patrick Scott directly or obliquely in a context that Mr. Hambourg finds to be at the least insulting, and at the most defamatory. Our present instructions go no further that to draw your attention to this matter, but we think you should know that if Mr. Scott continues to make reference to Mr. Hambourg in his column in your newspaper of the same character as in the past, consideration will be given to taking formal steps by way of an action for libel. Mr. Hambourg regards many of the references previously made by Mr. Scott as malicious and going beyond the fair comment that a newspaper columnist is entitled to make.[52]

Don Francks, who had performed occasionally in the House of Hambourg as a free-form jazz-talker-singer à la Lenny Bruce, was so upset at the way Scott had treated Clement that one morning he single-handedly invaded the *Globe and Mail* and occupied Scott's office. (It was the time of sit-ins.) Francks sat on the critic's desk, waiting for him to turn up. When Scott arrived Francks lectured him on the freedom of the press. "We artists," Francks orated, "also have our freedom."

Whether it was due to this lecture, or to one from the managing editor, Scott never mentioned Clement Hambourg again.

Grenville Street turned out to be the wrong location. Eventually, Clement's financial situation became desperate. His friends rallied and arranged a three-night benefit which yielded $2,200 to pay his debts.

In 1963 he gave up. "Ruth, my wife," he told a reporter, "is my only old age pension."[53]

But Clement was nothing if not resilient. On October 14, 1964, he appeared with Don Francks on the CBC variety program *Nightcap* in a mimed comedy skit à la Chaplin or Buster Keaton. Francks played "the usual horrible baritone" and Clement an elderly church pianist who had to raise himself by sitting on a telephone book. They performed *The Pansy in My Garden* by Amy Franfram, with a maximum of wrong notes and exchanges of furious looks, and ended with bravado, with the two artists leaving the stage glaring at each other.

"By 1965 the pioneer work of the House of Hambourg was over," Clement declared, "and Clement played the hotels and lounges as a solo variety pianist."[54] One of the lounges in which Clement played was The Room at the Back at the Regency Towers Hotel on Avenue Road. In his article "The Ninth Life of the Ninth Cat," Jon Ruddy wrote:

> Clement says: "The post-House of Hambourg position is this: Clement wants to go out of this life playing better and better."
>
> Music students came to hear the man who gave Pierre Salinger piano lessons. Some older people who wouldn't be caught dead in a jazz cellar decided he was a formidable pianist in these really quite *nice* surroundings. Veterans burst into tears when he played, very loudly, the *Warsaw Concerto*. Matrons sent

CLEM HAMBOURG
NIGHTLY AT THE PIANO

the boiler room

After the end of the House of Hambourg, Clement played piano in clubs (above) and appeared in commercials and advertisements. Below he appears as Scrooge for a meat company.

Piano firm gets tuned in with new-style commercial

SCENE ONE . . . the piano tuner slowly becomes carried away by sound of the Heintzman grand

SCENE TWO . . . his fantasy takes over and he sits down to play role of concert pianist

SCENE THREE . . . as the impromptu concert ends, his audience of one cleaning lady cheers

FINALE . . . the piano tuner who sat down to play takes a bow in response

Wondering how in the dickens to make this Christmas Dinner an especially festive occasion? Take a tip from Ebenezer Scrooge and send the nearest small boy to Bittner's to order a plump, fabulous Bittner Christmas Goose. Rich, elegant and delicately flavourful, a goose from our hand-picked gaggle turns the meal into the traditional gourmet event of Christmas Past. Your Bittner Butcher will cheerfully supply stuffing and cooking hints for this town's finest fresh frozen Geese or Ontario Fresh Turkeys. So get your name on Bittner's Christmas list soon!

What a difference a few cents a pound makes.

Bittner's

Clement played a piano tuner in a television commercial for Heintzman pianos. (Courtesy Chris Yaneff)

up requests for "a little unadulterated Bach," scribbled on their paper coasters.

Old Clement Hambourg leans back at the piano, points his sharp nose at the ceiling, beams out over the drinkers, waves at somebody coming in the door, says "He was wonderful, wasn't he, old Bach? Now Chopin, his B minor thing, his octave thing, is quite a smacker. Yes! Oh JOLLY good!" He laughs loudly – it is a sound of pure joy – looks down at the keys for a long minute, raises his arm swiftly and *attacks* the keys.[55]

Everyone had warm feelings towards Clement. John Fineberg, the owner of the Regency Towers Hotel, helped by putting "a little money" in the 45 rpm record of the *Rhapsody in Blue* that Clement and Norm Amadio produced in 1965. No doubt this was also useful as publicity for the Room in the Back. As Jon Ruddy put it, "Clement is charging around Toronto on foot, wearing a black bowler, tapping a black knarred cane, sometimes towing a Chihuahua on a leash, making arrangements for distribution, promotion, display."[56]

Ruthie designed ties. The Regency Towers Hotel commissioned four hundred decorated with the company crest for the staff, business associates and favoured customers. She also made six thousand Canadian flags. After his term at the Regency Towers came to an end, Clement played the piano for several years during Sunday dinner hour at Julie's, of all places – the restaurant in the old Massey mansion on Jarvis Street where the Hart House String Quartet had played in 1926 when Vincent Massey's father, Chester Massey, was dying.

Many of Clement's old friends in show business gave him work. Stan Jacobson, by now producer of *The Wayne and Shuster Show*, cast him in bit parts whenever he could. When CBC producers needed a striking-looking old man they gave him work.

In August 1971 a lump in the back of Clement's jaw was diagnosed as cancer. By now he was seventy-one. There were several operations. He had reason to fear he would lose the use of his left arm, which would have ended his career as a pianist. All operations, except the last one, which was "believed at first to be for a minor ailment," were successful.[57]

Between operations, he played at the Cav-A-Bob Restaurant, a downtown spot popular with the office crowd. Helen McNamara, who covered the jazz scene for the *Star*, was there: "When the Norm Amadio band was on the stand, Clement could be seen dancing, go-go style. 'I love it,' he said. 'It keeps me in shape.'"[58]

His new career, not only as an extra for charitable producers but as a serious actor in television, films, commercials and as a model in advertising, soon became more important than his musical activities. It had actually begun before his operations – operations which "would have kept lesser mortals out of commission for ever."[59] By now a frail old man with a white mane of hair, weighing a mere 137 pounds, he played a part in Eric Till's *A Fan's Notes* and was the subject – together with the American sculptor Louise Nevilson, also in her seventies – of a documentary about aging for the CTV television network.[60] He was an amiable, benevolent Santa Claus, "humble and alive," the documentary director Peter Thurman said, "amazingly cultured."[61] The film explored "how he surmounted age with achievement."[62] "Sharing, caring and daring" were the words Don Francks used to describe him.

He performed as a concert pianist for Burl Ives in *The Man Who Wanted to Live for Ever* and was seen in the "Kleenex Canadiana Collection" advertisements which appeared in *Weekend Magazine, Readers' Digest* and the *Star Weekly*. In television commercials he played a piano tuner who gets carried away by the beautiful sound of a Heintzman piano – evidence, for the last time, of the perhaps more than coincidental Hambourg-Heintzman connection – and performed in musical roles for the Simpson-Sears mail-order house. In a 3M commercial he was an orchestra conductor.

In his final years Clement and Ruthie lived in penthouses on Church Street, south of Maitland, and just behind the King Edward Hotel. In both places Ruthie practised her skills as costume maker and creator of flourishing roof gardens.

"She's nursed me through my second childhood," Clement said.

He never complained, even after several cancer operations. "I never lost hope," he said. "Look at Beethoven, stone deaf and dying, but he could write the *Missa Solemnis*. Who am I to complain?"[63]

On February 3, 1973, Clement Hambourg died.

> The ninth life of the ninth cat, son of the great Michael, brother of the great Mark, the great Jan, the great Boris, out of the shadow of them all, under the white light. Smashing out – Bach, Beethoven, Mozart, Walton, Albéniz, Scarlatti, Gershwin, Debussy, Ravel, Hindemith, Handel, Chopin, Schumann, Bartók.
>
> Radical phrasing.
>
> The last of the Hambourgs.[64]

APPENDIX A

The Bach Solo Violin Sonatas, by Jan Hambourg

From the British publication The Monthly Musical Record, *November 1934, Vol. 64, No. 761, p. 293.*

Since the year 1802 well over twenty editions of Bach's three sonatas and three partitas have appeared. Why then in 1934 yet another edition? For many years I was engaged in studying the interpretation of these works, without finding a single edition that satisfied me. I had therefore no alternative but to prepare an edition primarily for my own use, which I started in 1926. Patient study of all the available editions revealed that, apart from minor differences, they were basically almost identical.

I was not able to procure the 1802 edition, published by Simrock, but there is reason to believe that it was the origin of the many errors and fallacies that have accumulated in subsequent editions. The only other edition not included in my study was that of the *Bach-Gesellschaft*, edited by Dr. A. Dörffel. This collated the two original texts but does not attempt to solve the many practical difficulties which confront the violinist. In addition, its prohibitive price prevent its being used as an everyday edition.

The instrument for which Bach composed his sonatas and partitas has not changed in any way since they were written in 1717-1723. The violin bow, however, did change radically when François Tourte (1747-1835) altered the length and curve and established the modern type of bow. The bow generally used in Thuringia about 1729 was more or less in the shape of a half moon. It enabled performers to play and sustain chords on three or four strings simultaneously, both *forte* and *piano*, though the tone was much inferior to that produced by the modern bow.

It is important to remember that with the old bow it was impossible to execute light bowings such as *spiccato, sautillé* or *staccato,* solid or flying. The frequent indications of *spiccato* to be found in the twenty-odd editions which I have studied are therefore entirely erroneous. Aesthetically also these markings are unjustified, since they are incompatible with the architectural structure of the music, in exactly the same way as the baroque eighteenth century altar would be out of place in Chartres Cathedral. This has been realized by Pablo Casals, who has not used *spiccato, staccato* or *sautillé* in his interpretation of Bach's unaccompanied cello suites for the last thirty years....

Schweitzer, who rightly stresses the fact that Bach was a violinist as well as an organist, draws particular attention to the polyphonic character of these works:

> The Sonatas and partitas are so arranged that each sonata is followed by a partita. In both of them we hardly know what to admire more – the richness of the invention, or the daring of the polyphony that is given to the violin. The more we read, hear and play them, the greater our astonishment becomes.

To explain what I have tried to do in my edition (now published by Oxford University Press), in addition to rectifying the errors, I may be allowed to quote from my preface.

The chief endeavour in this edition of Bach's sonatas and partitas for solo violin is to enable the violinist to preserve the thematic or melodic line unbroken in the most intricate chord passages, such as are to be found in the three fugues. Serious musical students are perpetually perplexed by the numerous disappearances, presumably unaccountable, of the main theme in the C major fugue.

The reason for this is that in a three-part or four-part chord played on the violin in the usual way the highest voices are given special prominence, as they are the last notes heard, whereas on many occasion in Bach's compositions for solo violin the main theme is to be found in the lowest voices of the chord.

The only solution I see to this important problem, which is practicable for the violin as played with the present-day bow, is to employ a modification of a technical innovation of Jean-Marie Leclair (1697-1764). Leclair directs that certain three- or four-part chords should be played from the highest string down....

Technically this method of playing three-part chords gives no more difficulty than the usual method. The four-part chords, however, require a short period of special study.

In conclusion, a word about the text. There are two original sources. The first is now in the Berlin Royal Library. The second, which gives revised bowing marks, is a manuscript in the possession of the widow of Dr. Wilhelm Rust's grandson in Bonn. The first of these is printed in small type in Marteau's edition (published by Steingraben) and the second in small type in Joachim's edition. I have based the text of my edition on a collation of these two. [1]

APPENDIX B

Recordings

Compiled by Rev. Claude G. Arnold, c.s.b., University of St. Michael's College, Toronto, including discography generously provided by Donald Manildi, Curator, International Piano Archives, University of Maryland.

Mark and Boris Hambourg both made 78 r.p.m. records, Mark as piano soloist, Boris as both soloist and cellist of the Hart House String Quartet. In addition, Mark made a number of rolls for the reproducing piano.

When Mark and Boris began to record for the gramophone, the process used was acoustical, the artist with his instrument being stationed before the large end of a megaphone-like horn whose small end disappeared through a wall beyond which a technician supervised the engraving of the sound vibrations gathered by the horn on the surface of a rotating wax disc. This is the way all cylinder and disc records were made until the microphone replaced the recording horn (1925/26). Mark took immediately to the new, electrical process and Boris was joined by the other members of the Hart House Quartet.

The following record list, compiled from a variety of sources, intends to show all the published recordings by these two Hambourg brothers. The arrangement is alphabetical by composer and work, and chronological by recording (where more than one version of a piece was produced). In a few cases recording dates are given (day [when this is known], month and year: "3.i.10"; "xi.29"); otherwise, the date assigned is that of the first issue (in the form "xii/30"). Where these data are lacking, the year of first appearance can be conjectured (e.g. "1934"). The record numbers given are those of the first issue; only in a formally organized discography (research for which remains incomplete) can the complexities of reissues and of comprehensively accurate dating be fully presented.

Guide to Disc Sizes

"His Master's Voice" (U.K.)

Single-sided:
5500	10-inch
7800	10-inch
05500	12-inch
07800	12-inch
08000	12-inch

Double-sided:
B-Prefix	10-inch
C-Prefix	12-inch
D-Prefix	12-inch
E-Prefix	10-inch

"His Master's Voice" Victor (Canada)

Double-sided:
24000	10-inch

Victor (U.S., Canada)

Single-sided:
60000	10-inch

Mark Hambourg, piano

"His Master's Voice" discs (listed by composer)

Reissue on LP/CD

ANONYMOUS
(2) Sea Shanties (arr. Rutland):
   (a) Shenandoah; (b) Billy Boy
   B2935 *(Bb15457-2)*, 1/2 side each   1929

ARNE, Thomas Augustine (1710–1778)
Sonata in B Flat
   D692 *(Cc1869-2)*, 1/2 side   ix.22

BACH, Johann Sebastian (1685–1750)
Christmas Oratorio, BWV.248
   10, Pastoral Symphony (piano 4-hands,
     arr. Lucas)
   (w. Michal Hambourg)
   B8276 *(OB5387-1)*   1934
In dir ist Freude (Chorale Prelude, BWV.615)
   (piano 3-hands, arr. Vivian Langrish)
   (w. Michal Hambourg)
   B8152 *(OB5494-1)*   1934
Italian Concerto, BWV.971
   1, Allegro
   05630 *(H03482af)*   ii/20
Jesu, joy of man's desiring (No.10 from Cantata
   No.147; arr. piano 3-hands by Mark Hambourg)
   (w. Michal Hambourg)
   B8276 *(OEA590-2)*   8.xi.34
   (Recorded at a party in the Savoy Hotel, London,
   held in honour of the twenty-fifth anniversary
   of Hambourg's first recording for HMV.)
My heart ever faithful (No.2 from Cantata No.68;
   arr. Cyril Scott)
   B4180 *(OB2605-2)*   1932
Prelude and Fugue in D, BWV.532 (arr. Eugen
   d'Albert)   Pearl GEMM CD 9147
   D595 *(Cc683-1/84-1)*   xi.21   (Prelude *[Cc683-1]* only)
Toccata and Fugue in d, BWV.565 (arr. Tausig)
   C1704 *(Cc16915-2/16-2)*   ix/29

BEETHOVEN, Ludwig van (1770–1827)
Concerto no.3 in C, Op.37
(w. Symphony Orchestra/Dr Malcolm Sargent)
   C1865/68 *(Cc17876-2, Cc17873-1/74-2/75-2,*   Past Masters PM-26 (LP)
   Cc17877-2/78-2/79-1/80-2)   xi.29   Pearl GEMM CD 9147
Minuet in G, G.167
   B3798 *(Bb21088-2)* 1/2 side   1931
Die Ruinen von Athen, Op.113
   Turkish March (arr. Anton Rubinstein)
   05630 *(H03483af)* 1/2 side   v/19   Pearl GEM 108 (LP)
   B4261 *(OB2794-4)*   1932
Sonata no.3 in C, Op.2, no.3
   4, Finale: Allegro assai
   05599 *(H02325f)*   iii.17
   D1073 *(Cc7802-2)*   iv/26   OPAL CD 9839
Sonata no.8 in c, Op.13
   C2051/52 *(Cc19369-3/70-2/71-3/73-3)*   xii/30
Sonata no.12 in A Flat, Op.26
   C2117/18 *(Cc21076-2/77-1/78- /79-)*   v/31

Recordings

Sonata no.14 in c sharp, Op.27, no.2
  (a) Abridged Recording
  Part 1 (2, Allegretto; 3, Presto agitato [I])

05521 *(3968f)*	3.i.10
05544 *(z7033f)*	25.i.13
D66 *(H01127ac)*	x.15

  Part 2 (3, Presto agitato [II])

05520 *(3968f)*	3.i.10
D66 *(H01128ac)*	x.15

  (b) Complete Recording

C1549/50 *(Cc13837-1/38-1/39-1)*	ix/28
C2551/52 *(2B3911-1/12-2/13-2)*	vi/33

Sonata no.18 in E Flat, Op.31, no.3
  2, Scherzo

5572 *(Y16260e)*	1913

Trio in G, Op.1, no.2
  4, Presto
  (w. Marjorie Hayward, violin & C. Warwick Evans, cello)

08075 *(H02732af)*	vii.17

Variations on Paisiello's "Nel cor più"

C1550 *(Cc13840-2A)*	ix/28
C2552 *(2B3916-1)*	vi/33

Bizet, Georges (1838–1875)
L'Arlésienne: Minuet (arr. Rachmaninov)

B8139 *(OB2261-1)*	1934

Blow, John (1649–1708)
  Fugue in C

05572, 1/3 side	i/16

Brahms, Johannes (1833–1897)
Hungarian Dance no.5 in F sharp

C2007 *(Cc19922-1)*, 1/2 side	x/30

Waltz in A Flat, Op.39, no.15

C2007 *(Cc19922-1)*, 1/2 side	x/30

Bull, John (ca.1562–1628)
King's Hunting Jigge

05572, 1/3 side	i/16

Byrd, William (1542/43–1623)
Lord Salisbury's Pavane

05572, 1/3 side	i/16

Chaminade, Cécile (1857–1944)
Automne, Op.35, no.2

C2064 *(Cc20252-2)*	ii/31

Chopin, Frederic (1810–1849)
Andante spianto (from Andante spianto & Grande Polonaise in E Flat, Op.22)

05552	iv/14

Ballade no.1 in G, Op.23
   C1290 *(CR661-2/62-2)* ix.26
Ballade no.3 in A Flat, Op.47
   C2243 *(Cc21090-7/91-4)* xi/31
Berceuse in D Flat, Op.57
   C1730 *(Cc15466-4)* x/29
(12) Études, Op.10
   No.5 in G Flat
   05575 *(Z8503f)*, 1/2 side iii/16
   C1778 *(Cc16918-2)*, 1/2 side xii/29
   No.6 in E flat
   C1778 *(Cc16918-2)*, 1/2 side xii/29
(12) Études, Op.25
   No.1 in A Flat; No.2 in F; No.3 in F
   C1778 *(Cc16917-6)* xii/29
Nocturnes
   No.2 in E Flat, Op.9, no.2
   C1416 *(Cc11384-2)* xii/27   Pearl GEMM CD 9147
   C2587 *(2B3909-2)* x/33
   No.12 in G, Op.37, no.2
   C1307 *(Cc9508-1)* ii/27
   C2516 *(2B3918-2)* ii/33
   No.15 in F, Op.55, no.1
   C1921 *(Cc18811-2)* v.30   Pearl GEMM CD 9147
   No.18 in E, Op.62, no.2
   05562 *(AL8071f)* xi.14
   C1454 *(Cc12001-2)* iii/28
Polonaises
   No.3 in A, Op.40, no.1
   D486 *(H04160af)* xii.19
   C1292 *(CR656-1A)* ix.26
   No.4 in c, Op.40, no.2
   D580 *(Cc420-2)* viii.21
   No.9 in B Flat, Op.71, no.2
   05547 *(H01132ac)* x.15
   C1451 *(CR1315-2)* vi/28
   C2579 *(2B3927-1)* ix/33
Préludes, Op.28
   No.6 in B, No.7 in A and No.3 in G
   B3328 *(Bb18813-1)*, 1/2 side each 1930
   No.15 in D Flat
   B3328 *(Bb18812-2)* 1930
Préludes, Op.28
   No.17 in A Flat
   C2064 *(Cc20253-1)* ii/31
Waltzes
   No.3 in A, Op.34, no.2
   C1892 *(Cc18996-2)* vii/30
   No.4 in F, Op.34, no.3
   C1790 *(Cc17306-4)*, 1/2 side v/30
   No.5 in A Flat, Op.42

Recordings

05611 *(H02328af)*	xi.16	
C1499 *(Cc12005-3)*	vii/28	

No.6 in D Flat, Op.64, no.1

05575 *(Z8503f)*, 1/2 side	1915	
C1451 *(Cc12004-2)*, 1/2 side	vi/28	
C2579 *(2B3928-2)*, 1/2 side	ix/33	

No.7 in C sharp, Op.64, no.2

B3798 *(Bb21089-1)*	1931

No.10 in B, Op.69, no.2

C1790 *(Cc17306-4)*, 1/2 side	v/30

No.11 in G Flat, Op.70, no.1

D580 *(Cc423-2)*, 1/2 side	viii.21
C1451 *(Cc12004-2)*, 1/2 side	vi/28
C2579 *(2B3928-2)*, 1/2 side	ix/33

COUPERIN, François (1668–1733)
Les Barricades mystérieuses (Couperin)
    Le Carillon de Cythère (Couperin)

D644 *(Cc685-1)*, 1/2 side each	xi.21

DEBUSSY, Claude Achille (1862–1918)
Danse

D534 *(H04349af)*	iii.20

Jardins dans la pluie (Estampes, no.3)

B2990 *(Bb15464-4)*	1929

(La) Plus que lente – Valse

D534 *(H04348af)*	iii.20
C1892 *(Cc18995-1)*	vii/30

Pour le piano: 1, Prélude

05632 *(H03485af)*	x.18

Prélude à l'après-midi d'une faune (arr. Leonard Borwick)

E362 *(Bb3787-2/88-2)*	xii.23

Préludes, Book I
  10, La Cathédrale engloutie

C1303 *(CR530-4A)*	i/27
C2667 *(2B3929-2)*	vii/34

Suite Bergamasque
  3, Clair de lune

B2935 *(Bb15460-1)*	1929

DELIBES, Léo (1836–1891)
Coppélia: Valse lente (arr. Dohnányi)

C2505 *(2B2793-2)*	xii/32

Naïla Valse (arr. Dohnányi)

C2247 *(2B601-2)*	xii/31

Sylvia: Pizzicati

B2818 *(Bb13853-1)*	1928

DOHNÁNYI, Ernst von (1877–1960)
Rhapsody in C, Op.11, no.3

C2600 *(2B3900-1)*	xi/33	Past Masters PM-26 (LP)

DVOŘÁK, Antonín (1841–1904)
Humoresque in G Flat, Op.101, no.7
    5594 *(Ho2560ab)*   iv.17
    B2685 *(Bb11387-6)*   v/28
Slavonic Dance in E, Op.72, no.2
    C2007 *(Cc19921-2)*   x/30   Pearl GEMM CD 9147

d'ERLANGER, Frédéric (1868–1943)
Étude concertante no.2
    B3638 *(Bb19373-6)*   1930

FALLA, Manuel de (1876–1946)
Fantasia Baetica
    D766 *(Cc2448-4/49-1)*   i.23   Pearl GEMM CD 9147

GLUCK, Christoph Willibald von (1714–1787)
Mélodie (from the "Scène des Champs-Elysées,"
Orphée et Eurydice, Act II; arr. Sgambati)
    C1817 *(Cc17304-2)*   iii/30   OPAL CD 9839

GOSSEC, François Joseph (1734–1829)
Tambourin (arr. Garratt)
    B3798 *(Bb21088-2)* 1/2 side   1931

GRAINGER, Percy (1882–1961)
Country Gardens
    B2478 *(BR968-4)*   1927
    B4437 *(OB3910-1)*   1933
Shepherd's Hey
    B3172 *(Bb17317-2)*   1929

GRIEG, Edvard (1843–1907)
Norwegian Bridal Procession, Op.19, no.2
    05578 *(Ho1405ac)*   xii.15
    D68 *(Cc1169-3)*   iii.22

HAMBOURG, Mark (1879–1960)
Volkslied
    B4261 *(OB2791-2)*   1932

HANDEL, George Frederic (1685–1759)
The Harmonious Blacksmith (No.4, Air and
Variations from Suite no.5 in E)
    05561 *(Ho1608ac)*   iii.16   Pearl GEM 108 (LP)
    D72 *(Cc2452-2)*   i.23
    C1303 *(CR529-1)*   i/27
    C2667 *(2B5388-4)*   vii/34

LISZT, Franz (1811–1886)
Au bord d'une source (No.4 from Années de
pélerinage, 1ière année)
    C1454 *(Cc11796-2)*   iii/28
    C2600 *(2B3920-2)*   xi/33

Recordings

Auf Flügeln des Gesanges (after Mendelssohn)
    C1439 *(Cc12002-2)*   iii/28   Pearl GEMM CD 9147
    B8139 *(OB5389-2)*   1934
La Campanella (No.3 of [6] Grandes études de Paganini)
    05579 *(H01612ac)*   iii.16
    C1636 *(Cc13854-2)*   iii/29
Chant Polonais (after Chopin, Op.74, no.12)
    C2247 *(Cc20251-1)*   xii/31
Concerto Pathétique
    (w. Michal Hambourg, 2nd piano)
C2675/76 *(2B6096-1/97-1/98-1/99-1)*   viii/34   Pearl GEMM CD 9147
Consolation no.3 in D Flat
    B4180 *(OB2536-1)*   1932
Étude de concert no.3 in D Flat
    D692 *(Cc2451-2)*   i.23
Faust: Waltz (after Gounod)
    C2242 *(2B389-6/90-5)*   x/31
Hark, hark, the lark (after Schubert)
    B2990 *(Bb15470-2)*   1929
Hark, hark, the lark (piano 4-hands, arr. Elsie Horne)
    (w. Michal Hambourg)
    B8152 *(OB5495-1)*   1934
Hungarian Rhapsodies
  No.1 in E
    C2761/62 *(2EA567/68, 2EA581)*   vii/35
  No.2 in C Sharp
    C1276 *(CR531-2/32-1)*   ix/26
    C2508 *(2B3925-2/26-1)*   i/33
  No.3 in B Flat
    C2762 *(2EA569-)*   vii/35
  No.4 in E Flat
    C2447 *(2B3324-1)*   ix/32
  No.5 in E
    C2758 *(2EA580-2)*   vii/35
  No.6 in D Flat
    B8319, 2 sides   1935
  No.7 in C
    C2758 *(2EA581-3)*   vii/35
  No.8 in F sharp
    B2667 *(Bb11388-1/89-4)*   v/26
  No.9 in E Flat
    C2446/47 *(2B3325-3/26-3/27-4)*   ix/32
  No.10 in E
    B3268 *(Bb18512-2/13-2)*   1930
  No.11 in A
    B2753 *(Bb11390-1A/91-3)*   1926
  No.12 in C sharp
    C1891 *(Cc18997-2/98-2)*   vii/30
  No.13 in A
    C2672 *(2B6100-1/01-1)*   xi/34

    No.14 in F
      C1661 *(Cc15468-6/69-5)*   31.i.29   Arabesque 8011 (LP)
      C2645 *(2B5273-2/74-1)*   iii/34
    No.15 ("Rakóczy March")
      C1439 *(Cc12003-1)*   iii/28
Liebestraum no.3 in A Flat
    05580 *(H01609ac)*   iii.16
    C1307 *(Cc9511-1)*   ii/27
    C2516 *(2B3917-2)*   ii/33
Waldesrauschen (Étude de concert no.1, G.32)
    C1416 *(Cc11385-2)*   xii/27
    C2587 *(2B3901-2)*   x/33
Wedding March and Elfen Chorus ["Dance of
    the Elves"](after Mendelssohn)
    D859 *(Cc2716-2/17-2)*   xi.22
Widmung (after Schumann, Op.25, no.1)
    C2248 *(2B323-6)*   i/32

MENDELSSOHN, Felix (1809–1847)
Songs without words
    No.1 in E, Op.19, no.1
      B4162 *(OB2606-1)*   1932
    No.6 in g, Op.19, no.6
      B2433 *(BR971-2)*, 1/2 side   v/27
      B4409 *(OB3924-2)*, 1/2 side   1933
    No.18 in A Flat, Op.38, no.6
      B4162 *(OB2607-2)*   1932
    No.30 in A, Op.62, no.6
      B2433 *(BR970-2)*, 1/2 side   v/27
      B4409 *(OB3923-3)*, 1/2 side   1933
    No.34 in C, Op.67, no.4
      5641 *(H02565ab)*   iv.17
      B2433 *(BR971-2)*, 1/2 side   v/27
      B4409 *(OB3924-2)*, 1/2 side   1933
    No.45 in C, Op.102, no.3
      B2433 *(BR970-2)*, 1/2 side   v/27
      B4409 *(OB3923-3)*, 1/2 side   1933
Trio no.1 in d, Op.49
    3, Scherzo
    (w. Marjorie Hayward, violin; C. Warwick
    Evans, cello)
      08055 *(H02731af)*   vii.17

MOSZKOWSKI, Moritz (1854–1925)
Étude in G Flat, Op.24, no.1
    05530 *(3966f)*   3.i.10   Pearl GEMM CD 9147
    C1817 *(Cc17510-2)*   iii/30

MUSSORGSKY, Modest (1835–1881)
Sorochintsy Fair: Gopak
    B2818 *(Bb11383-6)*   1928

Recordings

POLDINI, Ede (1869–1957)
Étude in A
    5573 *(Y16259e)*   1913

POULENC, Francis (1899–1963)
Nouvelette no.1 in C
    B3638 *(Bb19920-1)*   1930

RACHMANINOV, Sergei (1873–1943)
Polichinelle, Op.3, no.4
    C1730 *(Cc15463-2)*   x/29
Prelude in C sharp, Op.3, no.2
    05574 *(Ho8499f)*   1915
    D1073 *(Cc7808-2)*   iv/26
    C1292 *(CR657-2)*   xii/26
Prelude in G Flat, Op.23, no.11
    05592 *(Ho2324af)*, 1/2 side   v/17

RAVEL, Maurice (1875–1937)
Gaspard de la nuit
  1, Ondine
    D644 *(Cc422-2)*   viii.21
Sonatine
    D1001 *(Cc3783-3/84-1)*, 2 sides   vii/25

RIMSKY-KORSAKOV, Nikolai (1844–1908)
The Snow Maiden: Dance of the Buffoons (arr. Mark
    Hambourg [?]; labelled "Midnight Sun: Waltz")
    B2657 *(Bb11797-2)*   iii/28

RUBINSTEIN, Anton (1830–1894)
Étude in F, Op.23, no.1
C2818 *(2EA2441-3)*   ii/36   Past Masters PM-26 (LP)
Melody in F, Op.3, no.1
B2657 *(Bb11380-4)*   iii/28
B4385 (OB3898-1)   1933
Valse (Allemagne), Op.82, no.5
C2818 *(2EA2440-3)*   ii/36

SAINT-SAENS, Camille (1835–1921)
Quartet in B Flat, Op.41
  3, Scherzo
  (w. Marjorie Hayward, violin; Frank Bridge,
  viola; C. Warwick Evans, cello
    08054 *(Ho2725af)*   vii.17

SCARLATTI, Domenico (1685–1757)
Pastorale e Capriccio (arr. Tausig from L.413 and
    L.375)
    05528 *(3970f)*   3.i.10
    D68 *(Ho1131ac)*   x.15
Sonata in A, L.241
    B4076 *(OB2535-2)*   1932

Sonata in G, L.349
   B4076 *(OB2534-2)*   1932
Sonata in G, L.499 ("Cat's Fugue")
   05551 *(Z7280f)*   iii/14   OPAL CD 9839

SCHUBERT, Franz (1797–1828)
Impromptu in E Flat, Op.90, no.2
   C2380 *(2B537-2)*   iv/32
Impromptu in A Flat, Op.90, no.4
   C2380 *(2B538-4)*   iv/32
Impromptu in A Flat, Op.142, no.2
   C2200 *(2B396-1)*   ix/31
Marche militaire in D, Op.51, no.1
   D486 *(H04162af)*   xii.19
   C1499 *(Cc12006-2)*   vii/28

SCHUMANN, Robert (1810–1856)
Andante and Variations in B Flat, Op.46
   (w. Michal Hambourg, 2nd piano)
   C2634 *(2B5271-3/72-6)*   i/34
Arabeske, Op.18
   C2248 *(2B398-3)*   i/32
Fantasiestücke, Op.12
   3, Aufschwung
   C1636 *(Cc15458-2)*   iii/29
Kinderscenen, Op.15
   7, Traumerei
   B2685 *(Bb11381-2)*   v/28
Novelette in F, Op.21, no.1
   C1921 *(Cc18509-4)*   viii/30   Past Masters PM-26 (LP)
Quintet in E Flat, Op.44
   3, Scherzo
   (w. Marjorie Hayward & Herbert Kinze, violins;
   Frank Bridge, viola; C. Warwick Evans, cello)
   08053 *(H02724af)*   vii.17
Romance in F Sharp, Op.28, no.2
   B3172 *(Bb15465-2)*   1929
Schlummerlied, Op.124, no.16
   B2635 *(Bb11382-3)*   ii/28
   B4385 *(OB3897-2)*   1933
Waldscenen, Op.82
   7, Der Vogel als Prophet
   05630 *(H03483af)*, 1/2 side   v/19   Pearl GEM 108 (LP)

SCOTT, Cyril (1897–1971)
Caprice chinois
   5642 *(H05459ae)*   xii.19
   B2635 *(Bb11386-3)*   ii/28
English Waltz
   C1790 *(Cc17316-3)*   v/30

Recordings

Scriabin, Alexander (1872–1915)
Étude in C Sharp
    05592 *(H02324af)*, 1/2 side   v/17

Sévérac, Déodat de (1873–1921)
Où l'on entend une vieille Boîte à Musique
    D580 *(Cc423-2)*, 1/2 side   viii.21

Sgambati, Giovanni (1841–1914)
Vecchio Menuetto, Op.18, no.2
    05549   i/14
    C2200 *(2B397-1)*   ix/31

Strauss II, Johann (1825–1899)
Küss-Walzer, Op.400 (arr. Schütt)
    05548 *(Z7286f)*   xii/13   OPAL CD 9839
Neu Wien, Op.342 (arr. Dora Bright)
    C2505 *(2B3899-5)*   xii/32

Tchaikovsky, Peter Ilyitch (1840–1893)
Chanson triste, Op.40, no.2
    B3811 *(OB321-1)*   1931
Concerto no.1 in b flat, Op.23
(w. Royal Albert Hall Orchestra/Sir Landon Ronald)
    D1130/33 *(CR736-1A/37-1/38-1A/39-1,*
    CR732-2A/33-1A/34-1A/35-1)   xii/26
Humoresque, Op.10, no.2
    5634 *(H03315ab)*   xi.16
    B3811 *(OB322-1)*   1931
Trio in a, Op.50
    2, Tema con variazioni
    (w. Marjorie Hayward, violin & C. Warwick Evans, cello)
    08067/68 *(H02727af, H02730af)*   vii.17

Wolf-Ferrari, Ermanno (1876–1948)
The Jewels of the Madonna
    Intermezzo, Act III
    B2478 *(BR969-4)*   1927
    B4437 *(OB3908-1)*   1933

Reproducing piano rolls

Bach, Johann Sebastian (1685–1750)
Prelude and Fugue in D, BWV.532 (arr. Eugen d'Albert)
    Welte 928

Beethoven, Ludwig van (1770–1827)
Sonata in C, Op.2, no.3
    4, Finale
    Welte 929

Chopin, Frederic (1810–1849)
Étude in D Flat, Op.10, no.5
    Ampico 55502F : 22911D

Mazurka no.13 in a, Op.17, no.4
   Welte 931
Polonaise no.9 in B Flat, Op.71, no.2
   Triphonola 51508

GRAINGER, Percy (1882–1961)
Country Gardens (No.22 from "British Folk-Music Settings")
   Triphonola 59918

HAMBOURG, Mark (1879–1960)
Volkslied
   Duo-Art 5652

HENSCHEL, Sir George (1850–1934)
Mazurka, Op.48
   Triphonola 51514

HENSELT, Adolf von (1814–1889)
Étude, Op.5, no.4 ("Ave Maria")
   Duo-Art 59088

LESCHETIZKY, Théodor (1830–1915)
La Source, Op.36, no.4
   Duo-Art 56999
Souvenirs d'Italie, Op.39, no.5
   Triphonola 51511

LISZT, Franz (1811–1886)
Étude de concert no.3 in D Flat
   Ampico 55574H : 41911F
Hungarian Rhapsody no.11 in A
   Triphonola 51516
Polonaise no.2 in E
   Welte 936

NETTO, Barrozo
Berceuse in e
   Triphonola 59921

RAVEL, Maurice (1875–1937)
Jeux d'eau
   Triphonola 51512

RIMSKY-KORSAKOV, Nikolai (1844–1908)
The Snow Maiden: Dance of the Buffoons
   Triphonola 59920

RUBINSTEIN, Anton (1830–1894)
Album de Peterhof, Op.75: 8, Nocturne
   Duo-Art 56540
   Triphonola 51510
   Welte 933
Le Bal, Op.14, no.4
   Artecho 2002
   Welte 934

Recordings

Barcarolle no.4 in G
   Triphonola 51509
Étude in F, Op.23, no.1
   Triphonola 51515
Polka Boheme, Op.82, no.7
   Duo-Art 6014

SCHUMANN, Robert (1810–1856)
Faschingsschwank aus Wien, Op.26:
   No.1; Nos.2-4; No.5
   Triphonola 51505, 51506, 51507

SCOTT, Cyril (1897–1971)
Lotos Land, Op.47, no.1
   Triphonola 51313

TCHAIKOVSKY, Peter Ilyitch (1840–1893)
Chanson triste, Op.40, no.2
   Duo-Art 59579

TURINA, Joaquin (1882–1949)
Danzas fantasticas: 3, Orgia
   Triphonola 59922

VILLA-LOBOS, Heitor (1887–1959)
Prole do Bebe: Polichinello
   Triphonola 59919

Boris Hambourg, Cello

Reissue on LP

Cello solo

CADMAN, Charles Wakefield (1881–1946)
   From the land of the sky-blue water
   HMV 7893

HARTY, Sir Hamilton (1879–1941)
Butterflies
   (w. Gerald Moore, pf.)
   HMV B3302 *(Bb18006-2)*   1930

IRELAND, John (1879–1962)
The Holy Boy (arr. cello and piano)
   (w. Gerald Moore, pf.)
   HMV B3302 *(Bb18005-2)*   1930

POPPER, David (1843–1913)
Papillon
   (w. Grace Smith, pf.)
   Victor 60064   1912   National Library of Canada C-256 (LP, 7")

SCHUMANN, Robert (1810–1856)
Kinderscenen, Op.15
   7, Traumerei
   (w. Grace Smith, pf.)
   Victor 60065   1912

TCHAIKOVSKY, Peter Ilyitch (1840–1893)
Chant sans paroles in F, Op.2, no.3
HMV 07860

As member of the HART HOUSE STRING QUARTET
(w. Géza de Kresz and Harry Adaskin, violins; Milton Blackstone, viola)

ANONYMOUS
À St.-Malo (arr. Sir Ernest MacMillan)
   HMV Victor 24004   1927
Angel Gabriel (arr. Alfred Pochon)
   HMV Victor 24002   1926
Drink to me only with thine eyes (arr. Pochon)
   HMV Victor 24001   1926
Notre Seigneur en pauvre (arr. MacMillan)
   HMV Victor 24004   1927

BEETHOVEN, Ludwig van (1770–1827)
Variations on Mozart's "Là ci darem la mano",
   WoO 28 (arr. Press)
   HMV Victor 24003, 2 sides   1927

BOCCHERINI, Luigi (1743–1805)
Menuet célèbre (the 3rd movement from
   Quintet in E, Op.13, no.5)
   HMV Victor 24001   1926

FOSTER, Stephen Collins (1826–1864)
Old Black Joe (arr. Pochon)
   HMV Victor 24002   1926

HAYDN, Franz Josef (1732–1809)
Quartet in F, Op.20, no.5
   HMV Victor 24009/10/11   1930

Notes

Mark Hambourg: Greatness of Spirit

1. This chapter is based in part on Mark Hambourg's autobiography *From Piano to Forte: A Thousand and One Notes*, Cassells & Co., London, 1931, and on his book of essays *The Eighth Octave*, Williams and Norgate, London, 1951.

2. *The Guardian*, August 29, 1960.

3. *The Eighth Octave*, p.153.

4. Michael Hambourg's Scrap Book, the Clement Hambourg Papers, National Library of Canada, Ottawa. This passage is based on a translation by L. Sverdlova of Russlan Inc.

5. Autobiography, p.11.

6. *Eighth Octave*, p.118.

7. *Eighth Octave*, p .22

8. Vasily Safonov (1852-1918), the son of a Cossack general, was a student of Leschetizky and a teacher of Josef Lhevinne (1874-1944).

9. It is possible that members of the Hambourg family were already living in London. If so, Mark does not mention them in any of his writings. He does mention a cousin, Charles Hambourg, who became a conductor and cello teacher, and who was born in London in 1895.

10. Autobiography, p.60.

11. Autobiography, p.14.

12. *Encyclopaedia Judaica*.

13. Mikhail Beizer, *The Jews of St. Petersburg*, The Jewish Publication Society, Philadelphia-New York, 1989, p.xvIIII.

14. Catherine Drinker Bowen, *Free Artist: The Story of Anton and Nicholas Rubinstein*, Random House, New York, 1939, p.3.

15. Catherine Drinker Bowen, p.8.

16. Salo W. Baron, *The Russian Jew under Tsars and Soviets*, Macmillan, New York, 1964, p.136.

17. Nicolas Slonimsky, *Perfect Pitch*, Oxford University Press, p.16.

18. Nicolas Slonimsky, *Lexicon of Musical Invective,* Coleman-Ross, New York, 1953.

19. Ibid, p.17.

20. Leopold Auer, *My Long Life in Music*, Lippincott, 1923, p.567.

21. *The Eighth Octave*, p,13.

22. Harold C. Schonberg, *The Great Pianists*, Simon and Schuster, New York, 1963, p.284.

23. Quoted in Schonberg, p.301.

24. Schonberg, p.301.

25. The Polish-born Natalie Janotha (1856-1932), a student of Clara Schumann, became court pianist in Berlin.

26. Bernard Shaw, *Music in London 1890-94*, Constable and Company, London, 1932, vol 1, pp 55.

27. Bernard Shaw, *How to Become a Musical Critic*, Constable and Company, London, p.195.

28. Introduction by Paul Avrich to Kropotkin's *The Conquest of Bread*, New York University Press, 1972.

29. David Garnett, *The Golden Echo*, Chatto and Windus, 1953, p.13.

30. Shaw, "A Word about Stepniak," *To-morrow,* January-June 1896, p.103-4.

31. December 30, 1895.

32. December 29, 1895.

33. Autobiography, p.35.

34. Fiona MacCarthy, *William Morris: A Life for Our Time*, Faber and Faber, 1994, p.450.

35. John Slatter (editor), *From the Other Shore: Russian Political Emigrants in Britain, 1880-1917*, Frank Cass, London, 1984, p.70.

36. Ibid, p.69.

37. Autobiography, p.28.

38. Most of the information about Vera Volkhovsky is taken from the article "Bertrand Russell and the Volkhovsky Letters 1920-1926," *Russell, the Journal of the Bertrand Russell Archives,* vol. 2, no.2, winter 1982-83. Surprisingly, Vera is not mentioned in Ray Monk's biography of Bertrand Russell, The Free Press, 1996, which deals extensively with Russell's personal relationships.

39. Caroline Moorehead, *Bertrand Russell: A Life*, Sinclair-Stevenson, London, 1992, p.319.

40. Ray Monk, *Bertrand Russell*, The Free Press, 1996, p.586.

41. Richard Garnett, *Constance Garnett: A Heroic Life*, Sinclair-Stevenson, London, 1991, p.350.

42. Schonberg, p.117.

43. *Eighth Octave*, p. 38.

44. Keir Hardie (1856-1915), British labour leader.

45. The chapter devoted to it in Richard Ellman's biography *Oscar Wilde* is called "Irishman Among the Moscovites." Vintage Books, Random House, New York, p.120

46. In 1886 the steel magnate Andrew Carnegie had published *Triumphant Democracy*. In 1889 Carnegie wrote "what is reckoned to be the most influential

magazine article of his era." Titled simply "Wealth," his essay said the really rich should live modestly and do for their poorer brethren "better than they would or could do for themselves." Karl E. Meyer in the *Globe and Mail*, Toronto, February 23, 1997.

47. Whitelaw Reid (1837-1912) later became American ambassador in London.
48. Autobiography, p.41.
49. Schonberg, p.291.
50. *Eighth Octave*, p.51.
51. Autobiography, p.61.
52. Schonberg, p.204.
53. Autobiography, p.46.
54. Schonberg, p.207.
55. There are thirteen entries of Leschetizky's compositions in the *Gramophone Classical 1996 Catalogue*, among them arabesques, arias, barcaroles, mazurkas and meditations.
56. Artur Schnabel, *My Life and Music*, Longmans, London, 1961, p.33.
57. Austin Roy Keefer, "Leschetizky's Pianistic Philosophy," *Étude*, November 1948, p.673.
58. Schonberg, p.296.
59. Schnabel, p.25.
60. Mary Lawton, *A Life with Mark Twain*, Harcourt, New York, 1925, pp.165-66.
61. Carl Dolmetsch, *Our Famous Guest: Mark Twain in Vienna*, University of Georgia Press, 1992, p.102.
62. Austin Roy Keefer, p. 673.
63. *Eighth Octave*, p.153.
64. The princess married Prinz Karl von Hohenzollern-Sigmaringen, who became King Carol I of Rumania. As queen she published more than twenty books under the name of Carmen Silva: carmen – song; silva – forest. They were books of her own poetry and also translations of Rumanian folk-tales into German. She was a friend and patron of the composer-violinist George Enesco, one of the teachers of Yehudi Menuhin.
65. Autobiography, p.50.
66. Autobiography, p. 67.
67. Autobiography, p. 67.
68. *Eighth Octave*, p.82.
69. *Eighth Octave*, p.75.
70. Autobiography, p.62.
71. Autobiography, p.98.
72. *Eighth Octave*, p.12.
73. *Eighth Octave*, p.83.

74. February 24, 1898.

75. February 23, 1898.

76. February 24, 1898.

77. It is remarkable that Saint-Saëns appeared too modern for this lifelong friend of Brahms. The friendship dated from the time the twenty-two-year-old Joachim introduced himself to Brahms, who was two years younger. The remarkable occasion was a concert by the Hungarian violinist Ede Remenye (1828-1898) and the pianist Brahms, who were playing Beethoven's Kreutzer Sonata in Göttingen. Suddenly faced with an instrument tuned half a tone too low, Brahms transposed the piano part, *which he played by heart,* from A to B flat. Joachim was deeply impressed by this amazing achievement. He himself, the foremost violinist of his age, was an extraordinary musician. At the age of thirteen he played the Beethoven concerto at the Philharmonic in London under the direction of Mendelssohn.

Ede Remenye was Queen Victoria's favourite violinist. Whenever he was in England, he had to be "on call" in case the Queen wanted him to play. His friend Franz Liszt began to compose a violin concerto for him but never finished it. *Grove's Dictionary of Music* observes that Remenye confused "true Magyar" music" with gipsy music, with the result that his friends Liszt and Brahms, in their "Hungarian" compositions, did the same thing.

78. In 1844 the pianist Ignaz Moscheles invited Alfredo Piatti to his house. His friend Felix Mendelssohn was staying with him. Piatti was to play a sonata with Mendelssohn. Piatti assumed it was the Sonata in B flat and prepared it. But when he arrived Mendelssohn brushed it aside and produced a new sonata in D major, then only in manuscript. Margaret Campbell, *The Great Cellists*, Trafalgar Square Publishing, 1988, p.111.

79. Autobiography, p.91.

80. The link between Melba and Lemmone was "an example of how indestructible a platonic friendship can sometimes be." It lasted, as Lemmone recalled in old age, until the final curtain came down on February 23, 1931, "when I was at the great diva's bedside at St. Vincent's Hospital, Sydney, when she died." John Hetherington, *Melba*, Faber and Faber, London, 1967, p.39.

81. Carline Thomas Harnsberger, *Mark Twain – Family Man*, The Citadel Press, N.Y., p.176. Authorities insist that one should not divide Mark Twain's name and refer to him simply as Twain, but because of the complexities of dealing with two Marks we shall break the rule here.

82. October 16, 1898.

83. "It had become increasingly obvious that the Party was in financial difficulties and that £2,000 was needed if all the delegates were to pay their fares back home. Lenin, Gorki, Plekhanov and others first visited the painter Felix Moscheles in the hope of acquiring the needed contribution to Party funds. They were un-

Notes

lucky, but the Central Committee of the German Social Democratic Party gave £300. A more important gesture came from Joseph Fels, an American soap maker of German-Jewish origin and a friend of George Lansbury. Fels was persuaded to visit the Brotherhood Church, listened to the debates for about twenty minutes and lent the Party organizers £1,700 on a loan bond signed by all the delegates after Lenin had guaranteed that the money would be returned. So it was. More than a decade later, when Krasin came to London after the First World War, he returned the £1,700, with interest, to Fels's heirs." Ronald W. Clark, *Lenin: The Man behind the Mask*, Faber and Faber, London, 1988, p.118.

84. Busoni (1861-1924) became a good friend of Mark's. German by choice, the *New Grove's Dictionary of Music and Musicians* writes, he remained abundantly Latin, his ambivalent nature striving to reconcile tradition with innovation.

85. Information provided on March 22, 1997, by one of the four daughters, Mrs. Nadine Mosbaugh, and, on several occasions, by Eugene Kash.

86. Henri Vieuxtemps (1820-1881), violinist and composer.

87. *Musical Courier*, February 1903.

88. *Eighth Octave*, p.123.

89. Toronto *Mail and Empire*, February 1903.

90. Baron Frédéric d'Erlanger (1868-1943), described in *The Oxford Companion to Music* as having composed "operas and most other things."

91. As a matter of fact, Tolstoy had developed an interest in music early in life. In his late period (1889) he wrote a short vitriolic anti-sex novel about the destabilizing effect of the Kreutzer Sonata. A man is driven insane by jealousy and murders his wife. "How can that first presto be played in a drawing room among ladies in low-necked dresses?" the protagonist asks. "To hear that played, to applaud and then to eat sweets and talk about the latest scandal? Such things should only be played on certain important occasions, and then only when certain actions answering to such music are wanted." *Tolstoy's Short Fiction*, W.W. Norton, 1991, p.218 and 441.

92. Maria Gay (1879-1943), mezzo-soprano, definitely sang Carmen in Brussels, Covent Garden, La Scala and Buenos Aires – and no doubt in many other opera houses as well.

93. *Eighth Octave*, p.127.

94. Percy Grainger (1882-1961), Australian-born American pianist and composer.

95. Cyril Scott (1879-1970), English composer.

96. Jacques Thibaud (1880-1953). The trio was active from 1930 to 1935.

97. The Clement Hambourg Papers, National Library of Canada.

98. Toronto *Globe*, June 16, 1916.

99. Conversation with Galia's daughter, Mrs. Stella Ryan, February 27, 1996.

100. *Eighth Octave*, p.85.

101. *Eighth Octave*, pp.85-86.

102. Jan Kubelik (1880-1940), Czech violinist and composer, was acclaimed in Vienna as a second Paganini. He was the father of the composer and conductor Rafael Kubelik.

103. Autobiography, p.184.

104. Sir William M. Whyte (1843-1914) played a significant role in the opening of the Canadian West.

105. Sir William Cornelius van Horne (1843-1915), president of the CPR.

106. Sir Augustus Nanton (1860-1925), president of the Dominion Bank, whose outstanding services helped finance Canada's part in the First World War.

107. Sir Daniel McMillan (1846-1933) was lieutenant-governor of Manitoba from 1900 to 1911.

108. Sir Ralph Champneys Williams (1848-1927) was governor of Newfoundland from 1909 to 1911.

109. *Eighth Octave*, page 97.

110. December 14, 1914.

111. Mischa Elman (1891-1967) had his first spectacular success in Berlin at thirteen. He settled in the U.S. in 1911. Altogether two million of his records were sold.

112. Dame Maggie Teyte (1888-1976), the English soprano and great interpreter of French music whom Debussy selected to succeed Mary Garden as Mélisande.

113. Lionel Tertis (1876-1975) was one of the foremost viola players of his time. He had to overcome much prejudice before the viola was finally accepted as a solo instrument.

114. Defauw visited Mark again in London after the invasion of France in June 1940. He had been conductor of the Brussels Conservatory Orchestra, had got across France in his car and left it on the quayside in Bordeaux with the engine still running in his frantic hurry to board the ship, which was just leaving. It was the second time he had to flee his country.

115. Benno Moiseiwitsch (1890-1963) was the father of Tanya Moiseiwitsch, well known in Canada for her long career as designer at the Stratford Shakespeare Festival.

116. Mieczyslaw Horszowski, June 23, 1892–May 22, 1993.

117. Schnabel, p.25.

118. Arthur Rubinstein (1886-1982), *My Young Years*, Alfred Knopf, N.Y. 1973, p.444.

119. Mathew Norgate and Alan Wykes, *Not So Savage*, Jupiter Books, London, p.27.

120. *Eighth Octave*, p.131.

121. Autobiography, p.287.

122. Gerald Moore (1899-1987), *Am I Too Loud?* Hamish Hamilton, London, 1962, p.33.

123. Prohibition was legislated by Order in Council under Wartime Emergency

Powers on April Fool's Day 1918. In November 1919 the weaker Temperance Act was passed and gradually liquor came back.

124. *Eighth Octave*, p.128.

125. *Eighth Octave*, p.56.

126. Viscount Richard B.H. Haldane (1856-1928).

127. Earl of Oxford and Asquith (1852-1928), prime minister of England 1908-1916.

128. *Eighth Octave*, p.80.

129. *Eighth Octave*, p.80. The work was composed in 1919 and dedicated to Arthur Rubinstein, who gave its first performance in New York in 1920. Mark misspelled the name *Baëtica,* no doubt assuming, quite reasonably, that it meant *poetic*. However, *Bética* is an ancient name for the province of Andalusia.

130. Autobiography, p.213.

131. Autobiography, p.300.

132. Norgate and Wykes, *Not So Savage*, p.27.

133. *Eighth Octave*, p.76.

134. *Eighth Octave*, p.73. The film, made in 1932, was part of the Musical Memories series made by Universal.

135. The film was made in 1941 by British National. "A rich young man poses as a tramp to save a dosshouse from destruction. Naive drama with a social conscience remade from the 1932 talkie *Dosshouse*." *Halliwell's Film Guide 1995* (tenth edition), Harper Perennial, p.228.

136. *Eighth Octave*, p.106.

137. Charles Hambourg (born in London in 1895) conducted the British Symphony Orchestra and taught conducting and the cello at the Metropolitan Academy of Music. He was the son of one of Michael's two brothers, both of whom were pianists. On October 5, 1960, Charles and his wife attended the Memorial Service for Mark at St. Sepulchre's Church, Holborn Viaduct.

138. *Eighth Octave*, p.116.

139. Frieder Weissmann, American conductor, refugee from Germany, born near Frankfurt in 1898.

140. *Globe and Mail,* May 6, 1949.

141. May 16, 1946. Another part of this review will be quoted at the end of the chapter on Boris.

142. *Eighth Octave*, p.158.

143. Letter of August 29, 1960, the Clement Hambourg Papers, Music Division, National Library of Canada.

Jan Hambourg: Epicure, Violinist, Scholar

1. Gerald Moore, *Am I Too Loud?* Hamish Hamilton, London, 1962, p.23.

2. *Tea and Anarchy: The Bloomsbury Diary of Olive Garnett 1890-1895*, Bartlett's Press, London, 1989, p.183, entry for May 17, 1895.

3. The Amati might be worth $400,000 today, the Guarneri close to $350,000; thus in 1910 they were relatively inexpensive. The astronomical rise in the value of old violins of quality in recent years is due, in addition to the proliferation of superb performers in the West, to the enormous demand for them in the Far East.

4. Pauline Donalda (originally Lichtenstein), Montreal soprano and teacher, 1882-1970; Edmund Burke, Toronto bass, 1876-1970; Kathleen Parlow, violin virtuoso, chamber musician and teacher, 1890-1963.

5. Sir Gilbert Parker (1862-1932), Canadian-born novelist and politician, champion of imperialism.

6. *Canadian Courier*, September 1910.

7. Elizabeth Moorehead, *These Two Were Here: Louise Homer and Willa Cather*, University of Pittsburgh Press, 1950.

8. E.K. Brown, *Willa Cather: A Critical Biography*, Knopf, 1953, p.112.

9. Letter to author, April 2, 1996.

10. Yehudi Menuhin, *Unfinished Journey*, Knopf, New York, 1977, p.77.

11. James Woodress, *Willa Cather*, University of Nebraska Press, 1987, p.86.

12. Joan Acocella, in the *New Yorker*, November 27, 1995, p.71.

13. *Miss Cather's Business as an Artist*, New York Herald Tribune Books, Sept.11, 1927.

14. John J. Murphy, *Critical Essays on Willa Cather*, G.K. Hall & Co., Boston, 1984, p.31.

15. Elizabeth Moorehead (see above) wrote about "the bedroom they shared," while Kathleen D. Byrne and Richard C. Snyder stated they had separate bedrooms, in *Chrysalis: Willa Cather in Pittsburgh, 1896-1906*, Historical Society of Western Pennsylvania, Pittsburgh, p.40.

16. *New Yorker*, November 27, 1995.

17. Hermione Lee, *Willa Cather: A Life Saved Up*. Virago Press, London, 1989, p.11.

18. Marion Marsh Brown and Ruth Crone, *Only One Point of the Compass*, Archer Editions Press, p.85.

19. Willa Cather, *Song of the Lark*, Houghton Mifflin, Boston, 1913, p.407.

20. *New Yorker*, November 27, 1995, p.56.

21. James Schroeter, ed., *Willa Cather and her Critics*, Cornell University Press, Ithaca, N.Y., 1967, p.7.

22. *New Yorker*, November 27, 1995, p.57.

23. Interview with Mrs. Stella Ryan, St. Albans, Hertfordshire, February 27, 1996.

24. Richard Giannone, *Music in Willa Cather's Fiction*, University of Nebraska Press, 1968.

25. Edith Lewis, *Willa Cather Living: A Personal Record*, Knopf, New York, pp.47-48.

Notes

26. David Daiches, *Willa Cather: A Critical Introduction*, Collier Books, New York, 1962, p.28.
27. Hermione Lee, p.51.
28. Byrne and Snyder, p.32.
29. Edith Lewis, p.53.
30. Dorothy Canfield Fisher (1879-1958), quoted by E.K. Brown in *Willa Cather*, Knopf, New York, 1953, p.96.
31. Hermione Lee, p.58.
32. Ibid.
33. *New York Times*, April 5, 1916.
34. Woodress, p.277.
35. Elizabeth Sergeant, *Willa Cather: A Memoir*, University of Nebraska Press, 1953.
36. Marion Marsh Brown and Ruth Crone, p.69.
37. Sharon O'Brien, *Willa Cather*, Oxford University Press, 1987, pp.239-240.
38. James Schoeter, *Willa Cather and her Critics*, Cornell University Press, Ithaca, 1967, pp.376-377.
39. Loretta Wasserman, "Cather's Semitism," in *Cather Studies*, vol. 2., edited by Susan J. Rosowski, University of Nebraska Press, 1993, p.17.
40. Leon Edel, "A Cave of One's Own," *Critical Essays on Willa Cather*, G.K. Hall & Co., Boston, 1984, p.203.
41. Loretta Wasserman, p.15.
42. Hermione Lee, p.227.
43. Leon Edel, p. 213.
44. Willa Cather, *Later Novels*, The Library of America, The Literary Classics of the United States, New York, p.202.
45. Interview, June 22, 1996.
46. Marion Marsh Brown and Ruth Crone, p.83.
47. Letter to the author, September 12, 1996. Meeting Jan was not Philip Clark's only adventure in Paris. He was a chartered accountancy student at the time. While buying a small wooden sculpture in a shop, he fell in love with the salesgirl. Two years later he married her. She became Paraskeva Clark (1898-1986), the well-known Toronto painter, who was born in St. Petersburg. When she came to Canada in 1931, the *Toronto Star* wrote on January 29, 1983, "Toronto was at least twenty years behind the times. 'It was a dead place,' she said. 'Nothing but the Group of Seven… the bloody Group of Seven.' Abstract art didn't arrive here until the advent of Painters Eleven in the 1950s. Clark's 1937 canvas *Petroushka* is considered her greatest achievement. Certainly, the work is the most eloquent and persuasive statement of her deeply-held anti-Capitalist sentiments." Paraskeva Clark was the subject of the National Film Board film *Portrait of the Artist* as an Old Lady, made in 1982.

48. Harry Adaskin, *A Fiddler's World*, p.183.
49. Menuhin, pp.77-78.
50. Robert Magidoff, *Yehudi Menuhin*, Robert Hale & Co., London, 1973, p.64.
51. In Isabelle Hambourg's letter to Willa Cather about Sammy Hersenhoren there is this passage: "He [Sammy] had a wonderful hour at the Gare Saint Lazare with Ferruccio and B. They came in to see him. Ferruccio's dream is to return to New York. He finds New York just right for him. Just big enough perhaps! Sammy always speaks of our house at Ville d'Avray as the old homestead!"
52. Menuhin.
53. Menuhin, p.78
54. Clement Hambourg's notes written by hand on October 7, 1972.
55. In late 1942 or 1943, the young violinists Morry Kernerman and Hyman Goodman visited Jan in his London apartment. Both were in the RCAF and both later had distinguished careers, primarily in the Toronto Symphony Orchestra. Hyman Goodman died in 1994. Kernerman remembers that Jan seemed to be working on an edition of the Bach partitas and asked him to help him work through some difficult passages. He was deeply impressed by Jan's devotion and seriousness.
56. This is the opinion of Jaak Liivoja-Lorius, Toronto music writer and former head of the musical instruments department at Christie's in London.
57. Albert Schweitzer, *J.S. Bach*, Black, London, 1935, vol. 1, p.387.
58. December 1934, vol.64, no.762, p.231.
59. January 1935, pp.34-35.
60. George Kates (ed), *Willa Cather in Europe*, Knopf, 1956.
61. Edith Lewis, *Willa Cather Living*, Knopf, 1953, p.88.
62. Woodress, p.288.
63. Woodress, p.338.
64. *New Yorker*, November 27, 1995, p.63.
65. Edith Lewis, p.153.
66. Edith Lewis, pp.158-159.
67. An essay in *Not Under Forty*, published in 1936.
68. Elizabeth Sergeant, p.259.
69. Edith Lewis, p.170.
70. Menuhin, p.130.
71. Edith Lewis, p.170.
72. E.K. Brown, p.329.
73. Thanks are due to Lucas's daughter Jessica in Sèvres, France, for permission to publish these two extracts.
74. Thanks are due to S..C. Hunter (Record Agent), in Hatch End, Pinner, Middlesex, England, for finding the will and sending a copy of it to the author.
75. Galia died on December 9, 1947.
76. It seems that Jan gave his Amati his wife's name.

Notes

Boris Hambourg: The Complete Musician

1. This section is in part based on extensive interviews with Marcus Adeney, Boris Berlin, Helmut Blume, Rachel Cavalho, Miriam Bassin Chinsky, Frank Fusco, Eugene Kash, Morry Kernerman, Eleanor Koldofsky, William Krehm, Paul Scherman, Stanley Solomon, Lou Taub, Ezra Schabas, Gloria Sheard, Joseph Sheard, Robert Spergel, Vincent Tovell, and on the books Harry Adaskin, *A Fiddler's World*, November House 1977, Maurice Solway, *Recollections of a Violinist*, Mosaic Press, 1984, Ezra Schabas, *Sir Ernest MacMillan*, University of Toronto Press, 1994, and Mária Kresz and Peter Király, *Géza de Kresz and Norah Drewett*, George Hencz, 1989.

2. A. R. Mullens, *Maclean's Magazine*, June 1, 1931.

3. Elie Spivak, (1902-1960) violinist, concertmaster of Toronto Symphony Orchestra 1931–1948.

4. Gerald Moore, *Am I Too Loud?* Hamish Hamilton, London, 1962, p.23.

5. Ed Hausmann, "Who Remembers 194 Wellesley?" *Star Weekly*, January 6, 1968.

6. Margaret Campbell, *The Great Cellists*, Trafalgar Square Publishing, 1988, p.95.

7. This must have been at an early stage of BBC experimental television broadcasting at Alexandra Palace.

8. Morry Kernerman (born 1925) was assistant concertmaster in the Toronto Symphony Orchestra 1972-1991.

9. The cellist Marcus Adeney, born 1900, was a member of the Toronto Symphony 1928-1948. He taught at the Hambourg Conservatory 1928-1951.

10. Paul Scherman, conductor and violinist, born 1907, was assistant conductor of the Toronto Symphony Orchestra from 1947 to 1955 and in the early 1950s participated as violinist in the Casals Festivals in Prades, France. The author interviewed him at length shortly before he died in 1996.

11. "Who Remembers 194 Wellesley?"

12. It is possible that one reason why Professor Michael Hambourg chose to come to Toronto was that other members of his extended family had preceded him. Ivan Hambourg – not his son Jan – is buried in the same grave as Michael and Catherine Hambourg in Mount Pleasant Cemetery.

13. "Who Remembers 194 Wellesley?"

14. Maria Tippett, *Making Culture*, University of Toronto Press, 1990, p.99.

15. Ezra Schabas, *Sir Ernest MacMillan*, p.74.

16. Harry Adaskin, *A Fiddler's World*, p.83. Adaskin (1901-1994) wrote two autobiographical works, *A Fiddler's World* (Memoirs to 1938), November House, 1977, and *A Fiddler's Choice* (Memoirs to 1980).

17. Mark Hambourg autobiography, p.269.

18. October 10, 1931.

19. Lou Taub, born in 1904, is a Toronto lawyer and an enthusiastic amateur violinist and chamber musician. He studied at the Hambourg Conservatory between the ages of ten and twelve.

20. Frank Fusco played the violin in the Toronto Symphony Orchestra for fifty years, from 1928 to 1978, from the days of Luigi von Kunits to those of Andrew Davis.

21. Maurice Solway, *Recollections of a Violinist*, pp.22-23. Colonel Gooderham was knighted in 1935 but died before the investiture.

22. Adaskin, *A Fiddler's World*, p.98.

23. Ezra Schabas, *Sir Ernest MacMillan*, p.56, and chapter 5, beginning p.69.

24. *Canadian Courier*, September 1910. This is part of the interview with Jan Hambourg quoted earlier.

25. Adaskin, *A Fiddler's Choice*, p.108.

26. Gerald Moore, *Am I Too Loud?* Hamish Hamilton, London, 1962, p.22.

27. William Dendy and William Kilbourn, *Toronto Observed*, Oxford University Press, 1986, p.115.

28. Walter Michel and C.J.Fox, *Wyndham Lewis on Art*, Funk & Wagnalls, New York, 1969, p.11.

29. "Wyndham Lewis: His Theory of Art and Communication," *Shenandoah*, summer-autumn 1952.

30. Credit for some of the Wyndham Lewis material cited must go to the article by C.J. Fox "Through Toronto's Fire and Ice," *The Beaver*, December 1996-January 1997.

31. Letter to J.M. Dent, November 22, 1941, *The Letters of Wyndham Lewis*, Methuen and Co., 1963, p.310.

32. Ibid, letter to R.D. Jameson, February 14, 1942, p.317.

33. Wyndham Lewis, *Self-Condemned*, McClelland and Stewart, 1974, p.179.

34. Adaskin, *A Fiddler's Choice*, p.149.

35. Ibid, p.18.

36. Hyman Goodman, concertmaster and occasional soloist with the Toronto Symphony Orchestra 1948-1967.

37. Archives, Arts and Letters Club.

38. Boris Berlin, born 1907, is one of Canada's most prominent piano teachers and author of more than twenty pedagogical works. He held the position of piano teacher at the Hambourg Conservatory from 1925 to 1927, and, in an interview with the author on May 13, 1996, spoke of Boris Hambourg with insight, admiration and affection.

39. Giuseppe Carboni (1866-1934), composer and choirmaster, was voice director at the Hambourg Conservatory.

40. The Australian-born pianist Rachel Cavalho taught at the Hambourg Conservatory for a short time after arriving from England in the late forties, long after

it had passed its peak. She had a distinguished career as an independent teacher in Toronto, devoting much of her time to promoting the teaching and performance of contemporary Canadian music.

41. One of Norah Drewett's most eminent students was Ida Krehm, Ernest Bloch's chosen pianist for the premiere in 1950 of his *Scherzo fantastique.*

42. Ernest Farmer (1886-1975), composer and pianist, had studied with Max Reger in Leipzig. Luigi von Kunits called him "a theory teacher of rare originality." Farmer also taught at the Toronto Conservatory. Among his students were Ida Krehm, Gerald Moore and Colin McPhee.

43. Broadus Farmer (1890-1959) had studied with Jan and taught the violin to Albert Pratz and Hyman Goodman. He also taught at the Toronto Conservatory.

44. In 1926 Boris invited the tenor Eduardo Ferrari-Fontana (1878-1936), who was born in Rome, to come to Toronto to teach. He had sung in some of the the world's greatest opera houses under the baton of Nikisch, Saint-Saëns, Toscanini and Weingartner.

45. Emil Gartner conducted the Jewish Folk Choir in Toronto.

46. Glenn Gould was the most famous student of Alberto Guerrero, who also taught at the Toronto Conservatory of Music. Others were William Aide, John Beckwith, Helmut Blume, Ray Dudley, Stuart Hamilton, Paul Helmer, Horace Lapp, Bruce Mather, Gerald Moore, Oskar Morawetz, Arthur Ozolins and R. Murray Schafer. Guerrero (1886-1959) was born in Chile and, as conductor of Santiago's first symphony orchestra, had introduced to Chile the music of Ravel and Debussy.

47. Redferne Hollinshead (1885-1937) also sang at the Timothy Eaton Memorial Church.

48. The greatly admired bass-baritone Campbell McInnes, who played a major role in Toronto's musical life for many years, and who sang Christus in Sir Ernest MacMillan's annual performance of *St. Matthew Passion,* was the ex-husband of the successful English novelist Angela Thirkell (1890-1961), the author of the popular novel *Wild Strawberries.* "He turned out to be a violent drunk.... Angela ran away from him in 1917 and they divorced, publicly and painfully, when she was twenty-seven." Hermione Lee in the *New Yorker,* October 7, 1996, p.90. In 1918 she married again and in 1920 went to Australia. After the failure of her second marriage she returned to England. She did not publish her first novel until 1933. Thirkell was estranged from her second son Colin – Graham was the older – who in the fifties became "the Kerouac of West London."

49. The Russian violinist, mystery-man and musical guru Yasha Paii (this may not have been his real name) may or may not have been a student of Leopold Auer. Kernerman, who was then in his early teens, thinks Paii was an excellent teacher. He "had a way about him," spoke excellent English and had (perhaps) written a number of books on violin technique. Paii was a believer in unorthodox medicine, unusual at the time, and at the beginning of every lesson, Kernerman re-

members vividly, like an amateur chiropractor, "cracked his neck."

50. Marcel Ray (1912-1987) played the cello in the Toronto Symphony Orchestra 1936-1947 and 1962-1969. He was also a gifted instrument-maker, photographer and writer.

51. Reginald Stewart (1900-1984), conductor, pianist and teacher, studied with Mark Hambourg, Arthur Friedheim and Nadia Boulanger. From 1921 to 1924 he taught at the Canadian Academy, and in 1921 he toured Western Canada with the Hambourg Trio. In the thirties he and Ernest MacMillan – both Bach lovers and superior performers – acknowledged each other as rivals. Stewart was the founder of the Promenade Symphony Concerts (1934-1956), which he conducted during the summer.

52. William Krehm, born 1913, economist, businessman and amateur violinist, studied at the Hambourg Conservatory in the 1920s. As a music critic in the late 1940s he often invited Boris to attend concerts with him. For a time his sister, the prominent pianist Ida Krehm, studied with Norah Drewett, who also taught at the Hambourg Conservatory.

53. Apart from conducting the Royal York Hotel Concert Orchestra from 1929 to 1938, Rex Battle led the *Singing Stars of Tomorrow* from 1943 to 1956 on CBC Radio.

54. There are a number of versions of this story, depending on which of the elderly musicians who remember John Langley one talks to. This version is a collage.

55. Letter to the author, September 12, 1996.

56. Augustus Bridle, *The Story of the Club*, The Arts and Letters Club, Toronto, 1955, p.12.

57. Michael J. Piva, *The Condition of the Working Class in Toronto – 1900-1921*, University of Ottawa Press, 1979, p.111.

58. From the program, in the Baldwin Room at the Metropolitan Reference Library, Toronto.

59. Toronto *Globe*, June 20, 1916.

60. Toronto *Globe*, June 22, 1916.

61. Conversation in the mid-eighties with Banuta Rubess, author of *Boom, Baby, Boom*, a play about Clement Hambourg's House of Hambourg.

62. Morton Shulman, *Coroner*, Fitzhenry and Whiteside, Toronto, 1975, p.123. Dr. Shulman, as coroner, reversed this practice.

63. It was overgrown with grass but was raised at the author's request in August 1996.

64. Adaskin, *A Fiddler's World*, p.103.

65. Solway, p.31. The spelling is Solway's.

66. Letter to the author from Murray Adaskin, Victoria, B.C., September 12. 1996.

Notes

67. Adaskin, *A Fiddler's World*, p.100.
68. October 16, 1931.
69. Adaskin, *A Fiddler's Choice*, p.105. Spelling Adaskin's.
70. *Toronto Telegram*, October 2, 1947.
71. Mark Hambourg autobiography, p.268.
72. "Who Remembers 194 Wellesley?"
73. Sir Sigmund Samuel had amassed a fortune in the sheet metal business in the early part of his life and spent the rest of it financing buildings at the University of Toronto and the University of Western Ontario, and collecting Canadiana and other treasures on an impressive scale. The Royal Ontario Museum contains many of his contributions. Samuel gave his house in Forest Hill unconditionally to the province of Ontario, in the hope that it would become the official residence of the lieutenant governor. He died in 1962 at the age of ninety-four, having been born only a hundred and fifteen days after Confederation. His father, Lewis Samuel, had been a founding member of the Holy Blossom Temple, and in 1954 Sigmund was made an honorary life member. He was among the handful of wealthy Jews who had achieved eminence in the larger community, in contrast to the period after 1945, when there would be many. Neither Sir Sigmund Samuel nor other Jewish philanthropists at the time were particularly interested in music.
74. "Who Remembers 194 Wellesley?"
75. Ibid.
76. *North Toronto Town Crier,* April 1997.
77. Graham McInnes, *Finding a Father*, Hamish Hamilton, London, 1967, p.119.
78. *The Group of Seven, Revelations by Members of the Arts and Letters Club*, The Arts and Letters Club, Toronto, p.1.
79. F.B. Housser, *A Canadian Art Movement,* Macmillan of Canada, Toronto, 1926, p.11.
80. Lovat Dickson, *The Museum Makers,* Royal Ontario Museum, 1986, p.58.
81. Ian Montagnes, *An Uncommon Fellowship*, University of Toronto Press, 1969, p.13.
82. "This arrangement held for some time, but as with all gifts or bequests carrying long-term stipulations, the rule had to be changed to keep pace with the growth of the city and its prosperity." Lady Eaton, *Memory's Wall,* Clarke Irwin, Toronto, 1956, p.58.
83. Claude Bissell, *The Young Vincent Massey*, University of Toronto Press, 1981. p.73.
84. Wyndham Lewis, *America, I Presume,* Howell, Soskin & Co., New York, 1940. W.K. Rose (ed.), *The Letters of Wyndham Lewis,* New Directions, 1965, p,.277.
85. Tippett, p.122.
86. Raymond Massey, *When I Was Young,* McClelland and Stewart, Toronto, 1976, p.268.

87. *Toronto Star,* July 26, 1924.

88. This and many other quotes in this chapter are taken from Mária Kresz (the de Kresz's daughter – she dropped the "de") and Péter Király, *Géza de Kresz and Norah Drewett, Their Life and Music on Two Continents*, George Hencz, 1989.

89. Kresz and Király.

90. Kresz and Király.

91. Mária Kresz, as well as being her father's biographer, had a distinguished career in ethnography and from 1943 until her death in 1989 was curator at the Ethnographic Museum of Budapest.

92. Solway, p.37.

93. Adaskin, *A Fiddler's World*, p.110.

94. *Toronto Star,* July 26, 1924.

95. Adaskin, *A Fiddler's World*, p.117.

96. Ibid, p.112.

97. *Maclean's,* June 1, 1935.

98. Adaskin, *A Fiddler's World*, p.119.

99. Ibid, p.120

100. Bissell, p.176.

101. Bissell, p.64.

102. Permission for quotations from the Vincent Massey Papers has been granted by the Master and Fellows of Massey College, University of Toronto.

103. *Musical Courier,* November 26, 1925.

104. *The Jew in Canada,* Jewish Publications Ltd., 1926, p.529.

105. Conversation with Boris Berlin, May 13, 1996.

106. December 27, 1931.

107. Adaskin, *A Fiddler's World*, p.235.

108. Most of the information in this section is drawn from twelve volumes of scrapbooks Milton Blackstone donated to the University of Toronto on December 3, 1952. They are stored in the Edward Johnson Music Library. The passages devoted to the Hart House String Quartet in the unpublished Ph.D. thesis *The String Quartet in Canada* by Robert W.A. Elliott, written in 1990, were also based in part on this material and have been useful to the author.

109. October 26, 1925.

110. Montagnes, p.75.

111. *Maclean's,* March 1, 1931.

112. *Musical Courier,* July 6, 1928.

113. Mark Hambourg autobiography, p.282. Ravel's Piano Concerto in G major was composed in 1931. Ravel played it at the première in the Salle Pleyel in Paris on January 14, 1932, and subsequently performed it in twenty cities in four months, though in declining health.

114. *Musical Courier,* January 26, 1928.

115. Adaskin, *A Fiddler's World*, p.170.
116. *Toronto Star*, March 28, 1928.
117. Ibid.
118. Quoted by Gilles Potvin in *Musical Canada, Words and Music Honouring Helmut Kallmann*, University of Toronto Press, 1988, p.157.
119. Ibid.
120. *Ottawa Citizen*, March 8, 1930.
121. *Daily Express*, October 9, 1929.
122. *Toronto Telegram*, October 11, 1929.
123. Beverley Baxter, Canadian-born journalist, who revamped the *Daily Express* for Lord Beaverbrook and in 1935 was elected to the British House of Commons. He had a column in *Maclean's Magazine*.
124. Kresz and Király, p.94.
125. The cello must not be confused with another Servais cello, now in the Division of Cultural History at the Smithsonian in Washington, D.C. It is also named after the famous Belgian cellist Adrien François Servais (1807-1866), but was built by Stradivari, not Guarneri. Servais' friend Princess Youssoupoff ordered it to be sent to him from St. Petersburg, but before it could be dispatched the princess died. However, the Servais family still managed to purchase it. After Adrien François' death his son Joseph, also a fine cellist, inherited it. In due course Prince Caraman-Chimay, an excellent player and a collector of rare instruments, bought it. Unfortunately, he became "the victim of odious publicity" when his American wife eloped with a gypsy violinist who died of the bubonic plague in Alexandria. Eventually, after a number of detours, an American philanthropist donated it to the Smithsonian. The author is indebted to Mr. Gary Sturm at the Smithsonian for this information.
126. Bissell, p.177.
127. Ibid, p.176.
128. Kresz and Király, p.103.
129. March 19, 1929.
130. June 1935.
131. Ibid, p.21.
132. Carl F. Flesch, *And do you also play the violin?*, Toccata Press, London, 1990, pp 207-8.
133. *Toronto Star*, April 29 1935.
134. Canadian Press, June 1, 1935.
135. *Ottawa Morning Citizen*, January 18, 1937.
136. *Das Echo*, Vienna, April 18, 1937. Translation by the author.
137. *Die Stunde*, Vienna. April 18, 1937.
138. Interview with Milton Blackstone, *Toronto Telegram*, April 28, 1938.
139. Adaskin, *A Fiddler's World*, p.268.

140. Ibid, p.248.
141. *Globe and Mail*, May 9, 1938.
142. *Toronto Star*, March 28, 1938.
143. Vincent Massey Papers.
144. Godfrey Ridout, *Fifty Years of Music in Canada? Good Lord, I was there for all of them*, W.J. Keith and B.Z. Shek, eds., University of Toronto Press, 1980, p.120.
145. Dudley Dell, in *Mayfair*, June 1946.
146. Helmut Blume (born in Berlin in 1914) later became dean of music at McGill University, Montreal.
147. *Globe and Mail*, May 16, 1949.
148. Archives of the Arts and Letters Club.
149. Archives of the Arts and Letters Club.

Clement Hambourg: The Black Sheep

1. This section is in part based on interviews with Archie Alleyne, Norm Amadio, Madeline and Ed Bickert, Dennis Burton, Ron Collier, Don Cullen, Gary Ferrier, Don Francks, Nic Gotham, Paul Grosney, Hagood Hardy, Gwen Iveson, Stan Jacobson, Moe Koffman, Genevieve MacAulay, Phil Nimmons, John Norris, Banuta Rubess, Ron Rully, Gloria Sheard, Joseph Sheard, Harry Somers, Norman Symonds, Don (D.T.) Thompson and Peter Thurman.

2. *Canadian Courier*, September 1910.

3. Pierre Salinger was for most of the last two decades a senior ABC News correspondent and investigative reporter, and then, until 1995, vice-chairman of the public relations firm Burson-Marsteller.

4. Telephone conversation with the author, November 1996.

5. Their son, the violinist Dr. Klement Hambourg, is now professor emeritus of music, Lebanon Valley College in Annville, Pennsylvania. He was born in Ottawa in 1928, taught strings in the Peterborough school system, and in 1967 was the founding conductor of the Peterborough Symphony Orchestra.

6. The U.K. General Registry Office, in a letter to the author June 26, 1996.

7. Ed Hausmann, "Who Remembers 194 Wellesley?" *Toronto Star*, January 6, 1968.

8. Ross Harkness, *J.E. Atkinson of the Star*, University of Toronto Press, 1963, p.198.

9. H.A. Fricker (1868-1943), conductor and organist, successor of A.S. Vogt as conductor of Mendelssohn Choir.

10. Leo Smith (1881-1952), composer, cellist, teacher and writer.

11. "Who Remembers 194 Wellesley?"

12. Harold Town, *Albert Franck: Keeper of the Lanes*, McClelland and Stewart, Toronto, 1974, p.19.

13. Obituary, *Toronto Star*, February 6, 1973.

Notes

14. Flutist, saxophonist, clarinetist, composer, arranger Moe Koffmann was born in Toronto in 1928 and in 1948 won a CBC "Jazz Unlimited" poll as best alto-saxophonist. He became one of Canada's most prominent and celebrated personalities in jazz and popular music. Among his first important musical experiences was playing in the House of Hambourg.

15. The composer, arranger, conductor and trombonist Ron Collier was born in Lethbridge, Alberta, in 1930. His jazz group performed at the Stratford Festival in 1957. In 1961 Collier was the first jazz composer given a Canada Council grant. Among his works for big band are *Requiem for JFK* (1964) and *Humber Suite* (1973). He taught composition and arranging at Humber College from 1972 to 1991. Carne Bray, bass player for the Ron Collier Quintet, was quoted in the *CBC Times* of September 5, 1959: "Good jazz, like any top flight musical composition, should be equivalent to an inspired sermon or a first-class lawyer's address to the jury. It should state an assumption, allow for logical development while being highly persuasive by relying on inventive techniques that pluck the heart string. Ron Collier does this to perfection."

16. Norman Symonds, born 1920, raised in Victoria, served with the Royal Canadian Navy during the war, and after the war, from 1945 to 1948, studied the clarinet and theory at the Toronto Conservatory. In the fifties he wrote jazz works employing classical forms, including *Fugues for Reeds and Brass* and two concertos for jazz octet. His *Concerto Grosso* was premiered and recorded in 1957 by Ron Collier's quintet with the CBC Symphony Orchestra under Victor Feldbrill. *The Nameless Hour* (dedicated to Albert Camus) was given a premiere in 1966 by the Toronto Symphony Orchestra under Victor Feldbrill, and, after revisions, was recorded under Ron Collier with Duke Ellington as soloist. Much of his later work is evocative of the vastness of nature. Symonds now lives in Victoria.

17. Listings in Toronto city directories.

18. Letter to the author, January 8, 1997.

19. Canadian Press story, July 17, 1957.

20. Letter dated March 16, 1945, Clement Hambourg Papers, National Library, Ottawa.

21. It was first produced at the du Maurier World Stage Festival at Harbourfront in Toronto, June 15-18, 1988, and first published in the *Canadian Theatre Review 58*. David Bolt played Clement and Kate Lynch Ruthie.

22. Don Francks or Iron Buffalo, actor, jazz musician, environmental activist and honorary Cree, sees Toronto as a an illustration of "the simple idea that cities become great by what they preserve" (David Gardner in *The Canadian Encyclopedia*).

23. Mark Miller, *Cool Blues: Charlie Parker in Canada 1953*, Nightwood Editions, London, Ont., 1989, p.56.

24. Clement Hambourg, quoted in the *Toronto Star*, May 17, 1956.

25. Rosemary Sullivan, *Shadow Maker: The Life of Gwendolyn MacEwen*, HarperCollins, Toronto, p.96.

26. Obituary, *Toronto Star*, February 6, 1973.

27. *Toronto Star*, May 17, 1956.

28. Mark Miller, *Jazz in Canada*, University of Toronto Press, 1982, p.96.

29. Tom Alderman in the *Ryersonian*, February 24, 1956.

30. There is reason to doubt, however, that Clement played it very well. In 1965, he and Norm Amadio made "a little record" of it together, on 45 rpm. According to Amadio, "they bluffed it out." In the publicity for the record it was stated that Clement had broadcast the solo version for the "International Radio Test" in 1926.

31. Story by Bert Petlock and Walter Curtin, *Weekend Magazine*, vol. 7, no.44, 1957.

32. Mackenzie Porter, "The Jazz-happy Tailor," *Maclean's Magazine*, December 21, 1957.

33. Personal note to the author.

34. Jon Ruddy, "The Ninth Life of the Ninth Cat," *Toronto Telegram*, July 31, 1965.

35. Ibid, p.95.

36. Alderman, *Ryersonian*, February 24, 1956.

37. *Toronto Star*, May 17th, 1956

38. Dennis Burton, born 1933 in Lethbridge, Alberta, achieved renown in 1965 for his "Garterbeltmania," Like his colleagues Joyce Wieland and Michael Snow, he is noted for the exploration of erotic themes in Canadian painting. "His paintings, figurative, abstract or calligraphic are full of dashing energy" (Joan Murray in *The Canadian Encyclopedia*).

39. Clement, as reported by Tom Alderman in the *Ryersonian*, February 24, 1956.

40. Don (D.T.) Thompson is not to be confused with the bassist Don W. Thompson.

41. Ed Bickert, born 1932 near Winnipeg, is noted for a reticence that belies his internationally recognized accomplishments on the guitar. He has frequently performed with most of the jazz musicians mentioned in this chapter and is universally respected and admired.

42. Hagood Hardy (1937-1996), one of Canada's most versatile and respected jazz musicians – and occasional politician – played the vibraphone in jazz clubs while studying science and economics at the University of Toronto in the mid-fifties, and also played at the House of Hambourg. He became very fond of both Clement and Ruthie and spoke about them to the author with deep affection four weeks before he died of cancer late in 1996.

43. Canadian Press story, July 17,.1957.

44. *Weekend Magazine*, vol.7, no. 46.
45. Alderman, *Ryersonian*, February 24,. 1956.
46. Ibid.
47. David Lewis Stein, *Toronto Star*, April 10, 1971.
48. *Toronto Telegram*, February 4, 1969.
49. Personal note to the author.
50. Archie Alleyne, born 1933 in Toronto, later accompanied many jazz stars, including Billie Holiday, Lester Young, Coleman Hawkins and Ben Webster, and played in local studios in jazz bands with Ron Collier and Don (D.T.) Thompson. During his years as the house drummer at the Town Tavern in the fifties he was considered Toronto's premier drummer.
51. October 10, 1961. Clement Hambourg Papers, National Library of Canada.
52. Letter from Newson and Sheard, October 1, 1964. Clement Hambourg Papers, National Library of Canada.
53. Obituary, *Toronto Star*, February 6, 1973.
54. Autobiographical note written October 7, 1972.
55. Jon Ruddy, "The Ninth Life of the Ninth Cat," *Toronto Telegram*, July 24, 1965.
56. Ibid.
57. Obituary, *Toronto Star*, February 6, 1973.
58. Helen McNamara in "That's Show Business," October 23, 1972.
59. Ibid.
60. This was part of the series of documentaries made by Hobel-Leiterman for CTV under the title of *Here Come the Seventies*.
61. Telephone conversation with the author.
62. Autobiographical note written October 7, 1972.
63. Obituary, *Toronto Star*, February 6, 1973.
64. Ruddy, "The Ninth Life of the Ninth Cat," *Toronto Telegram*, July 24, 1965.

Index

Page numbers in italics refer to pictures or captions

Academy of Radio Arts 208
Acocella, Joan 84-85
Adaskin, Harry 97, 114, 119, 121, 123, 128, 130, 134, 138-141, 157-159, *160*, 164, 165, *169*, *171*, 172, 178-179, 182, 184-185, 186, 191, 192
Adaskin, Murray 97, 130, 131, 137, 141, 157
Adeney, Marcus 116, 129, 145, 261 n
Aeolian Hall (London) 60, 114
Aide, William 263 n
Aird, Sir John 203
Albéniz, Isaac 232
Albert Hall (London) 52
Alberta Lounge (Montreal) 210
Alexander II 10, 16
Alexander III 10
Alexandra, Queen 40
Alleyne, Archie 226, 271 n
Amadio, Norm 207, 223, 230, 231, 270 n
Amalfi (Italy) 191
Amati (Nicoli) violin 71, 80, 101, 110, 260 n
Amherst (Nova Scotia) 164
Anderson, Maxwell 89
Ansermet, Ernest 186
Art Gallery of Ontario (Toronto) 148, 152
Art Museum of Toronto. *See* Art Gallery of Ontario
Arts and Letters Club (Toronto) 113, 131, 133, 134, 149, *150*, 151, 178, 194, 197

Asquith, Herbert Henry (Earl of Oxford and Asquith) 67-68, 257 n
Asquith, Margot Tennant (Countess of Oxford and Asquith) 67-78, 190
Association Hall (Toronto) 132
Auer, Leopold 12, 263 n
Australia 33-36, 43, 66, 81, 114
Avenue Theatre Stock Company (Pittsburgh) 87

Bach, Carl Philip Emmanuel 192
Bach, Johann Sebastian 45, 79, 101, 102, 205, 230, 233-235
Bad Pyrmont 113
Balzac, Honoré de 103
Banting, Frederick 192
Barras, Paul François Jean Nicolas 96
Barrymore, Ethel 146
Bartók, Bela 166, 172, 185, 232
Bassetto, Corno di 15
Bassin, Samuel 147
Battle, Rex 130, 139, 264 n
Bauer, Harold 129
Bax, Arnold 187
Baxter, Beverley 176, 267 n
Beauchope, Maria. *See* Hambourg, Maria
Beauharnais, Josephine de 96
Becker, Hugo 113
Beckwith, John 263 n
Beethoven Saal 56
Beethoven, Ludwig van 4, 25, 36, 49, 61, 66, 70, 72, 102, 117, 168, 177, 232
Belgium 103
Beneš, Eduard 21
Berkman, Alexander 87-88

Berlin (Germany) 36, 45, 56, 63, 81, 113, 256 n
Berlin (now Kitchener, Ontario) 19
Berlin *Hochschule* 27
Berlin Philharmonic 155
Berlin, Boris 129, 207, 262 n
Bernard, Samuel 96
Bickert, Ed 208, 219-220, 221, 223, 270 n
Bickert, Madeline 208, 220
Birmingham 22, 50, 117
Bissel, Claude 163, 178
Blackstone, Milton 139, 158-159, 163-164, *169*, *171*, 179, 180, 183, 185, 186, 194, 266 n
Bloch, Ernest 182, 263 n
Blume, Helmut 129, 196, 263 n, 268 n
Blüthner (piano-makers) 33
Bombay 66
Bonaparte, Napoleon 96, 174
Bonn 72
Boom Baby Boom 209-10, 213
Borodin, Alexandr 190
Bösendorfer Saal (Vienna) 32
Boston 166
Boulanger, Nadia 264 n
Boult, Sir Adrian 190
Bournemouth (England) 60, 71
Boyce, George 129
Brahms, Johannes 30-32, 37, 56, 121, 254 n
Brailowsky, Alexander 25, 62
Brant, Felix 19. *See also* Volkhovsky, Felix
Brantford 116
Bray, Carne 269 n
Bridge, Frank 187, 190
Bridle, Augustus 120, 131, 134, 166, 173
Brighton 71
British Broadcasting Corporation 68, 71, 114, 175, 261 n
Broadwood piano 50
Browning, Robert 23

Bruce, Lenny 227
Bruckner, Anton 121
Brussels 45, 47
Budapest 196
Buenos Aires 67
Buffalo, Iron 269 n
Bülow, Hans von 23, 117
Burke, Edmund 80, 258 n
Burne-Jones, Sir Edward 50
Burns, John 18
Burton, Dennis 219-220, 226, 270 n
Busoni, Ferruccio 39, 45, 58, 69, 255 n

Café St. Michel (Montreal) 210
Cairo 66
Calgary 55
Calverley, Amice 182
Cambridge (England) 75
Camus, Albert 269 n
Canadian Academy of Music 119, 121
Canadian Bank of Commerce 151
Canadian Broadcasting Corporation 94, 192, 195-196, 208, 210-211, 220, 225, 228
Canadian Legation 174
Canadian National Exhibition 202
Canadian National Railways, radio department 166
Cape Town 49, 51, 66
Caplan, Dave 213
Caraman-Chimay, Prince 267 n
Carboni, Giuseppe 129, 134, 262 n
Carnegie, Andrew 24, 39, 252-253 n
Casals, Pablo 57, 102, 129, 234
Cather, Willa 82-95, *90*, 96, 103-109, 110, 260 n
Cav-A-Bob Restaurant (Toronto) 231
Cavalho, Rachel 129, 262 n
Cellar Club (Toronto) 225
CFCA 173, 203
Chabrier, Emmanuel 173
Chaliapin, Feodor 172
Chamber Music Society 159

Index

Champlain Society 152
Chaplin, Charlie 228
Chausson, Ernest 40
Chicago 38
Chinsky, Miriam Bassin 146-147
Choir of the Young Peoples' Socialist League 132
Chopin, Frédéric 45, 49, 230, 232
Churchill, Winston 51, 56
City Hall (Cape Town) 49
Clark, Paraskeva 259 n
Clark, Philip 97, 259 n
Clemens, Clara 28, 37
Coates, Eric 113
Cocteau, Jean 96
Cohen, Nathan 226
Coke, Galia (*née* Hambourg) 8, 15, 18, 20, 22, 54, 85, 110, 122, 147, 176, 202, 260 n
Coke, Reginald Grey 15, 123
Coke, Stella (*see* Stella Ryan) 147
Coke, Sylvia 147
Coke, Thomas William (*see also* Earl of Leicester of Holkham) 15, 123
Coliseum (London) 61
Collier, Lizzie Hudson 87
Collier, Ron 207, 214, 219, 225, 269 n, 271 n
Colonial Tavern (Toronto) 207, 215
Congo 66
Connaught, Duke and Duchess of 55
Conservatoire, Moscow 6-7, 12, 132
Conservatoire, St. Petersburg 4, 11-12, 132-133
Conservatoire, Voronezh 4-5
Conservatory Orchestra (Massey Hall, Toronto) 141
Cornfield, Bob 139
Cortot, Alfred 58
Covent Garden (London) 75
Cromwell, Oliver 221
Cuba 190
Cullen, Don 223

Czaplinski, Henri 129, 136-143, *144*, 154, 157
Czerny, Karl 27, 56

d'Erlanger, Baron Frédéric 44, 255 n
d'Indy, Vincent 40
David, Ferdinand 102
Davis, Andrew 262 n
Dawson, Ken 206
de Beauvoir, Simone 224
de Falla, Manuel de 182
de Grey, Lady 40
de Kresz Hambourg Trio 114
de Kresz, Géza 114, 129, 130, 155-159, *160*, 161, 166, *169*, *171*, 177, 179-183, 185-186
de Kresz, Nora. *See* Drewett, Norah
de Lenclos, Ninon 213
de Ridder, Allard 195
de Ridder, Pauline 195
Death Comes for the Archibishop 104-107
Debussy, Claude 40, 173, 177, 232, 256 n, 263 n
Defauw, Désiré 60, 256 n
Delius, Frederick 23, 187
Delmont, Gordon 207
Deyrolle, Maison 96
Diamond Jubilee of Confederation 167
Dixon, George 123
Dohnányi, Ernst von 185-186
Donalda, Pauline (*née* Lichtenstein) 80, 258 n
Drewett, Norah 114, 129, 155-156, 157, 158, *160*, 165, 179, 186, 263 n, 264 n
Dreyfus affair 41
Dudley, Ray 263 n
Dukes, Ashley 176
Dumas, Alexandre (pére) 97
Duncan, Isadora 219
Dunedin (Scotland) 52
Dusseau, Jeanne 190

Earl of Leicester of Holkham. *See* Coke, Thomas William
East London (South Africa) 49
Eastbourne (England) 60
Eaton Auditorium (Toronto) 74, 151, 182, 196
Eaton family 118
Eaton Operatic Society 151
Eaton, Jack 151, 176
Eaton, Lady Flora (*née* McCrea) 151, 161
Eaton, Mrs. R. Y. 176
Edel, Leon 92
Edward VII 40, 53
Edward VIII (Duke of Windsor) 70, 143, 175
Egypt 33, 66
Einstein, Albert 63
Elgar, Edward 187
Eliot, T.S. 91
Elisabethville (now Lubumbashi, Democratic Republic of Congo) 66
Ellington, Duke 207, 269 n
Elman, Mischa 12, 58, 129, 130-131, 256 n
Enesco, Georges 39
Erard's (piano-makers) 33
Euclid Hall (Toronto) 126

Faith, Percy 94
Farmer, Broadus 129
Farmer, Ernest 129, 263 n
Fauré, Gabriel 40, 173
Feldbrill, Victor 269 n
Fels, Joseph 39, 255 n
Ferrari-Fontana, Eduardo 129, 263 n
Feyer, George 222
Field, John 7
Fineberg, John 230
First Floor Club (Toronto) 225
Fisher, Dorothy Canfield 87, 88, 259 n
Fitzgerald, F. Scott 91
Fitzgerald, Katherine 202

Flaubert, Gustave 103, 107
Flesch, Carl 185-186
Flonzaley Quartet 58, 146
Florence, Evangeline 33
Forbes, Sydney A. 226
Forsyth, W. O. 64, 119, 134
Franck, Albert 206
Franck, César 40, 156, 177
Francks, Don 210, 215, 226, 227-228, 231, 269 n
Franfram, Amy 228
Frankfurt 45, 81, 113
Fremantle 66
Frick, Henry Clay 87
Fricker, H. A. 204, 268 n
Friedberg, Carl 58
Friedheim, Arthur 264 n
Friedman, Ignaz 3, 25
Friends of Russian Freedom 19
Fritchey, Clayton 202
Furtwängler, Wilhelm 45, 186
Fusco, Frank 120, 262 n

Gabrilowitsch, Ossip 12, 25, 28, 36, 37, 183
Gallaghan, Morley 127
Garden, Mary 256 n
Garnett, Olive 79, 86
Gartner, Emil 129, 263 n
Gay, Maria 44, 255 n
Gelber, Jack 226
George V, King 188
Gericke, William 37
Gershwin, George 172, 232
Gillespie, Dizzy 211
Gladstone, Herbert 39
Glasgow (Scotland) 40
Glasgow Exhibition 39
Glazunov, Alexander 11-12
Godinne-sur-Meuse 50, 81, 113, 155
Goldman, Emma 87
Gooderham and Worts distillery 119, 139

Index

Gooderham family 118, 124, 140
Gooderham, Lady 119
Gooderham, Sir Albert 119, 120, 138-139, 187, 262 n
Goodman, Hyman 129, 260 n, 262 n, 263 n
Goossens, Eugene 182
Gorki, Maksim 254 n
Görlitz, Hugo 52
Gotham, Nic 209
Göttingen 254 n
Gould, Glenn 68, 151, 263 n
Graham, William 50-51
Grainger, Percy 45, 255 n
Grand Duchess Elena 11
Grand Duke Constantine 7
Green, Nathan 137
Greene, Lorne 208
Griffith, Eleanor 129, 147
Grosse Musikverein (Vienna) 31
Group of Seven 149-150, 159, 196, 259 n
Grünfeld, Alfred 8
Guarneri (Giuseppe) violin 80, 101, 138-140, 178, 258 n, 267 n
Guarneri, Andrea 177
Guarneri, Servais (violin) 177-178
Guedalla, Sir Philip 190
Guerrero, Alberto 114, 125, 129, 263 n
Guiccardi, Countess 70
Guidente, Giovanni Floreno 178
Guildhall School of Music 46

Hagen, Betty Jean 186
Hahn, Paul 114
Haldane, Lord Chancellor 67
Halifax (Nova Scotia) 54-55, 166
Hall of the Nobles (Moscow) 7
Hall of the Nobles (Voronezh) 5
Hambourg Concert Society 146, 173
Hambourg Conservatory of Music (Toronto) 39, 81, 93, 94, 104, 114, 120, 123-124, *125*, 128, 130, 132, 134, 146, 149, 154, 157, 166, 182, 188, 196-197, 201, 203, 261 n
Hambourg Conservatory of Music (London) 46, 133
Hambourg String Quartet 113
Hambourg Trio 113-114, 116, 187-190, *189*, 201
Hambourg, Bernard 15. See also Hambourg, Boris
Hambourg, Boris 5, 15, 18, 20, 22, 33, 39, 45, 47, 54, 65, 74, 81, 88, 93, 110, 111-198, *115*, *144*, *150*, *169*, *171*, *189*, 201, 232, 236, 264 n
Hambourg, Catherine 122, 133, 134-136, 140, 143, 202, 261 n
Hambourg, Charles 71, 251 n, 257 n
Hambourg, Clement 46, 75, 88, 93, 101, 114, 122, 129, 133, 173, 192, 199-232, *216*, *222*, *229*,. 270 n
Hambourg, Dorothy (Dolly) (*née* Muir MacKenzie) 50–52, 54-56, *59*, 71, *73*, 81, 143, 147, 156, 176, 190, 227
Hambourg, Dr. Klement (son of Clement) 268 n
Hambourg, Galia. See Coke, Galia
Hambourg, Isabelle (*née* McClung) 81-84, 87-89, *90*, 91, 99, 103, 106, 108, 191, 201, 260 n
Hambourg, Ivan 135, 261 n
Hambourg, James 15. See also Hambourg, Jan
Hambourg, Jan 5, 15, 18, 20, 22, 33, 35, 45, 46, 47, 50, 71, 77-110, *83*, *95*, 113-114, 122, 133, 143, 145, 155, 159, 187-188, *189*, 201, 202, 208, 232, 260 n, 261 n
Hambourg, Luba 46, 75, 109, 110, 122, 133, 135, 202, 208-209, 227
Hambourg, Manya 122, 133, 135, 202
Hambourg, Maria (Borina) (*née* Beauchope) 143-146, *144*, 148, 176, 183, 191, 197-198, 202
Hambourg, Mark 1-76, 26, *73*, 79, 81,

86, 88, 110, 113-114, 116, 117, 122, 123, 133, 143, 147, 148, 156, 168-172, 175, 176, 183, 187, *189*, 190, 196, 197, 201, 202, 214-215, 227, 232, 236, 256 n, 257 n, 264 n
Hambourg, Max 15, 20, 79. *See also* Hambourg, Mark
Hambourg, Michael 4-6, 8-9, 11-13, 20, 25, *26*, 46-47, 53-54, 117, 118, 122-125, 130, 131-134, 135, 148-149, 201, 202, 232, 261 n
Hambourg, Nadine. *See* Marshall, Nadine
Hambourg, Ruth (Ruthie) (*née* Nadine) 208-210, 211, *216*, 218-219, 224, 225, 227, 228, 230, 231, 270 n
Hamilton 109
Hamilton, Stuart 263 n
Handel, George Frideric 232
Hanslick, Eduard 121
Hardie, Keir 18, 23, 252 n
Hardy, Hagood 207, 220-221, 270 n
Harisay, Erwin 39
Harisay, Vino 114
Harris, Peter 219
Hart House (Toronto) 152-154, 166, 195
Hart House String Quartet 65, 114, 116, 130, 139, 158, 161-187, *169*, *171*, 174, 181, 184, 187, 188-196, 230, 236
Hart House Theatre (Toronto) 154, 161, 166, 195
Hawaii 43
Hawkins, Coleman 271 n
Haydn, Franz Joseph 102, 162
Hecht, Ben 226
Heifetz, Jascha 12, 101, 102, 173
Heinl, Frank 178
Heinl, George 178
Heintzman (piano-makers) 123, 214-215, *229*, 231
Helmer, Paul 263 n
Hemingway, Ernest 91, 93, 126
Henstridge, Ian 226

Hepburn, Katherine 31
Herbert, Victor 38, 121
Hersenhoren, Jeanie 94
Hersenhoren, Samuel 94, 95, 99, 260 n
Herzen, Aleksandr (Ivanovich) 19
Herzovna, Katrina 4
Hess, Dame Myra 71, 129
Hindemith, Paul 182, 204-205, 232
Hitler, Adolf 58, 190, 194
Hoch Konservatorium (Frankfurt) 45, 113
Hofmann, Josef 16, 36, 58
Holiday, Billie 209, 271 n
Hollinshead, Redferne 129, 263 n
Honegger, Arthur 182
Honolulu 43
Horowitz, Vladimir 12
Horszowski, Mieczyslaw 25, 62, 256 n
Hotel Martin (New York) 38
Hotel Metropole (Vienna) 37
Houghton, Alanson 175
House of Hambourg (1184 Bay Street, Toronto) 205-207, 209, 211
House of Hambourg (142 Bloor Street, Toronto) 215, *216*
House of Hambourg (159 Cumberland, Toronto) 213, 215-225, *222*
House of Hambourg (Grenville Street, Toronto) 225-228
House of Hambourg Theatre 226
Housser, F. B. 149
Howard, British Ambassador and Lady Isabella 175

Jackson, A. Y. 127
Jacobson, Stan 225-226, 230
Janopoulo, Tasso 46
Janotha, Natalie 15, 252 n
Jazz Artists Club (Toronto) 215
Joachim, Joseph 34-35, 40, 102, 177, 254 n
Johannesburg 49, 66

Index

Johnson, Edward 151
Joyce, James 39
Julie's (Toronto) 230

Kash, Eugene 255 n
Kayaloff, Yasha 142
Kaye, Maury 226
Keaton, Buster 228
Kennan, George 19
Kernerman, Morry 114, 116, 129, 260 n, 263 n-264 n
King Edward Hotel (Toronto) 139, 159, 172
King, Prime Minister William Lyon Mackenzie 194
Kingston 166, 181
Knabe (piano-makers) 37
Kneisel Quartet 38
Knorr, Ivan 113
Kodály, Zoltán 185
Koffman, Moe 207, 221, 269 n
Koldofsky, Adolph 157, 192-193
Koldofsky, Eleanor 151
Kontski, Antoine de 25
Kossuth, Lajos 19
Kostelanetz, André 12
Kosy, György 166
Kramer, Gidon 102
Krasin, Viktor 255 n
Krauss, Clemens 45
Kravchinskii (*see also* Stepniak, Sergei) 17
Krehm, Ida 263 n, 264 n
Krehm, William 130, 264 n
Kreisler, Fritz 39, 58, 129, 172, 182
Kresz, Mária 156, 266 n
Kropotkin, Prince Peter 13, 16-18, 20, 22, 132
Kruschev, Nikita 209
Kubelik, Jan 36, 52, 256 n
Kubelik, Rafael 256 n

Lahore 66

Lambert, Constant 176
Lambert, Maurice 176
Landowska, Wanda 192
Langley, John 130, 264 n
Lansbury, George 255 n
Lapp, Horace 263 n
Lascelles, A. F. and Mrs. 190
Lavallée, Calixa 174
Lavut, Martin 226
Leclair, Jean-Marie 235
Lee, Hermione 84
Leeds 22
Lemmone, John 36, 254 n
Lenin, Vladimir Ilich 17, 38-39, 254 n
Leschetizky, Theodor 25-32, 26, 35, 36, 56, 61-62, 87, 129, 133, 155, 251 n, 253 n
Lethbridge (Alberta) 188
Levey, James 74, 179, 183, 186-187, 196
Levi, Hermann 23
Lewis, Edith 104-108
Lewis, Sinclair 82
Lewis, Wyndham 126, 127, 128, 153
Lhevinne, Josef 251 n
Liivoja-Lorius, Jaak 260 n
Liliuokalani, Queen 43
Lind, Jenny 117
Lismer, Arthur 149
Liszt, Franz 27, 28, 31, 32, 56, 61, 65, 254 n
Little Symphony (Toronto) 182
Llewellyn, Sir William 190
London (England) 8, 13-18, 21, 32-33, 34, 36, 38, 40, 44, 46-48, 57-58, 61, 64, 70-71, 88, 109, 113, 117, 133, 175, 187, 190, 201, 207, 212, 251 n, 254 n, 260 n
London (Ontario) 166
London Academy 46
Longsworth, Speaker and Mrs. 175
Los Angeles (California) 38, 207
Lotus Club (New York) 60
Lucas, Clarence 35, 41, 109

Lucas, Jessica 109
Lunch Hour concerts at the National Gallery (London) 71
Lyric Theatre (London) 15
Lytton, Earl and Countess of 190

MacDermot, Galt 153
MacDermot, Terence W. L. 153
MacDonald, Alistair 175
MacDonald, Ishbel 190
MacDonald, J. E. H. 149-150
MacDonald, Ramsay 39, 67
MacEwen, Gwendolyn 211
MacMillan, Sir Ernest 64, 118, 120, 122, 166, 173, 177-178, 187, 197, 204, 263 n, 264 n
Macpherson, Jessie 198
Mahler, Gustav 32
Malipiero, Gian Francesco 182
Manchester 117
Manchester Hippodrome 3, 56
Manet, Edouard 41
Mansfield, Katherine 143
Marchand, Colonel 41
Marsellus, Louie (character in *The Professor's House*) 91-93
Marshall, Nadine (*née* Hambourg) 76
Marshall, Tom 76
Marx, Eleanor 18
Mary, Queen 188
Massey Commission 115
Massey Hall (Toronto) 43, 68, 114, 123, 146, 148, 151, 152, 158, 168, 183, 187, 188, 201, 211, 215
Massey, Alice (*née* Parkin) 152, 159, 162, 164-165, *171*, 174, 182, 187
Massey, Chester 154, 165, 230
Massey, Hart Almerrin 152, 168
Massey, Hart Parkin Vincent 164, 165
Massey, Lionel 164
Massey, Raymond 154, 165, 190
Massey, Vincent 114-115, 149, 152-155, 159, 161-162, *171*, 176-187, 190, 191, 210

Mather, Bruce 263 n
Matthews, Howard 226
Mavor, James 134
May Day 132
Mayer, Daniel 14, 33
Mazzini, Giuseppe 19
McClung, Isabelle. *See* Hambourg, Isabelle
McClung, Samuel A. 81, 87, 99
McCowan, George 226
McCrea, Flora. *See* Eaton, Lady Flora
McDonell, Arch 226
McFarland, Colonel G. Frank 161, 163, 177, 180-181
McGill University 64
McInnes, Graham 147-148
McInnes, James Campbell 129, 147, 159, 263 n
McLuhan, Marshall 127
McMillian, Sir Daniel 53, 256 n
McPhee, Colin 263 n
Melba, Nellie 36, 254 n
Melbourne 36, 52
Melody Mill (Toronto) 215
Menard, Dorian 41
Mencken, H. L. 85
Mendelssohn Choir 118, 151, 152
Mendelssohn, Felix 22-23, 102, 254 n
Mendelssohn-Bartholdi, Felix 195
Menter, Sophie 32
Menuhin, Hephzibah 99, 107-109
Menuhin, Yaltah 99, 107-109
Menuhin, Yehudi 82, 99-100, 101, 102, 107-109, 129, 253 n
Metropolitan Opera (New York) 151
Mexico 190
Mezentzev, General 17
Miejasz, Dainis 219
Milan 190
Miller, Donna 219-220
Miller, Mark 210-211
Milstein, Nathan 102
Minc Club (Toronto) 225

Index

Mingus, Charlie 211
Mischakoff, Mischa 140
Mitchell, Attorney-General and Mrs. 175
Moiseiwitsch, Benno 25, 62-63, 69, 256 n
Moiseiwitsch, Tanya 256 n
Montreal 54, 166
Moody, Fanny 33
Moore, Gerald 64, 79, 113, 123, 124, 256 n, 263 n
Moose Jaw 53
Morawetz, Oskar 263 n
Morenzo, Paul 123, 134
Morley, Glen 116
Morocco 66
Morris, Willam 18
Mosbaugh, Nadine 255 n
Moscheles, Felix (Uncle Lix) 22-24, 25, 30, 38, 39, 56, 254 n
Moscheles, Grete 23-24
Moscheles, Ignaz 22-23, 24, 56, 254 n
Moscow 6-7, 18, 44
Mottl, Felix 23, 49
Mozart, Wolfgang Amadeus 45, 102, 205, 232
Muck, Karl 23
Muir Mackenzie, Dorothy (Dolly). *See* Hambourg, Dorothy
Muir Mackenzie, Lord T. A. 50-51, 57, 59, 67
Music Lovers' Club (Toronto) 197
Mussolini, Benito 190

Nadine, Ruth. *See* Hambourg, Ruth
Nanton, Sir Augustus 53, 256 n
Naples 191
Natal 49
National Gallery of Canada (Ottawa) 152
Nevilson, Louise 231
Nevin, Ethelbert 86-87
New Glasgow 164
New York 37-38, 41, 52, 57-58, 60, 88, 96, 103, 108, 110, 133, 135, 166, 168, 207, 260 n
New Zealand 43, 52, 114, 143
Newfoundland 53
Ney, Elly 25
Niagara Falls (Ontario) 174
Nicolas II 10
Nikisch, Arthur 23, 49, 156, 263 n
Nimmons, Phil 221, 225
Nixon, Richard 209
North Africa 33
Nova Scotia 164

Odessa 9
Oistrakh, David 102
Olympic Theatre (London) 33
Orford Quartet 122
Ottawa 35, 55, 166, 167
Oxfordshire 67
Ozolins, Arthur 263 n

Paderewski, Ignace 14, 25, 33, 49, 72, 129, 133
Paganini, Niccolò 256 n
Paii, Yasha 129, 263 n-264 n
Painters Eleven 259 n
Pale of Jewish settlement 9, 12
Papritz, Eugénie 8, 13
Paris 40-41, 44, 46, 63, 93-94, 96-97, 98, 99, 104-105, 106, 178, 187, 196, 207, 259 n, 266 n
Paris Cinema (London) 71
Park Plaza Hotel (Toronto) 215, 220, 224
Parker, Charlie "Bird" 211
Parker, Sir Gilbert 80, 258 n
Parkin, Alice. *See* Massey, Alice
Parkin, Sir George 152
Parkman, Francis 106
Parlow String Quartet 94
Parlow, Kathleen 80, 258 n
Parnassus Sunday Concerts (London) 110

Pellatt, Sir Henry 126, 132
Perry, P. J. 226
Peterson, Oscar 210, 221
Philadelphia 39, 121, 141, 154
Philadelphia Orchestra 142-143
Phipps, Henry 24
Piatti, Alfredo 34-35, 254 n
Picquart, Colonel 41
Pinchot, Mr. and Mrs. Gifford 175
Pinder, Paul Gibson 215-218
Pinsent, Gordon 226
Pisa 190
Pittsburgh 38, 82, 86, 88, 121
Plekhanov, Georgi Valentinovich 254 n
Pleyel and Gavreau (piano-makers) 33
Poland 44
Pompei 191
Poore, Vincent 110
Port Hope 165
Porter, Katherine Anne 82
Potocki, Countess 44
Pound, Ezra 91
Powell, Bud 207, 211
Prague 81, 121
Pratz, Albert 140, 263 n
Preston, Bernard 129, 137
Prince of Wales. *See* Edward VIII
The Professor's House 91-93
Prom Concerts (Toronto) 72
Promenade Symphony Orchestra 215, 264 n
Proust, Marcel 82
Pulborough 71

Quebec City 130, 105-107, 167
Queen's Hall (London) 40, 49, 69, 71, 109

Rapallo 191
Rapee, Erno (pseudonym of Henri Czaplinski) 142
Ravel, Maurice 68, 168-174, 203, 204, 232, 263 n, 266 n
Ray, Marcel 129, 264 n
Redouten Saal (Vienna) 30
Regency Towers Hotel (Toronto) 228, 230
Reger, Max 263 n
Regina 53
Reid, Whitelaw 24, 253 n
Remenye, Ede 254 n
Respighi, Ottorino 182
Richter, Hans 23, 24, 31, 32, 49
Rideau Hall (Ottawa) 167
Ridout, Godfrey 195
Rimouski 54-55
Rio de Janeiro 67
Rivière du Loup 55
Roach, Max 211
Roberts, Charles G. D. 148
Robespierre, Maximilien François Marie Isidore de 96
Robinson, John 113
Rockhead's Paradise (Montreal) 210
Rodin, Auguste 56
Rodriguez, Percy 226
Roma, Lisa 173
Romanelli, Luigi 139
Rome 190-191
Roosevelt, Theodore 41-42, 43
Rosé Quartet 32
Rosé, Justine 32
Rosenthal, Moriz 14, 133
Ross, David 123
Ross, Dr. J. F. W. 124
Rotary Club (Budapest) 179
Roy Thomson Hall (Toronto) 122
Royal Conservatory of Music (Toronto) 119, 186
Royal Ontario Museum (Toronto) 148, 151, 265 n
Royal York Hotel (Toronto) 130, 139
Royal York Hotel Concert Orchestra 264 n

Index

Rubess, Banuta 209, 213
Rubie, Les 226
Rubinstein, Anton 4, 10, 16, 27, 28, 35-36, 40, 41, 48, 49, 56, 117, 132-133
Rubinstein, Arthur 31, 62, 256 n, 257 n
Rubinstein, Nikolay 4, 8, 10
Rubinstein, Roman 10
Rudolph Wurlitzer Company 177
Russell, Bertrand 20-21, 252 n
Russia 4-8, 9-13, 44
Ryan, Stella (*née* Coke) 85, 147

Safonov, Vasily 6-7, 251 n
St. James Hall (London) 22, 34
St. Paul, Marquise 41
St. Petersburg 9, 13, 27
Saint-Saëns, Camille 40, 41, 173, 254 n, 263 n
Salinger, Pierre 202, 228, 268 n
Salisbury (now Harare) 66
Salle Pleyel (Paris) 266 n
Salzburg Festival 45
Samuel, Lewis 265 n
Samuel, Sir Sigmund 146, 265 n
San Francisco 38, 166
Sand, George 223
São Paulo 67
Sargent, Sir Malcolm 190
Sartre, Jean-Paul 223-224
Satie, Eric 173
Sauer, Emil von 14
Savage Club (London) 60, 62-63, 69, 75 148-149, 190
Scalatti, Alessandro 232
Schablinsky, Heinrich 141
Schafer, R. Murray 263 n
Scherman, Paul 129, 134, 136, 137, 261 n
Schnabel, Artur 25, 27, 28
Schönberg, Arnold 173, 182, 192
Schubert, Franz 168
Schumann, Clara 29, 31, 58, 252 n
Schumann, Robert 45, 102, 232

Schweitzer, Albert 101, 102, 102, 234
Scott, Cyril 45, 255 n
Scott, Hazel 221
Scott, Patrick 227-228
Sergeant, Elizabeth 89, 107
Servais (cello) 267 n
Servais, Adrien François 267 n
Servais, Joseph 267 n
Ševčík, Ottakar 121
Ševčík String Quartet 192
Shadow on the Rock 104-105, 108
Shaw, George Bernard 15-16, 17, 23, 32, 219
Sheard, Joseph D. 167-168, 220, 227
Shostakovich, Dmitri 182
Sidney (Nova Scotia) 164
Silva, Carmen 253 n
Silver Rail (Toronto) 215
Silverman, Fanny 129
Simpson's Arcadian Room (Toronto) 139
Simpson, Wallis (Duchess of Windsor) 70
Simpson-Sears (Toronto) 231
Sinclair, Walter 168
Slonimsky, Nicolas 11
Smith, Leo 204
Smith, Robert 219
Snow, Michael 270
Solway, Maurice 120, 129, 137, 157
The Song of the Lark 84-86
Sorrento 191
South Africa 33, 49-50, 51, 65-66, 114
South America 67
Southern Rhodesia (now Zimbabwe) 66
Spanier, Herb 212
Spencer, Joyce 226
Sperdakos, George 226
Sperry, Dodie 219
Spivak, Elie 113, 114, 116, 197, 261 n
Star Concert Company (Sydney, Australia) 34

Steinway (piano-makers) 33, 57
Steinway Hall (London) 15
Stepniak, Sergei 13, 16-18, 20, 23-25, 30, 79
Stern Conservatorium 155
Stewart, Reginald 114, 129, *144*, 215, 264 n
Stokowski, Leopold 121, 142
Stradivari, Antonio 267 n
Stradivarius (violin) 71
Stratford Shakespeare Festival 256 n
Strauss, Johann 37
Stravinsky, Igor 173, 210, 219
Stringer, Arthur 148
Sullivan, Rosemary 211
Sydney (Australia) 34
Symonds, Norman 207, 208, 269 n
Szeryng, Henryk 102
Szigeti, Joseph 39, 102, 172

Tandy, Rechab 134
Taub, Lou 120, 134-135, 262 n
Tchaikovsky, Peter Ilich 4, 132-133
Tempest, Dame Marie 190
Terry, Ellen 23
Tertis, Lionel 60, 256 n
Teyte, Maggie 58, 256 n
Thibaud, Jacques 39, 45, 46, 58, 255 n
Thibaud-Cortot-Casals Trio 45
Thirkell, Angela 263 n
Thirkell, Colin 263 n
Thirkell, Graham 263 n
Thomas, Theodore 38
Thompson, Don T. 219, 270 n, 271 n
Thurman, Peter 231
Till, Eric 231
Tolstoy, Count Leo (Nikolaevich) 16, 44, 255 n
Tolstoy, Countess 44
Toronto 39, 43, 46, 53-55, 64, 67, 68, 72, 74, 75, 79-80, 87, 93, 94-96, 103, 113-132, 140, 145-149, 173, 186, 192-198, 201, 205-207, 210

Toronto Conservatory of Music (now Royal Conservatory of Music) 118-119, 122, 128, 145, 178
Toronto Symphony Orchestra 119, 120, 128, 131, 158, 182, 193-194
Torquay 71
Torrington, F. H. 119
Toscanini, Arturo 45, 263 n
Tours 110
Tourte, François 234
Town Tavern (Toronto) 207, 215
Town, Harold 205-206
Tristano, Lennie 207
Tudor Hotel (Toronto) 126
Turgenev, Ivan 107
Twain, Mark 28-29, 36-37, 183, 254 n
Tzara, Tristan 39

United States of America 190, 226, 256 n
University of New Brunswick 64
University of Toronto 118, 120, 152, 198, 265 n, 266 n. *See also* Hart House, Victoria College.
University of Western Ontario 265 n

van Holstein, Sir William 49
van Horne, Sir William Cornelius 53, 256 n
Vancouver 53
Varèse, Edgard 172
Varsity Arena (Toronto) 72
Vaughan, Sarah 221
Vert, Narcissus 16, 18, 22
Veuillot, Louis 96
Victoria 53
Victoria College (Toronto) 152
Victoria, Queen 254 n
Vienna 8, 25-32, 36-37, 65, 190, 194
Vienna Tonkünstler 155
Vieuxtemps, Henri 40, 255 n
Villa-Lobos, Heitor 182

Index

Ville d'Avray (France) 94, 95, *98*, 100, 104
Vilna (Lithuania) 12
Vincent, George 152
Vogt, Augustus 122, 134
Volkhovsky, Felix 13, 18-19, 132
Volkhovsky, Vera 18-21, 22, 24, 252 n
von Dohnányi, Ernst 186
von Hohenzollern-Sigmaringen, Prinz Karl (later King Carol I of Rumania) 253 n
von Kunits, Luigi 120-122, *125*, 134, 136-140, 154, 157, 159, 192, 215, 262 n, 263 n
Voronezh 4, 12

Walenn, Herbert 113
Walker, Sir Edmund 151-152, 161
Walter, Bruno 45
Walton, William 232
Wanderer's Hall (Johannesburg) 49
Warburg, Edward M. N. 192
Warrender, Lady Maud 190
Warsaw 44
Washington, D.C. 171, 174
Webster, Ben 271 n
Weingartner, Felix 32, 49, 263 n
Weissmann, Frieder 72-73, 257 n
Wells, H. G. 21
Wells, Paul 134
Welsman, Frank 131
West, Rebecca 82
White House (Washington, D.C.) 41, 43
Whyte, Sir William M. 53, 256 n

Wied-Neuweid, Prinzessin Elisabeth zu (later Queen of Rumania) 29, 155
Wieland, Joyce 270 n
Wieniawski, Henri 80
Wigmore Hall (London) 175
Wilde, Oscar 23-24
Willan, Healey 182, 204
Williams, Ralph Vaughan 187
Williams, Sir Ralph Champneys 53, 256 n
Willingdon, Lord Freeman Freeman-Thomas 167
Wilson, Mrs. Woodrow 175
Wimbledon 71
Windsor 181
Winnipeg 53
Winnipeg Auditorium 151
Wittgenstein, Paul 25
Wolff, Hermann 35-36
Walton, William 232
Women's Musical Clubs 166, 203

Yohe, May 33
Yorkville (Toronto) 224
Young, Lester 209, 271 n
Youssoupoff, Princess 267 n
Ysaÿe Quartet 183
Ysaÿe, Carrie 39
Ysaÿe, Eugène 39, 45, 47, 50, 58, *59*, 60, 80, 81, 99, 101, 103, 113, 129, 155, 156, 176, 188, 192
Ysaÿe, Théophile 59

Zimbalist, Efrem 12
Zola, Emile 16, 41, 103

ABOUT THE AUTHOR

Born in Frankfurt/Main, Germany, in 1919, Eric Koch learned to play the violin as a child. In middle age he added the viola. Many years ago, as he says, he reached a plateau as an excellent third-rate amateur. Among those he has played with are many who remember one or more of the Hambourg brothers.

PHOTO: TONY KOCH

Koch left Germany for England as a refugee in 1935. He went to Cranbrook School, Kent, and St. John's College, Cambridge. In May 1940 he was interned as an "enemy alien" and later shipped to Canada, where he remained interned until the end of 1941. He was released to continue his studies at the University of Toronto. He wrote about his experiences and those of his fellow "enemy aliens" in his well-known book *Deemed Suspect*. His career as a broadcaster began in 1944 when he joined the Canadian Broadcasting Corporation's International Service, later called Radio Canada International. From 1953 to 1967 he was a member of the CBC Public Affairs Department, where he was involved in the production of a large number of radio and television programs. He was Area Head, Arts and Science (1967-1971) and Regional Director in Montreal (1971-1977). He retired in 1979 to devote himself to writing. For the last eleven years he has taught a seminar on the politics of Canadian broadcasting in the Social Science Division of York University, Toronto.

His other books include *The French Kiss*, *The Leisure Riots*, *The Last Thing You'd Want to Know*, *Good Night Little Spy*, *Deemed Suspect*, *Inside Seven Days* and *Hilmar and Odette*.